Idlewild

'Idlewild is a brilliantly concieved and imagined novel. A wonderfully ironic grasp of a recent span of American culture, it is amusing, affecting and thought provoking'

Richard North Patterson – author of *Degree of Guilt*

'In this, his first novel, Mark Lawson asks two of the bigger "what ifs" of the past fifty years and comes up with some smart answers about the nature of fate and celebrity'

Elle

'Idlewild is inventive and full of worthwhile insights'

New Statesman and Society

'Slick and satisfying. It is recognizably a first novel, but one that makes you want to read the second and the third'

Independent on Sunday

Also by Mark Lawson in Picador

FICTION
Bloody Margaret: Three Political Fantasies

NON-FICTION
The Battle For Room Service: Journeys To All The Safe Places

Idlewild

Or Everything Is Subject to Change

MARK LAWSON

PICADOR

First published 1995 by Picador

This edition published 1996 by Picador
an imprint of Macmillan Publishers Ltd
25 Eccleston Place, London SW1W 9NF
and Basingstoke

Associated companies throughout the world

ISBN 0 330 34450 1

9 8 7 6 5 4 3 2 1

A CIP catalogue record for this book is available
from the British Library

Filmset by CentraCet Limited, Cambridge
Printed and bound in Great Britain
by Mackays of Chatham PLC, Chatham, Kent

For William Lawson

Contents

Kennedy, John Fitzgerald, 1917–63, 35th President of the United States (1961–63), b Brookline, Mass. . . . On Nov 22, 1963, President Kennedy was shot while riding in an open car in Dallas, Texas. He died half an hour later and was succeeded as president by Lyndon Johnson. The WARREN COMMISSION, appointed by Johnson to investigate the murder, concluded that it was the work of a single assassin, Lee Harvey OSWALD. Kennedy's death shocked the nation and many felt that had he not died at the age of 46 he would have gone on to achieve real greatness as a president.

The Columbia Encyclopaedia, fifth edition, 1991

First, how can the complexity of the universe and all its trivial details be determined by a simple set of equations? Alternatively, can one really believe that God chose all the trivial details, like who should be on the cover of *Cosmopolitan*? The answer seems to be that the uncertainty principle of quantum mechanics means that there is not just a single history for the universe but a whole family of possible histories. These histories may be similar on very large scales, but they will differ greatly on normal everyday scales. We happen to live on one particular history that has certain properties and details. But there are very similar intelligent beings who live on histories that differ in who won the war and who is Top of the Pops.

Stephen Hawking, *Black Holes and Baby Universes*

Monroe, Marilyn, 1926–62, American movie actress, b Los Angeles Norma Jean Baker. Raised in orphanages and first married at 14, Monroe became a world-famous sex symbol, and, after her death, a Hollywood legend. She was noted for her distinctively breathy singing style and seductive film roles. . . . Her suicide at 36 only increased her mystique.

The Columbia Encyclopaedia, fifth edition, 1993

Q: What was the original name of John F. Kennedy International Airport in New York?
A: Idlewild.

The Big American Quiz Book, 18th edition, 1989

Part One

THE MINUS GAME

1: Night Noise

At 3 a.m., he wakes, and hears sounds downstairs: the click of the latch and the clap of a solid shoe on the stoop.

Even now, after more than thirty years of this strange life, there is the involuntary reflex of fear: the inside night-light from our warrior past – for feet or paws outside the hut – which humans still possess, as late as 1993, despite the invention of doors, and locks, and property.

But, in less than thirty seconds, he remembers to relax. One of his first appreciations of the sheer weirdness of public life in the late twentieth century was the understanding, in a broken moment of the night not unlike this one, that for him, as for no normal home-owner, noise below in the early hours meant reassurance: the percussion of round-the-clock protection.

The guard is changing downstairs, which makes it 3 a.m. or 6 a.m., without even looking at the clock, and it is too tomb-dark to be the later time, even in winter. An agent clumsier than others has bumped the step, and then forgotten to stop the winter wind bench-pressing the door.

In his mind, he summons the offender as a big guy, the kind who once dropped his piece on ambush drill, and nearly failed the Academy, who the others keep making roll-eyes at just out of vision, and who will eventually be moved to desk-work after some botched job, when the White House needs a Secret Service scalp.

He demonizes the maker of the noise, because he does not welcome interruptions in the night. Once, in a bitchy profile in a glossy-sleazy magazine, a 'friend' was quoted as saying of him: 'Would you want to have his dreams?'

A *friend*? The quote was mainly a more poetic way of talking of him as haunted and failed, which has been for quite some time the standard line on him. But the comment is not wrong. In folklore, night is the time of ghosts, but the old statesman has found this also to be true of life.

There was another line, in the same magazine piece or a different one: 'He has walked behind too many coffins.' That was really just another toney phrase for the disappointment of his biography, but neither can he, at times, entirely deny it to himself. The family caskets alone would have kept even a dumb believer in fate or providence awake at night, and then there were those of the soldiers.

He soon begins, however, to feel less resentment at his divided night, for he realizes the need to piss, old age's wake-up call, and would therefore not have reached the dawn undisturbed, even without the elephantine agent.

He eases out of bed, ready for the twinge in his grizzled scar tissue from the November East Coast sea breeze, and drapes around him, over the nightshirt, a tattered flying jacket with the governmental crest.

In the passage, he passes an agent, who is slim and of nearly silent tread; not, he thinks, the one who made the row.

'Good morning, Mr President,' his protector almost whispers, although there is no other sleeper in the house to welcome this discretion. A mere night convention, then.

'Oh, uh, hi,' the old politician answers. 'Trouble, uh, sleeping.'

2: Ghosts

Nobody seems to be dead any more, she thinks, frisking the channels on her bedroom television set, unable to sleep. She is an habitual through-the-night viewer, her more or less constant insomnia worsened tonight by the humidity which seems to warn of another storm. The climate on the West Coast this November has suffered from a version of what fashionable psychoanalysis now calls multiple personality disorder: long dry spells sparking fires, then all-day rain-storms, shifting mud slides. Every other station she samples seems to hold a weatherman with an undertaker's smile.

And everything else is ghosts. She has just watched – on some cable outfit in the upper nineties – a few scenes from a film in which famous baseball players, long dead, regroup in some guy's paddock for a shady last game. One of the movie channels is running two features in tonight's schedule about dead men somehow escaping the grave to date their widows. Back-from-the-grave seems to be the plot of choice for any movie with an early nineties copyright line.

She writes a list in her mind of all the afterlife stuff she has seen in recent weeks. There was the one about the racist cop who gets the black man's heart in a transplant, and, with it, his spectral companionship. She caught on cable – or did Mrs M. rent it from the store? – another one, about the medical students inducing death and then resuscitation to bring back news from day trips to oblivion.

Every cast list these days seems to contain at least one of the half-dead. Even the peak-time sitcoms are full of zombies now. And she doesn't mean these things the bitchy way she would have done a few years back.

Her interest in this is partly professional. Over on the night table – in front of the pill bottles, for sleeping mainly, nothing recreational, which stand like a cylindrical version of a big city skyline – is the latest pre-shooting script of a movie called *She's Back!* She is slated to play the female of the title, in her first appearance for a decade, since the disaster of the film she never mentions, which began her latest lengthy exile from the business.

The character is a famous Hollywood actress – dead from some clean and unspecified disease in her sixties, which has left her spirit image strangely undisfigured – who is permitted to return to earth to supervise the production of a biopic about her. The script is vague about the reasons for the character's rain-check from heaven. 'We always knew studio bosses are god. Maybe God is a studio boss!' quipped *Variety*, including a plot résumé in one of its nearly weekly pieces during the last two years about the on-off status of the comeback.

She started studying the script tonight because she could not sleep, but the shallowness of the character depressed her. In the more than forty years since she began, her range of roles seems to have changed in nothing except age, apart from the one film she never mentions. She is always offered the sappy, not the sassy, roles. So, throwing the script aside, she tried the TV for distraction. But now she is worried about the glut of such back-from-death stories. Might the afterlife market be saturated, packed like a graveyard with ghosts, by the time they get theirs out? She remembers a review in the *Los Angeles Times* just this week of a new release about some dad-to-be, diagnosed with the big C, the tumour growing faster than the child, who makes a video so the kid will see him, though he will not see the kid.

What is it with America and death in the 1990s? Some of it, she guesses, must be Aids. She read an article once that put it well. This generation of artists – the term the writer used for people in the business – was more familiar with death as a daily threat and occurrence than any since the English war poets of 1914. And America – though surely no nation in the world had more churches or Bibles – had never really come to terms with death. Look at the Elvis and Kennedy stuff. She read only recently that the coming craze is the video gravestone, with a screen cut into the granite, like those back-of-the-seat TVs they have on some planes these days. The mourners press a button and the departed speaks their piece. There is a gag going round about some of the television veterans getting 'Back in a moment!' as an epitaph.

But, for her, there is already a version of this hell. The worst moments in the night are when she stumbles against her own ghost. Bored with a show, she button-punches to another number, and there she is: young, lovely, and funny. This is a cruelty of the movie business, particularly to women, for men care less about the contrast, although she knows that this remark is what they now call politically incorrect. Well, so it may be, but it is, she fears, all too psychologically true.

And, sometimes, escaping from her own old self, she keeps meeting, during her retreat across the airwaves, friends long dead, resurrected on celluloid. So does Hollywood contrive to reverse the natural processes of healing for those who work in it. And, if it isn't the ghost films, or the corpses of her friends come back on cable, then there are the biopics. The proper history ones – the kings and queens of England, Rome, or Greece – don't bother her. Contemporary re-creations, though, are often troubling. A number of the supposedly great public men she has known, loved, hated, fucked turn up in the night on cable re-runs, sometimes embodied by an actor she has known, fucked, hated, loved. Once recently, quite eerily, she chanced upon a Life Of in which she had slept with both the hero and the star. Sadly, their perform-ances with her had more in common than their cinematic match.

Tonight there was a still more awful haunting. Roaming between shows, she comes across an ad that kind of catches her. There's a woman, smart but sad, walking through some woods. 'I often think what he'd be doing now if he hadn't been killed,' the woman says. And this kid, at various sizes, keeps materializing beside her, as the voice goes on: 'He'd be starting school . . . He'd be class valedictorian . . . He'd be bringing home girls.'

So, she stays, guessing it's about gun control, which is one of her subjects. At the end, the child goes fuzzy round the edges and disappears, leaving the mother alone among the trees. And the actress is just thinking she should discover which anti-handgun lobbyists put this out, and maybe send them a letter of support and a donation on the famous-name notepaper she nearly never uses, when the voice of the woman in the park says, 'I wish I'd never had an abortion,' and they put up that line about life being a beautiful choice. And she stares at the screen for a long time, until the woman, and the park, have themselves gone fuzzy round the edges and been replaced by something else. For, if it is true that you should think as the woman in the commercial does, then her own past contains an entire family of possibilities, alternative histories.

There is no more sleep that night. Sometimes – and not just because of this movie she is making – her life feels like the third act of *Our Town*, one of the plays that she read back in the fifties when she was hanging around the Actors' Studio in New York, and then again, in the seventies, when she was thinking that she maybe ought to do some acting on the stage. But that was just another nothing project.

She always, though, remembers the scene: the ghosts come back to haunt the living in the little New England town, posthumous commentators with their asides from below. She knows the feeling. There are too many ghosts. Nobody seems to be dead any more, thinks the former starlet, the ex-sex-bomb, in her sixty-seventh year.

3: Dallas, November, 1963

The car, the blue Lincoln convertible two years old, turns on to Elm Street just short of half an hour after noon. On November 22nd, 1963, downtown Dallas is warm after morning rain.

Agent Greer, at the wheel, is holding to eleven miles per hour, slowed by the President's frequent declaration of his duty to be properly viewed, and by the snaky turns drawn up by Lawson, the agent who plotted the route for the motorcade.

The President is grinning right, the First Lady smiling left. Governor Connally, in the right-side jump seat up front, waves with alternate hands, the free one caressing his stetson, his personality prop. A man slowly raises an umbrella, for some reason, this sunny lunchtime, over by the Stemmons Freeway sign.

There is no rain, but the wind is brisk, and the First Lady puts a cautionary hand to her pink hat. 'You can't say Dallas doesn't love you, Mr President,' says Nellie Connally, craning back from the left-side jump. She indicates some real wind-mill-and-grin folks over on her side of the Lincoln.

The President is smiling left, across his wife, who shares the eyeline. There is a noise. The President is looking right, towards this kind of rise of grass. The Governor is shouting: 'Oh, no, no, no!' The First Lady whips her eyes right. A second noise. Greer brakes, looks back.

Father Huber tries to wipe the idea of privilege from his mind as he forces his seventy-year-old feet, at a speed they did not think to feel again, across the Tarmac outside Parkland Hospital's entrance and up its steps. In one hand, he carries

9

a small canvas bag, containing oils and ashes, and, in the other, a rolled stole.

To give communion to America's first Catholic president would be a privilege. Or to hear his confession, not that such a man as John Fitzgerald Kennedy would have done very much in his forty-six years that required absolution. A routine penitent, surely, in all but rank. But to administer to America's first Catholic president the final sacrament, that would not, will not, be a privilege. That would be a 'Why God?' sermon for this Sunday that he would not like to write.

He has expected to be met at the entrance, and rushed to the trauma room. But no one is waiting for him on the steps. He does not know whether to take this as evidence of chaos or of hope.

There comes to him a sudden sense of this moment as one of history's hinges. Events can swing to either side from here.

The priest approaches the reception desk and gives his own name, and that of the Secret Service agent – Ready – who made the faltering phone call to Holy Trinity. Father Huber is used to the summons to the bedsides of Texans wishing to die in the shadow of Rome – Trinity is the closest RC church to Parkland – but the caller is ordinarily a nurse. So he was awake to special terrors as soon as he heard the word 'Agent'.

'Huber? Huber? Hallelujah!' says the flustered admissions clerk. 'Now *you* we are expecting . . .'

She winds her eyes up and to the right. He follows her gaze, and is surprised to see a throng of priests. There are more reversed collars in proximity than in the coffee break of a theology conference. He realizes that nearly every Catholic priest in Dallas has driven to Parkland on hearing the news.

'Father Huber?' says the clerk, replacing the phone. 'The situation's a little unclear. Would you take a seat – if you can *find* one.'

Apart from the surge of clergy, the hospital lobby is busy with journalists and television crews. The old hands have scented and commandeered all available telephones: one in the blood bank, another in the cashier's office. There is a line beside each telephone like you might see for a dime-an-item closing sale at Macy's. The priest deliberately stands near enough to overhear a reporter filing copy.

'President Kennedy arrived here at Parkland Hospital at 12.35 p.m., comma, Central Standard Time, comma, after a desperate dash down Stemmons, sugar, tommy, elephant, mother, mother, omaha, nebraska, sugar, Freeway. Stop. Para . . .'

Fearful of being unable to separate the facts from the lists of spelling-out nouns, the priest eavesdrops on a radio reporter.

'The President is currently in Trauma Room One of Parkland Hospital's Major Medical section, under the care of a team led by Dr Malcolm Perry, a thirty-four-year-old surgeon. Mrs Kennedy is with him. Details of the President's condition are sketchy, although a large number of Roman Catholic priests have been called to the hospital, which clearly begins to raise the worst fears. Vice-President Lyndon Baines Johnson is *safe* and uninjured in a secure room at the hospital, awaiting developments . . .'

Huber finds a chair, and sits, eyes closed, trying to isolate his mind for prayer. The awesome calculation in the administration of extreme unction is whether or not the soul has fled the body at the time the priest arrives. But would it be proper for a humble priest to make the sacrament conditional – inserting the words *si capax* before *ego te absolvo* – in the matter of a president? Would there, on the other hand, be biblical or theological justification for the making of exceptions?

But the voices from a ruckus of reporters nearby keep stealing his thoughts.

'And then everyone runs up that hill behind the freeway sign.'

'The knoll.'

'What the fuck's a knoll?'

'The hill. I'd call it a knoll, a grassy knoll.'

'You grad school guys! I start writing words like "knoll", I'm Alaska bureau chief by Tuesday.'

'You keep it down, you boys. This is a fucking national tragedy. You know, I covered earthquakes before now, bodies knee deep, and I ain't ever *cried* on a story before.'

The priest's shoulder is touched, and he looks up.

'Father?' a young nurse says. 'Will you come with me?'

They corkscrew through the crowd, pursued by a brutal competition of voices.

'Miss, whaddayaknow about the President?'

'Father, this is the last rites, right?'

'When will there be another bulletin?'

They pass a NO LOITERING sign, and push through a set of kicked and blistered double doors. Behind these, they meet a pair of solemn and meaty Dallas cops, who, once the priest and nurse are past, plant their parted legs, spread their arms, and make a wall against the reporters, who roar betrayal.

Huber and the nurse have reached the surgical section of the Major Medical block. For a place that is the last sight seen by a million eyes, it makes a dispiriting picture. Those who enter will only know sunlight again if they recover, for there is none here. Strip-lights flicker. The linoleum is, unsubtly, nearly the colour of blood, and the tiles on the walls are a grimy light brown. Fading signs divide death's specialisms: Oncology, Triage, Pediatrics, Gynecology, X-Ray, Trauma. A continuous red arrow runs along the wall, at approximately stretcher level, to speed the direction of lives in crisis to the trauma rooms.

A right turn and they are in a deserted corridor.

'Is he . . .? Is he . . .?' the priest at last gambles to ask.

'Dr Perry and Dr Clark are operating right now,' the nurse says. 'It's brain work. Open skull. High risk.'

'But there's a chance?'

'Who knows? You go to church Sundays?'

The last remark, that might have been taken for rudeness or Southern anti-Catholicism, he puts down to the dislocation they all share that day.

She shows him to a seat, and says she will return with news.

4:   Los Angeles,
August, 1962

Many regard Los Angeles as hell and Saturday August 4th, 1962, has certainly been infernally hot. A preview of the flames of damnation has surrounded the players in the film industry all day. The only relief from the heat has been an alternative irritation: the unusual humidity which sluices the air.

The Hollywood Bowl this evening has been as hot as a Chinatown wok. So for Jacobs and his date, his fiancée, their chilled champagne, though still an indulgence, has a definite practical aspect. But it is the relative cool of the evening – 10.30 p.m. – when their date is terminated. They are trying to pick the individual strands out of a medley of Henry Mancini movie tunes – performed in the Bowl by an orchestra under the baton of the cinema maestro himself – when a stadium page boy arrives at the box.

'Mr Jacobs,' says the boy, an unknowing walk-on in a famous story, and one of the few who will never write a book or tell the press about the events of this handful of hours. 'An urgent call for you backstage. They say it's an emergency.'

The boy leads a path through the dark with his flashlight. The house phones are near the dressing rooms, beneath the orchestra pit, through which the muffled medley can still be heard.

'Jacobs,' snaps the man into the receiver, and the boy watches him as his face pales and his eyes seize. The page is standing at the polite, beyond ears, distance, but he is skilled at listening from there.

Family, he thinks. A death in the family. It is common

13

enough here for a spectator to be called away. It is sort of a rule that no one breaks into a ball-game or a concert with good news, except a dàme in labour, and this customer is asking the death questions – 'When?', 'How?', 'How is she?' – and giving the corpse responses: 'Shit!', 'Oh, no!', 'No, really?'

The boy has read, in some gee-whizz magazine, that, within a decade, men will wear little electronic packs in their jackets, like the doctors do in hospitals, to which their messages can be telephoned. Then there will be no tap on the shoulder in the dark. The bad news will cry and tremble at their hearts.

When the man replaces the telephone, he asks to be led back to his box. The boy says he hopes it wasn't terrible news, or anything, but this doesn't trick the customer into spilling it.

Jacobs is too distracted, as he rush-stumbles back to explain things to Natalie, to be aware of an irony, a nearly divine neatness. He – a movie publicist suddenly sucked into one of the saddest scenes in his industry's history – is acting out these moments to backing music; movie backing music. What sync! What sick sync!

He crouches beside his fiancée.

'Art, what was it?'

'This is serious, Natalie. Marilyn is dead . . .'

'Marilyn . . .?'

'Yeah. I don't know how long this will take. I'll call you . . .'

And he sprints away, the dives and rises of the movie background music covering his exit.

5:   History By Inches

'Okay. Stand down the padre,' says Perry. Pulling off his white plastic gloves, the fabric snagging and twanging, he looks for a moment like a child playing with pastry.

'Doctor?' queries the senior nurse.

'Stand down the padre,' he repeats, lightening his voice a little more to rescue a sentence that seemed neat to him first time.

Second pitch, it hits. The surgeon's low-key reference to the passing of the need for the last sacrament – deliberate understatement in the heat of great events – brings to the operating room for the first time since the President was admitted an atmosphere other than fear and the collective pressure of will. In the room, there is the rasp of stored breath jettisoned, and quiet sobbing sharply stopped. A nurse and a junior surgeon make the sign of the cross.

'Oh,' adds Perry, 'and tell Earl Rose he can go eat lunch.'

This reference to the Dallas County Medical Examiner, on standby at his office to perform the autopsy on the President, punctures any remaining uncertainty in the room. There is even an uncertain chuckle from the crowd around the operating table.

Over the subsequent years, one of the nurses will tell perhaps a hundred journalists, television interviewers, and other rapt historians of these few hours: 'It was then I knew. I had thought that morning never to hear laughter again.' *Laughter Again* will also form the title of her short memoir of this November morning, published by a small Texas press in 1964, and one of five books identified in the credits of a 1965

15

NBC made-for-television movie called *The President Is Living!*, screened in the week of Kennedy's second inauguration.

In the decades after the events, there will also be much comment – principally from the group who call themselves Dealey Plaza Researchers, pedantic re-examiners of every aspect of November 22nd, 1963 – about the light mood of Dr Perry at the end of the operation. 'He was reportedly "wandering round like Bob Hope, doing gags for the nurses",' one *New York Times* best-seller-list non-fiction writer will claim, a footnote to the quotation citing an unnamed source at Parkland Hospital. This version of the surgeon's behaviour will become evidence, for some Dealey Plaza Researchers, that little was at stake in the operation, that its seriousness was exaggerated by the doctors as part of the so-called 'staged assassination plot'.

But is this fair? Perhaps Perry's jocularity is a response to his gathering sense of the stakes for which he has just played: his jokes are an attempt to lighten history's load on him. Maybe he says, 'Stand down the padre!' because he cannot bring himself to say either, 'I have saved him!' or, 'God has let him live!' He – it is possible – cannot say these things because of their effect on the life he must subsequently lead. But the Dealey Plaza Researchers reject such psychological empathy and, many times in the next thirty years, will wake the surgeon in the middle of the night, having tricked their way once more to his unlisted number, with a question, accusation, or taunt.

Now, however, it is 14.06 p.m. Central Standard Time on November 22nd, 1963, and the President – radio code-name for this month, Lancer – is being wheeled to the recovery room. The maul of medics holding bags and cords around the stretcher is a parody of the press throng that more normally haunts him. The white linen of hospital employees alternates with the dark cloth of Secret Service agents: radio code-names Domino, Duplex, Dazzle, Dusty, and Dagger. They turn alertly at every creak or breeze near the trolley with apologetic and cathartic urgency.

The President's torn and bloodstained suit – along with the soaked and battered back-brace without which he could not endure public appearances – have been bagged and carried away by Forensics. The forms and files already taking root in the hospital system identify the patient as emergency room admission No. 24740. On the forms, under the heading 'Chief Complaint', is written 'GSW'. Gunshot wound.

In a corridor a few hundred metres away, a nurse approaches Father Huber, who sits, head down, eyes shut, his little case of oils and ashes wedged by his arms to his knees as if it is a box of priceless gems.

'Father?' says the nurse, with a genuine tenderness that suggests a schooling in either Catholicism or liberal tolerance, although both factions are minorities in Dallas at this time. The nurse is not the wide-assed wise-cracker who walked him down here, and he immediately suspects that her softer touch heralds the worst.

'Yes?'

Opening his eyes, the priest looks straight into the nurse's, and, seeing wetness and redness there, feels fear at the accommodation with his faith that he must shortly make. Could he get away, in Sunday's sermon, merely with the unknowability to humans of God's will?

'There is news?'

'We won't be needing you, Father. You can go home. Shall I call a cab for you?'

His first reaction is that he has been out-ranked. The Kennedys, he guesses, have flown in a family confessor from Boston. Or, perhaps more likely, it has been revealed to the Cardinal of Dallas and Fort Worth in a vision that extreme unction for a president of the United States should be administered, for theological reasons, by a member of the hierarchy.

The priest is disliking himself for these sins of pride and covetousness when he suddenly realizes that the nurse's tears are not those he has seen from mourners, but more resemble weeping at traumatic births with unexpectedly successful outcomes, when the frightened father has summoned the priest to keep the child from limbo, but the pulse suddenly doubles and the sacrament remains in its carry-case. Moist joy. That is what he is seeing.

'He lives?' asks the priest slowly, expecting rejection with every breath.

'Yes,' says the nurse. 'Yes. Somehow, *yes*.'

And the priest looks at her with something like alarm, startled at a prayer so clearly answered. Many times afterwards he will brood on – and will discuss with at least two television documentary crews – the fact that what he said to the nurse at that moment was, more or less, allowing for translation, a version, though admittedly interrogative, of the sacred phrase 'Resurrexit'. He is living.

Perry's robes are iridescent in the erupting flash-guns as he enters Classrooms 101–2, the area in the school reserved for student nurses – across the court from Major Medical – where the press have been penned. Such light is new to his eyes, for he has never before operated on anyone about whose fate more than one family cared. His ears are quite as unaccustomed to the sound, of overlapping voices seeking dominance.

He makes four starts at the sentence before they allow him to say: 'The President is living! The President is out of danger!'

The sudden hush and rush of flashing light produced by his words is seductive. The surgeon is all at once jumped by the knowledge that his words will be preserved down time. He is now a player in a greater game, called from the dugout of who-the-fucks to join the team of is-it-hims. He feels his bulletin bulking into a speech.

'Ladies and gentlemen,' he begins. 'Whatever levers we pulled back in 1960, we were all – every man and woman in that operating room – Democrats today!'

The laughter lifts him, and he begins to think of what a politician must feel when his words work on a crowd. He remembers that the President had come to Dallas to deliver a speech. The motorcade was incidental.

'Ladies and gentlemen, early indications are extremely

positive. The president is out of mortal danger and is expected to survive with all his faculties intact.'

But this sounds too clinical, too medical, he thinks, and images come to him of politicians, of Kennedy himself, and the sort-of-poetry they speak. And so he adds: 'We felt the prayers of all America were in that operating room with us today . . .'

The pencils of the reporters quicken at this, becoming nearly kitchen whisks, and the surgeon is strangely warmed by the endorsement of his story. He is secretly speaking for posterity now; indeed, experimenting with some of the vocal effects of Henry Fonda, a favourite actor.

He pauses, momentarily thrown by the thought of history taking shorthand from him.

'Ladies and gentlemen,' he finishes, his own features and Henry Fonda's now virtually merged in his mind's-eye picture of this event, 'an inch the other way . . . and the history of America would have been very different!'

6: Shooting Will Resume

On August 6th, 1962, the Monday edition of the *Los Angeles Times* reports, in a front-page story, turned onto three other pages:

MARILYN 'SUICIDE' MYSTERY
Actress hospitalized after midnight ambulance dash — publicist cites "post-operative complications" — drugs found at house — studio fumes over "latest crisis."

LOS ANGELÈS, August 5: Marilyn Monroe, the 36-year-old film actress who has come to embody sexual allure for millions around the world, lies here today in Cedars of Lebanon Hospital, her condition "serious but stable."

Meanwhile, statement and counter-statement, gossip and contradiction, claim her as either the victim of an unavoidable medical incident or the escapee — by minutes — from becoming the latest self-imploding victim of Hollywood's broken dream factory.

The crisis began at approximately 8:30 PM Pacific Standard Time on Saturday. Milton Rudin, Miss Monroe's attorney, telephoned Mrs Eunice Murray, the actress's housekeeper, at her mock-adobe hacienda house on Fifth Helena Drive, in the Brentwood district of Los Angeles. Mr Rudin had been alerted in a telephone call from Milton Ebbins, an independent film producer and friend of Miss Monroe's, that she had seemed "disoriented and unwell" in telephone conversations with friends earlier in the evening.

According to Mr Rudin, the housekeeper told him that Miss Monroe was experiencing a recurrence of a viral condition from which she had suffered in previous months, and had retired to her bedroom to rest. Mr Rudin asked her to check on Miss Monroe's condition.

"I am conscious that this was one of those moments in history when things go one of two ways," said Mr Rudin today. "If Mrs Murray hadn't checked on her—or had told me that she had done so when she hadn't—then you guys would be writing a very different story now."

When Mrs Murray returned from the actress's bedroom, she reported, in the words of Mr Rudin, "'Oh my God! She's face down naked on the bed and I can't wake her!'" (Mrs Murray confirms this description of the circumstances of her discovery of her employer, although her recollection is that her words were: "Oh, dear! Oh, dear! I think we've got a problem here!")

Ambulance Dash

The first of many mysteries already accumulating around this latest episode in the troubled career of Miss Monroe is why it was more than two hours before an ambulance was called to the Monroe bungalow. Mrs Murray said today that she felt unable to make a decision herself, because of her employer's status, and awaited the arrival at Fifth Helena of Mr Rudin and of Ralph A. Greenson, Miss Monroe's psychoanalyst. It was their decision, on finding the actress still breathing but apparently comatose, to call an ambulance.

Mr Rudin, Mr Greenson, and Mrs Murray all refused to comment today on whether they had contacted or consulted others during the period from the telephone conversation between the housekeeper and the attorney until the actress's departure for hospital. However, a senior film industry executive, speaking on condition of anonymity, said: "They called the studio. The studio called the shots. Go figure it. You find Donald Duck face down in a pond, you tell Walt Disney before you call Cedars. Same thing here."

Reported Dead

Certainly, at approximately 10:30 PM Pacific Standard Time, Arthur S. Jacobs, Miss Monroe's personal publicist, was paged to take a telephone call during a Henry Mancini concert he was attending at the Hollywood Bowl. Mr Jacobs refused to say today who contacted him.

Evidence of the initial confusion of the situation can be found in the fact that Mr Jacobs believed from the phone call that Miss Monroe was dead. (Early wire reports, around midnight, also reported Monroe's death.)

"I drove over there, writing her obituary in my head," said Mr Jacobs. "It was only when I reached Fifth Helena and saw an ambulance leaving the house that I realized she must be alive. She had to be."

Mr Jacobs was referring to a California statute that forbids the transport of corpses in ambulances.

Neurological Examination

Miss Monroe was admitted to Cedars of Lebanon Hospital at 11:08 PM Pacific Standard Time. The clinic has refused to release details of the actress's condition beyond the statement that she is in a "serious but stable" condition, is unconscious but able to breathe without artificial assistance, and that similar cases generally offer a prognosis of eventual full recovery. Hospital sources say that no surgery has taken place and that a neurological examination of the actress produced no negative results.

The only detailed comment on the cause of the actress's hospitalization has come from Arthur S. Jacobs, her publicist. Mr Jacobs attributed his client's collapse to "post-operative complications" resulting from a cholecystectomy (removal of gall bladder and gall stones), carried out at the Manhattan Polyclinic in July 1961, and from more recent surgery for endometriosis, a condition affecting women, in which womb tissue accumulates elsewhere in the abdominal cavity.

Cedars of Lebanon Hospital refused to comment on Mr Jacobs's diagnostic speculation, referring reporters to its standing statements on the actress's condition. The hospital made an identical response to requests to comment on rumors—frequent in Hollywood today—that the actress was the victim of a drug overdose, either accidental or deliberate.

However, an anonymous hospital source suggested that prescription quantities of the narcotics Nembutal, Secanol, morphine, and chloral hydrate were discovered in the actress's bedroom. And a Hollywood performer, who has recently worked with Miss Monroe, said, speaking on condition of anonymity: "A doctor told me that, on her latest movie, she was taking methamphetamines, a few vitamins, glucose to give an immediate lift, and a small amount of Librium to smooth out the effects of the uppers."

Speculation about the actress's susceptibility to an accidental overdose of drugs will center on her history of difficulties in sleeping. Miss Monroe, who has referred in several interviews to life-long problems with insomnia, has military-style blackout drapes on the windows of her Brentwood bedroom. According to friends and associates, she has for several years used chloral hydrate, a mild sleeping medication. This was among the substances, according to the anonymous hospital source, discovered in the actress's bedroom.

Powerful New Lover

Theories that the actress may have been attempting to end her own life through a deliberate overdose of prescribed medication gain strength from frequent rumor on the 20th Century Fox lot that Miss Monroe had recently been involved in an unhappy romantic relationship.

Another actress who has recently worked with Miss Monroe said, again speaking on condition of anonymity: "She had been in love again. But he was a married man—and it had gone badly wrong." The actress refused to identify the man in question but said: "Look at her husbands—the top sports star, the top intellectual. This new guy was in the same league—but he didn't play sports and he didn't write plays . . ."

Miss Monroe's first marriage was to James Dougherty, an aircraft mechanic, in 1942, when she was only 16 and known under the family name of Norma Jean Mortenson. However, her most celebrated weddings were to the baseball star Joe Di Maggio, and to the playwright Arthur Miller. The marriages ended in 1954 and 1959 respectively. Hollywood gossip is that—after these relationships with heroes of the athletic and literary world—the film star had become infatuated with a political celebrity. Recently, a New York gossip columnist, Dorothy Kilgallen, wrote in the *New York Journal American* that Marilyn Monroe was "proving vastly alluring to a handsome gentleman who has a bigger name than Joe Di Maggio in his heyday . . ."

Miss Monroe is not, however, known for moving in political circles. Perhaps her closest involvement with this world came in May of this year, when she sang "Happy Birthday!", in a famously daring dress, at a birthday gala for President John F. Kennedy in Madison Square Garden, New York.

Shooting Will Resume

Hospital sources stress that there is no reason why Miss Monroe should not make a full recovery, barring unforeseen medical complications. However, if her hospitalization should prove to have been the result of mental rather than physical distress, the position might be more complicated.

The professional career of the star is already in doubt. Persistent Hollywood rumors suggest that Miss Monroe's latest movie project—a 20th Century Fox comedy called *Something's Gotta Give*—will be cancelled by the studio, and the star's contract ended, after what one Fox insider described as "a polite interval." The source added: "Once they're sure she'll live, they'll drop her. That's the idea."

However, Arthur S. Jacobs insisted today: "Shooting will resume as soon as Miss Monroe is medically cleared to return to work. There is no question mark hanging over this project at all. If anything is hanging over it, then it is a parenthesis . . ."

Publicists for 20th Century Fox declined to comment on the status of the project, saying that to do so would be "unseemly in these circumstances."

Absences From Set

Something's Gotta Give—a remake of the 1939 RKO screwball comedy *My Favorite Wife*—has already been an epically troubled enterprise. The studio's exasperation at Miss Monroe's alleged tardiness, absences from set, frequent illnesses, and reported uncertain demeanor before the cameras, led to the cancellation of the film in early June.

Those on Miss Monroe's side say that the star, who has a history of respiratory ailments, was absent from the set because of a virus which triggered inflammation of the sinuses, and, on some days, raised the actress's temperature to above 100 degrees. Studio executives, though, suspected a "sick-out": a familiar Hollywood star-bargaining technique in which absence from set on medical grounds is used to renegotiate terms.

Last month, however, Miss Monroe was reinstated and *Something's Gotta Give* resumed production. The star's new contract with Fox also covered other work, including *The Jean Harlow Story*, a biopic based on the life of the early movie star Jean Harlow, who died young 25 years ago. Miss Monroe was to play the title role. At the same time, 20th Century Fox underwent substantial restructuring, with Daryl F. Zanuck replacing Milton S. Gould, the former Wall Street lawyer, as company president.

Something's Gotta Give

The strong indications today are that *Something's Gotta Give*, and Miss Monroe's relationship with Fox, cannot survive the latest interruption to a previously troubled project under the auspices of a company already stretched by the substantial overspend on the Joseph L. Mankiewicz epic *Cleopatra*, currently filming in Italy, starring Elizabeth Taylor and Richard Burton.

As Marilyn Monroe, aged 36, lies in Cedars of Lebanon today, and controversy gathers about the forces that brought her there, many in Hollywood are already wondering whether the title of her most recent movie might not provide an epitaph to, if not her whole career, then to this section of it—Something's Gotta Give.

7: I Want To Be An Airport!

As they wait for clearance to leave the house at Hyannis, for the drive to Boston airport, Jack notices that one of the detail of agents is a big guy he has not seen before, who bears a couple of scabby islands on his neck above a squeezed-on collar. A dangerous shaver; clumsy. He wonders if this might be the one who stumbled coming in and broke his sleep the night before.

'Sir, I hope I didn't wake you last night,' the guy says. 'Bit of an elephant's polka coming in. The guys are getting together for a foot transplant for me, they always say.'

'I didn't hear anything,' Jack says. 'You know, campaigning once, in '64, a schoolkid says, in one of these tenth-grade Q and As, "Do you have this dread of being woken up and told a nuclear war has started?" I said, "Most nights, it would take a nuclear war to wake me!"'

He has told this joke before, on *Oprah* and *Charlie Rose* and other talk shows with which he has broken his absences from the collective memory. On television, he employs the story to see off the inevitable question about whether he is troubled by bad memories, but the elaborate fiction gets a big laugh from the agents when repeated here.

He knows that this is the word on him among the Secret Service, comparing notes on postings. JFK – good talk and jokes, not bad travel, neat sailing at Hyannis, things to turn a blind eye to, of course, though less now that he's older.

One of the agents hears in his ear that they are cleared to leave, and confirms receipt to his sleeve. The limousine is drawn up to the rear of the modest sea-view clapboard house in Hyannis, a mile from the official Kennedy compound, which he bought in the eighties as an irregular refuge from the magazine photography and day-trip curiosity that the Kennedy home, the old 'Summer White House', attracts.

The main task of his Secret Service detail is to deny him daylight: to block all possible angles from one of the thousands of haze-brains in America keen to complete Lee Harvey Oswald's cock-eyed assignment, and keener than ever as November 22nd approaches each year, particularly the landmark anniversaries. Assassins are apparently fanatical about calendars. It is the perception of such maniacal sense of order that prompts most of the fears on Jack's behalf.

So he is scarcely given time to sniff the sharp November air before he is in the limousine, its side walls as fat as a bank vault, its windows tinted to turn away eyes and thickened to prevent more malevolent entry. Already in one of the front seats is Boomer.

Aged twenty-four, with a fussily clipped black beard which his face is far too young to make a proper case for, Boomer is a native of Pennsylvania, his curious name presumably Americanized by his forebears from one of those crunchy Dutch surnames full of crossed and squashed vowels. Boomer – a graduate of the Edward M. Kennedy School of Government at Harvard – is in his second year on Jack's staff.

Boomer takes the title of Chief of Staff, partly for reasons of the former president's self-esteem, partly for the purposes of his own future résumés. These young men, with senatorial or diplomatic futures sketched out for themselves, pass through every few years. Jack is careful about the recruitment, because, with the class stars from the politics courses drawn to the headline politicians of the day, he tends to attract what he calls the plane-crash applicants, the gawping and morbid and cruel. And any candidate Jack accepts must then be checked by the Secret Service, nervous of an inventive assassin taking the payroll route. But Boomer, everyone agreed, seemed to have a more or less normal balance between ambition, curiosity, and duty.

Leaning over from the front seat of the limo, Boomer hands Jack a folder.

'Good morning, Mr President. Today's schedule . . .'

'Good morning, David. Thank you . . .'

As they take Route 6 for Boston, Jack flicks back the cover, and finds the usual heavy sheets of A4 paper. His engagements for the next two days are laid out, as always, in Boomer's self- and employer-boosting parody of White House style.

Trip of Former President Kennedy – New York
15/16 November 1993

Monday 15th November

0700 EST – Leave Hyannis Port. Car. Accompanying staff: Mr D. Boomer. Agents Moose and Moped.

0900 – Arrive Boston Logan International Airport. Taken to private holding room.

0945 – Delta Flight 436 Boston Logan to Idlewild International Airport, New York. First class cabin fully reserved. Late boarding facilities.

1100 – Arrive Idlewild International Airport, New York. Priority deplaning. Private exit from airport.

1115 – Depart Idlewild for Plaza Hotel, New York.

1200 – Arrive Plaza Hotel. Official greet by chairperson and members of American Society of Lower Back Pain Sufferers. (ASLBPS.)

1210 – Drinks, informal circulation – Roosevelt Room.

1245 – Luncheon, Grand Dining Room.

1345 – Address to American Society of Lower Back Pain Sufferers.

1415 – Leave Plaza Hotel.

1430 – Arrive Radio City. Official greet by representatives of JFK Children of Courage Awards committee. Brief remarks.

1445 – Present JFK Children of Courage Awards 1993. Address.

1545 – Leave Radio City for Carlyle Hotel. Reservations Presidential Suite.

1600 on – Downtime. Private meetings.

0700 – Leave Carlyle Hotel.

0715 – Arrive NBC Studios, Rockefeller Plaza. Proceed
private holding room.

0745 – Live Interview NBC *Today* show. Interviewer:
Bryant Gumbel.

0830 – Leave NBC Studios for Idlewild International
Airport, New York.

And so on. Jack has a number of reactions to these plans.
The first is that nearly half an hour of informal circulation at
the lumbar pain lunch will be hard on his back. Indeed, how
bizarre, for this must surely be the case for a majority of those
invited. How strange, the more he thinks about it, that the
American Society of Lower Back Pain Sufferers should coun-
tenance vertical conviviality at its events. Perhaps he will
mention this in his address.

But he also feels relief that his two public events take
place indoors. This means that those he meets will almost
certainly be real people. At the few outdoor walkabouts he
has been permitted in recent years, every other hand he shook
led upwards to a crew-cut or suspiciously big shoulders, and
he guessed that these were agents playing spectators, because
of the paranoia of his protectors about crowds.

And, as today's events are held at sealed and vetted
premises, there is little risk of protest. Even now, twenty-five
years after Vietnam, Jack knows to fear, at public appearances,
the lost eyes and wasted faces of the war veterans, dragged
from his eyeline by the cops, but still able to reach his ears
with the cry: 'Hey, hey, JFK, how many kids did you kill
today?' This was the snarled chant that made him virtually a
prisoner in the White House in 1968.

Jack has little wish to play in his head the newsreel of his
second term, and he is happy to take the distraction Boomer
offers him, handing across the seat-back a second file.

'Mr President, if you'd like to look over the texts for this
afternoon . . .'

'David, I think I will. Be sure I get straight where the back stops and the ass begins . . .'

This remark wins a laugh from Boomer, and from agents Moose and Moped (the agents' radio code-names are picked from the dictionary in clumps, rotating through the months from A to Z). Jack feels inspired to prolong the moment.

'Now there's a line for the first speech,' he says. 'The Back Stops Here . . .'

There are three intersecting yelps of laughter.

'Who needs Sorenson?' says Boomer, referring to Jack's old White House speechwriter, who they still infrequently employ for occasions more substantive than today's.

But Jack inhales few pheromones from their response. It is impossible to be sure, as a famous man among employees, whether you are being humorous or being humoured.

At Boston Logan, they are steered so quickly through the building to the private holding room that Jack sees only the briefest flashes of terminal activity. A mother is loudly and grumpily reconstructing her family from elements that have strayed further than ordered from the gates. Violently coloured posters and T-shirts hang in gift stores. He catches sight of the young Marilyn Monroe heat-sealed on one piece of cloth.

The private holding room, in a quiet corner of the airport, has no VIP sign on the door, and Jack suddenly suspects that it is one of the grieving suites where relatives are sequestered after a disaster, well away from flying business.

Beside the gleaming moon rockets of hot coffee, regular and decaffeinated, on the table, the airline management have placed bottles of Irish spring water: a corporate response to the Kennedy name.

Sipping a glass, more from politeness than dryness, Jack watches CNN. Bosnia, gays in the military, gross domestic product up 2.8% in the third quarter, a Michigan doctor assisting the suicides of the terminally ill, two ten-year-olds on trial in England for the murder of a baby boy. And then: 'Today, the President . . .'

Boomer, Moose, and Moped stiffen. With former presidents, subsequent administrations are generally a no-fly zone, but their man has shown himself to be especially troubled by the present incumbent.

And, true to cue, he growls: 'I do not believe *that man* is in the White House . . .'

Jack is looking bullets at the grinning features, now being transmitted by CNN, of the winner of the 1992 election. The agents nod sympathetically, although one of them voted keenly for that candidate.

Boomer says: 'Sir, for someone like you to feel anger at someone like him is like using a rifle . . . to . . . to . . . kill a fly . . .'

Jack notices the mid-sentence hesitation, which is what generally happens when someone accidentally uses a weaponry metaphor in his presence.

'Sometimes you wonder what is supposed to be so great about democracy,' says Jack, fixing with his eyes the videotape gaze of the man the American public chose in 1992.

They board the plane, for security reasons, last, just before the suctioned walkway is shucked off. The first class cabin has been closed off from coach class scrutiny with dark blue drapes.

'Welcome aboard Flight 436,' crackles the captain. 'We know that air consumers have a range of flying options, and we are glad to be your company of choice today. Our flying time this morning will be sixty-five minutes into New York's Idlewild Airport . . .'

Jack remembers reading in the *New York Times* of gubernatorial plans to replace Idlewild – the long-used title for the airport, stripped from the village first removed by the runways – with the name of some celebrated American. There is talk of a statewide referendum. Idlewild is America's main aviation terminus, and a famous international destination, so they will be looking for someone bigger than old Mayor La Guardia, who got his baptismals above the domestic airport over in Queens. The early betting is on Elvis Presley, and the Republicans will get behind Ronald Reagan, but it is expected that Jack's dead brothers – Bobby and Ted – will attract some Catholic and Democrat support.

As they taxi at Boston Logan – a namecheck for an otherwise neglected hero of the Second World War – Jack reflects on this eccentric modern custom. This is how political evolution works. First, you are a man. Then, if you are lucky, you are a statesman. Finally, if you are really blessed, you are an airport. Dust to dust; but, for some, ashes to asphalt. When they die, they become a terminal.

Charles de Gaulle is immortalized in glass and concrete at Paris, remembered on a billion forward baggage tags as CDG. A mere mayor – Tom Bradley – is on the lips of a million pilots landing at Los Angeles. Old Mayor La Guardia, nominally rewarded for the New York domestic airport he built, is the first name learned by the city's immigrant cab drivers. None of the London hubs has been baptized. Is that because the English distrust the architectural cult of personalities? (Except, of course, for architects.) But Simón Bolívar, an epic traveller forced all his life to rely on horses, presides over jet flights right across South America. And who the fuck was Kingsford-Smith to merit Sydney's shining terminal as his epitaph?

It is obviously a lottery but why, as a two-term president, if one of inconstant reputation, should he not buy a ticket?

Flying towards New York's Idlewild, in November 1993, former President John F. Kennedy thinks, with a petulance only partially ironic: *I want to be an airport!*

8: Hasn't She Heard The Word Diet?

The young woman stands above the sidewalk grating on a New York street, the upwards eruption of hot air sculpting her skirt into a parachute and making every male in the audience wish to pull the rip-cord.

This image is held for a few seconds – the rush of the wind from the subway, the hello-to-pneumonia ruching of the skirt, the girl's smirk of unconcern – before a baby-doll voiceover says: 'Aphrodite – for twenty-four-hour protection – and no seven-hour itch!'

Perhaps film is too flimsy an art to be open to the possibility of blasphemy – and *The Seven Year Itch* was, after all, a comedy – but Jean felt a cold jolt the first time she realized that one of her most famous scenes had become an advertisement for sanitary wear, and she feels no easier seeing the celluloid heresy repeated; sleepless, again, on her bed in front of the television.

The girl in the advertisement is, Jean must concede, a reasonable version of her younger self. But that is no less unsettling. The curse of the celluloid sex symbol in later years is to suffer the chrysalis process in reverse. The dull slug is doomed to see the butterfly for ever pinned and sealed in cable re-runs and retrospective seasons.

Two weeks before, spotting a mistake in the pagination of an issue of the weekly magazine *America Now*, Jean guessed that a piece had been torn out, either by her housekeeper on her own initiative or, more likely, on the orders of Jean's analyst or press agent. She assumed it was an attempt to protect her from something offensive.

At the book store on La Cienega – in her usual rich nobody disguise of plate-sized tinted eyeglasses, bandanna, and fake fur coat – she found the magazine and flicked to the missing numeral. It was, as she had half expected, a bitch page written by one of the Hollywood gossip columnists. This one, whose column was called 'Studio Soup', began each catty paragraph with the trademark phrase: 'Don't tell anyone but . . .'

Those regularly written about eventually possess a radar that can pick their name from a page of prose blindfold in a darkened room. Jean has scarcely opened the magazine when she sees hers in the third item of 'Studio Soup':

WEIGHTY PROBLEMS AT FOX

"*Don't tell anyone but* . . . Marilyn Monroe is causing a few headaches to Fox executives who saw, at a private Burbank screening Friday, costume and lighting tests for MM's comeback movie *She's Back!*

It's La Monroe's first stint in front of the Fox cameras for three decades. The actress and the studio were, of course, involved in nearly twenty years of bitter litigation over *Something's Gotta Give!*, the movie abandoned due to MM's attempted drug overdose during shooting in 1962. And it's Marilyn's first film for anyone since the critical derision and empty theaters that greeted her disastrous 'serious movie' *The K Brothers* in 1982. ('The film I never mention,' as she refers to it.) Since then, she's been calling herself 'Jean' on her bankbook again and telling friends she was through with the movies.

So hopes were riding high for *She's Back!* It's a sort of Hollywood *Ghost*, with MM as a dead celluloid legend acting, in spectral form, as unofficial adviser to a modern movie biopic of her life.

What's worrying Fox chiefs is that Marilyn wasn't looking too ethereal on the test footage. In fact, as he watched the 66-year-old star, an alarmed studio flack was heard to remark: 'Hasn't she heard the word diet!'

My little whisperer says: 'Ok, she's off drugs, and that's cool. But, boy, has she gone onto food. Fox is gonna be glad of wide-screen cinema on this one!'

Word is that the joke of choice on the Fox lot right now is that Ms Monroe's next charitable venture – after her popular Marilyn Monroe Clinic For Repeat Drug Abusers in Colorado Springs – will be the Marilyn Monroe Clinic For Repeat Eaters . . . *But don't tell anyone I said that!*"

An assistant asked her snappily if she planned to buy that magazine. She did, reassured that the disguise survived the transaction.

She did not, to her slight surprise, feel harmed by the article. Perhaps it was because she had been allowed the defensive preparation of knowing that the coverage must be destructive, or it would not have been removed. But it was also the case that an actress whose agent had rebuffed thirty-five approaches in recent years to appear in a remake of *Sunset Boulevard* became progressively less vulnerable to taunts of decay.

Now, lying in her bedroom on Fifth Helena – a house she has never felt able to let go – Jean tries to consider her body as objectively as possible, first reversing the instinctive attempt of her stomach muscles to prettify the scene.

It is true that, because of her long exile from the industry, she did not at first remember the tendency of the camera to fatten those it films, so that she was definitely puffy in profile in the early tests. But she is twelve pounds lighter now.

She briefly considers litigation against the magazine, but the twenty years of Fox v. Monroe, over *Something's Gotta Give!*, for more or less a stalemate outcome (an apology for some things said and written about her, but no compensation), have made her leery of that route. And how, anyway, could she establish defamation here? Scales and tape measure in the court room?

In fact, what pained her most about the article – the magazine she bought on La Cienega lies open on the night table beneath the scripts – was not the reference to her weight, but the implied mockery of her recovery from drugs. Clean now for fifteen years, she is proud, although the gossip writers sneer at 'Saint Marilyn', of her campaign against substance abuse; happy to lend her name and backing to the Marilyn Monroe Clinic For Repeat Drug Abuse in Colorado Springs, with fund-raising for others at Seattle and Yaddo well advanced.

Jean hopes, in this connection, that her number three least favourite TV commercial of all time does not turn up during tonight's insomnia watch.

Number one, from which she has already flinched this evening, is the *Seven Year Itch* parody for sanitary napkins. Number two – which turned up a few moments ago, but from which she speedily switched channels – is the pro-life pitch, which she first thought sold gun control, in which the aborted foetus grows a ghost life as his mother strolls the woods. Number three, which she thankfully hasn't seen for several hours, is the coffee commercial in which a central casting American Family – mom, pop, junior – rises stretching from bed and cot in shafts of sunlight, while a voice sings: 'The best part of waking up is Fulger's in your cup!'

This, Jean thinks, is silly nonsense. The best part of waking up is waking up. Take a vote of those who don't.

As a precaution, she abandons the commercial break on the channel she is watching, and keys the number for CNN. The doctor assisting suicides in Michigan is still the top story, followed by the kids in Liverpool, England, accused of murdering a baby boy. Next up is footage of the President.

She flinches, ambushed by bad memories. Within a month of his inauguration in January 1993, he had invited her to a White House ball. She was seated next to an Israeli diplomat, whom she surprised with her knowledge of the. Gaza Strip, gleaned on one of her visits as a UN Goodwill Ambassador, the other element in the papers' 'Saint Marilyn' gibe.

At 1 a.m., the President was pressing sweatily at the door of the Lincoln Bedroom, suggesting sex. She told him he was married and she was old.

36

'D'you believe that?' the President said. 'I finally get to be president, and Marilyn Monroe's turned frigid . . .'

'Celibate,' she corrected him.

'Back home, celibate's just a fancy word for frigid,' the President slurred at the firmly closing door.

CNN, too, now brings down the shutters on the President, and Jean next sees pictures of Jack Kennedy handing out some prizes to sick kids. The teeth and hair and grin of legend are all holding down their roots in his septuagenarian face. Only when he walks across the stage to the lectern to begin his address – at which point CNN opts out for a bigger story – does his age truly show, in his freeze-frame pace and question-mark frame. But this, she suspects, has as much to do with Dallas and Addison's disease as his accumulated decades.

Oh, Jack, she thinks. *Black Jack. Did we ever think to see ourselves as we are now?*

It is 3.15 a.m. Jean tunes the television to mute – a small red line awaiting resurrection as a number – and reaches for her script. She flicks the rainbow pages of the brainstorm plot and dialogue revision. Now she is learning brown. You know you are working on a troubled project when they get to the colour of shit before shooting starts.

The conceit of *She's Back!* is that the ghostly star returned to earth – played by Marilyn Monroe – is being portrayed, in the biopic-within-the-film, by a hot new young actress, something of a lookalike for herself in early years. After some elementary tension, the older actress befriends the younger one, and instructs the rookie looker on how to avoid the career and life mistakes made by the dead legend. These homilies are generally to do with men. The director says he is a feminist, although this did not stop him truffling for a fuck from Jean's hot new young co-star.

Jean is trying to memorize a speech from a later sequence in which her character gets to play herself aged from forties to sixties in the biopic, passing herself off to the crew as the younger actress in layered make-up. The process by which this is possible is explained neither technologically nor theologically. The director says it is a metaphor. She has wondered aloud to him if ghosts would show up on celluloid – in another film she saw, they didn't – but he told her to put her Stanislavski down the john. And, more cruelly, referring to her old Method Acting mentor at the Actors' Studio: 'Lee Strasberg is dead.'

There is excitement at the studio about the fit between the scenario and Marilyn Monroe's own return to the screen. Indeed, one of the nearly two hundred titles the project seems to have gone through so far was *The Comeback*, until this resulted in copyright problems with the makers of an obscure British 1970s horror film.

The casting is also thematic. The hot new co-star actress looks not unlike the young Marilyn Monroe, while Jean fairly unavoidably resembles the older Marilyn Monroe.

When the starlet walked in for the lighting tests, the director turned to Jean and said: 'Marilyn, it's spooky. She's you when young!'

The slug and the butterfly, back to front.

9: The Day of the Skunk

In New York this afternoon, Meredith – known to the families and friends of his victims as 'the English assassin' – will find out how much he is to be paid for taking out his latest target.

On the morning flight from London Heathrow to New York Idlewild in early November 1993, he wonders if he is the only passenger who makes a particular analogy with the Traveller Refresher Kit just handed out in the business class cabin.

Making shapes with her mouth like a blow job waiting to happen, the stewardess gives each mid-price flyer a hessian bag, tied with cord, in the company colours. Inside are: a set of bottles containing aromatic lotions, supposedly phylacteries against jet-lag, a pair of furry over-socks, and a shallow oblong box in liveried plastic.

Clicking it open, he finds an inlaid tray of foam rubber, from which shapes are cut to hold a set of plastic implements. A cylindrical shaft with a screw-top can be attached to either a toothbrush head or a razor blade, each with ratcheted extensions, so that the shaft serves as a double-purpose handle. Pleased by the ingenuity of this, although doubtful of the influence of such touches on commercial loyalty, he suddenly realizes its inspiration. The Traveller Refresher Kit, in an industry obsessed with safety, is based on a hideaway rifle, an assassin's lethal briefcase.

Rocking his head against the frilled and logo-ed anti-macassar, he laughs aloud – a sound as pleasant, his many enemies have said, as a car alarm at 3 a.m. – at the irony of the connection.

'Everything all right, Mr Chichester?' asks the stewardess,

hurrying over, taking his bray of amusement for a howl of pain: a legitimate confusion, as has been said.

'Fine,' Meredith says. Mr Chichester is his alibi on this particular passenger manifest. Someone in his business – and who has already survived an assassination attempt – would be silly to be me-me-me in public. Sometimes, though, he imagines a plane crash – he is a gold member of seven frequent flyer schemes, under four different names, allowing discounts and upgrades on major routes across every continent – and all those who detest him, and the one or two who feel a little warmer, not knowing when the list is printed that he is dead.

The in-flight movie is one of those soppy comedies in which somebody comes back from the dead. He has already not watched it on an earlier flight this month, so he reads a book instead: one of many published about his latest target.

About thirty minutes before they begin the descent into Idlewild, he squeezes into the bulkhead rest room, removes the miniature rifle kit, hovers between the telescopic toothbrush and the foldaway razor, but decides to target his mouth rather than his face. In the foam rubber cutaway where you would expect the bullets to be, there is a sampler tube of a new improved whitener toothpaste. *Don't eat dirt*, he thinks.

In the foggy acoustics of the aircraft bathroom, he laughs again.

The formal closing of the contract takes place four hours later in a steamy, reeky trattoria on 40th and 8th.

'We have an account here,' explains his contact. 'A lot of the guys like Italian cooking.'

He wonders if the firm really does bring all its top guns here, or if a put-down is intended. He is no longer calling himself Chichester. He is here as Peter Meredith, his professional name, or one of them.

The contact is a big man, half his fleshy face immobile from some kind of seizure or disease, so that every facial gesture – smile or frown – is divided, backing on to a contradiction of itself, like one of those split-screen ads where

40

they wash the hair in the goodie and the baddie shampoo, and you end up with one half dull and one half fluffy.

Christ, thinks Meredith, he even *looks* like a gangster.

The contact is called, or calls himself, Fraternelli. Meredith guesses this is probably Italian for brotherly love, or something like it, but Fraternelli looks as if he could handle himself in a fight, or could have done before the business with the face.

At the beginning, Meredith was surprised to see Fraternelli at all, given that he had seemed strictly subsidiary at the preliminary meetings.

'Ah,' says Meredith, when Fraternelli, as it turned out to be, picks him out at the bar. 'Last time it was . . .'

'And, next time, maybe it's someone else,' says Fraternelli. 'So don't go sleeping with my picture under your pillow either. This is a cut-throat business. You don't ever begin a sentence with the word *tomorrow* . . .'

Fraternelli spoke of his insecurity of tenure with a Novocaine casualness Meredith could have done without on the edge of agreeing a deal with him.

But, over the *zabaglione*, the terms of the contract are set out, and are undeniably attractive financially. There is also the simple question of adrenalin. It is a long time since Meredith's last hit.

'You won't be the first to try,' admits Fraternelli. 'And some people say – we are aware of this – some people say: he is wounded already. Why finish him off? Well, because we want him finished off. We're looking for a direct hit. There have already been too many misses. As it is who it is – as it's Kennedy – we felt the sum of . . .'

He discloses the chosen zeroes. Meredith cannot hold back the charmless laugh which is the single thing for which he is known under each of his aliases.

'Don't miss,' says Fraternelli as they part.

Afterwards, Meredith walks across to Fifth, and up to Barnes & Noble, where he anxiously scans the bookshelves for any new stuff on Kennedy. It is a point of principle with him that one of the important distinctions between a quality operator like himself and the freelances, the lone-nut guys as he likes to call them, is that Meredith, or whatever name he is using, likes to know *everything* about a target. Sometimes, at airports, he worries about a security check exposing a hold-all packed with volumes on one man. To tell them that he was a biographer would probably not halt their suspicions.

On Barnes & Noble's 'New Non-Fiction' table, he can find nothing fresh about his intended victim, but he buys a tourist guide to Boston. Meredith enjoys New York: its long perspectives, the wide clean slices of brightness at the end of its big strict streets and avenues. But his quarry is in Boston.

10:   The Minus Game

Duke says 'Hiya!' when they meet by the water cooler, as they usually do, just before they go on duty, which may mean that he is playing things straight today. The time when he said 'Hello,' in the English way, as soon as they caught up with each other in the morning, Ford was on alert at once.

They have been in the car less than five minutes – chasing up a radio call for units to an incident at Tremont and West by the Common – and Ford already feels hungry. He fumbles for the packet – hoping that Duke, who is driving, will be too distracted by traffic to see – and hoists a miniature pretzel into his mouth, covering the action with a cough, like a high-security prisoner trying to take the cyanide pill.

'Gerry,' says Duke, 'I hope that's medication, not food.'

'Shit, Duke,' growls Ford, 'my guts could get a recording contract, the way they're singing at me already. My breakfast was so small, I had to look twice . . .'

Ford is currently under threat from a Boston Police Department ruling that the larger cops must reduce to a maximum waist measurement of 36 by the end of the year. Over his fifteen years of service, Ford has expanded to a whole size up from that. Already, as part of the initiative, each officer going on duty has to walk through a special door at the station, which has a plastic inner frame cut to the legitimate width, with a half-moon sliced from the right-hand side for the bulge of a holster and gun.

At the moment, Ford is going through sideways but, after the cut-off, or cut-down, date, this will be a disciplinary matter. The union has challenged the ruling on numerous grounds, including racism – lawyers argued that wideness was in the Irish genes of many of the force – but now the last two remaining recourses are Supreme Court or slim.

Ford has switched to diabetic pretzels, but they just don't give him the same kick, and he watches public television at nights because that way he misses the million little films on food by which the network shows all pay their way.

'You want a pretzel, Duke?' asks Ford, looking to spread the sin, though Duke must at the most be thirty-four around. But Duke is Greek-American. They're served in smaller portions than the Micks. The union attorneys have a point.

'Negative,' Duke replies, and Ford is suddenly tense.

Negative. Has he been watching too many cop shows on TV?

The controller stands them down from Tremont and West. The incident is over, happily or not. Duke kills the light and siren, and starts heading back west towards their regular patrol.

'What I'd give to have your waist,' Ford sighs.

'A, I'm . . . at duty, and, B, Kitty do . . . er hates me seeing boys . . .'

That *at* is the clue, plus the pauses Duke is taking, checking each breath before it burns. And, if you think about it, he should have said *one* and *two* and *doesn't like* there.

'O! O! O! O! O! O! O!' Ford shouts.

'You have to have an orgasm, Gerry, not on duty please.'

'I mean, I get it, Duke. You dropped the letter O.'

'Negative? No, I *don't think so*.' But he over-enunciates the O sounds there deliberately, and grins, and says: 'You're right. What can I say? Maybe I should say: *Yo!*'

Ford celebrates with another diabetic pretzel. Ever since they got to share a car – Officer Michael 'Duke' Dukakis and Officer 'Gerry' Ford – his partner has played this crazy game. The Minus Game, Duke calls it. The rule is that you remove one thing – maybe as small as a letter, perhaps as large as a major breakthrough invention of the century – from daily life. If Duke is playing when they are on duty, then Ford has to guess what has gone.

One time, for example, Duke was sick with the 'flu: one of those nearly nuclear viruses that seems to drift in from the

Communist world. The doctor writes him in for four days off. He is due back on a Tuesday. On the Monday, Ford calls him at home.

'Duke? Y'okay now?'

'I'm through it. Yes. I'm good.'

'See ya tomorrow then.'

'These days. These days.'

Ford doesn't get that but, when he asks Duke what he means, he just repeats it: 'These days . . . These days . . .'

On the Tuesday, Duke doesn't show for the shift. Ford calls and the machine is on. There's a message: a new announcement he hasn't heard before. Instead of the usual name and maybe a joke, or even a little piece of Greek music, you just get Duke's voice saying: 'I'm not here . . .'

It's past noon, and Ford is out on patrol with a replacement from the pool, when he guesses. Towards the end of the shift, Ford already has a quarter warming in his hand beside the wheel and, as soon as he can, he runs as fast as his bulk allows to a pay phone. The machine is still on, but he waits for the bleep and shouts: 'Penicillin! Fucking penicillin!'

There is a scrape as the receiver is raised, and Duke hollers: 'Ya got it!'

The kind of mind Duke seems to have is not perhaps an obvious one for a cop, and the force is never quite sure how to take him. He could have lost his job over the penicillin business, but the doc finds Duke interesting – perhaps, Ford sometimes jokes, as a future psychiatric study – and wrote a memo about a mix-up over just how many sick days he was due.

Ford himself – the second or third time the minus game was played on him – said: 'Duke, I don't want to sound down on cops. Hell, I *am* one. But do you ever think you're too smart for this gig?'

'People say this,' Duke admits. 'You shoulda gone to college, they say. Law school. Listen, Mama says I could have run for president. But mamas say that. You could waste your life with maybes . . .'

This is as close as they allow themselves to come to discussing their other selves. Duke is putting himself through night classes, learning law, a timeslip of the ambition his family had for him long ago. Ford, off-duty, stares at the smeared screen of a second-hand WP, writing a novel about a Boston priest-stroke-gumshoe, Father 'Beads' O'Reilly, so called because he fiddles through the rosary during deductions. He has reached page 168: the body in the confessional box. Ford read a piece in the *Boston Herald* about a guy called Wambaugh, a cop turned bestselling novelist, and he thinks, why not.

So officers Dukakis and Ford are men who have not lost sight of other possibilities. They live quite different lives at night.

'Hey, Gerry, you see the shift sheet?' asks Dukakis on this November day. 'All leave cancelled on the 22nd.'

'No shit? The Prez is coming?'

'Sanders? In Boston? We're the East Coast élite. You didn't hear his speeches? No, this is the Kennedy thing. At Holy Cross. Big mass for all the family dead. And thanksgiving for Jack's survival. Thirtieth anniversary of Dallas.'

'Thanksgiving?' grunts Ford, who was all over Newton Sanders when he came through to do a photo-opportunity with the Boston cops in '92, and was a Reagan Democrat before that. 'Anyway, who are we protecting? Kennedy's kind of a nobody now, isn't he?'

'You think? JFK. Thirty years after Dallas. Half the nuts in America will be trying to, well, close the loop . . .'

As the shift goes on, Ford looks more and more worn and pasty, although it is a quiet morning.

'Hungry?' Duke wonders.

'Does Old Ma Kennedy have a black dress?' Ford growls.

11: The State of the Union

It is another bad morning for the White House Chief of Staff. The President is again threatening to go public with his belief in reincarnation.

In the margins of the draft text for his first State of the Union address, the President has added, in his thick and undisciplined script, in the margins of the standard paragraph about how his policies tie up with the kind of guy he is, the words: 'I stand before you as myself, this self – but I was someone else before and I will be someone else again.'

'I'm not entirely sure that works,' says the Chief of Staff in a tone that is the equivalent in speech of a hand being placed in a flame, when they reach that passage in the 8 a.m. meeting. 'Union Address Draft – President, Boyd, Woodall', it says on the embossed daily schedule.

The Chief of Staff is Boyd. He has just passed his thirtieth birthday, a former political correspondent in the President's home state, unexpectedly summoned to the White House because the boss appreciated the tone of his campaign profiles, and distrusted those who had held such posts before. He has a fast-burner personality, his eyes enclosed by the charcoaled doughnuts of exhaustion, his office late-night pizza bill already the subject of jokes in the *Washington Post*.

'Works?' says the President, after looking at him for a long time.

'Er, grammatically,' adds Boyd.

'Gram-mat-ic-ally,' says the President slowly, using the favourite what-is-this-shit? repetition trick he applies to difficult questions on the Sunday morning television shout shows.

Boyd looks at Woodall for support. Woodall is the senior

media adviser to the White House: veteran of a dozen elections in America and elsewhere. He belongs to the profession now known as 'spin doctors', those who surgically remove unsightly growths from politicians' images, and transplant healthier parts into dying campaigns. He likes to say at dinner parties that, if Jesus Christ had authorized a big television spend and run hard against Roman domination, they could have turned that whole thing round in twenty-four hours.

'Bob may have a point, Mr President,' says Woodall, in his trademark near-whisper. His rivals gibe that he speaks this softly so that he can always pretend he hasn't said it if a remark plays wrong.

'The lines work splendidly, uh, intellectually,' Woodall continues. 'But, poetically, I wonder if we might not tinker with them . . .'

'Po-et-ic-al-ly,' says the President.

'Grammatically,' adds Boyd.

'You think Mr and Mrs America are gonna say: "Don't re-elect that guy. He broke his pledge on Webster's!"?' asks the President, ending with the stab of the right finger with which he likes to underline what he believes to be zingers in speeches and on television.

The President holds the draft text away from him and reads: 'Listen. "I stand before you as myself, this self – but I was someone else before and I will be someone else again." Tell me I don't know literature from chickenshit, but that sounds like grammar *and* poetry to me . . .'

Boyd and Woodall look at each other. One says grammar and the other says poetry, but the aim is the same. The tactic of the executive wing, when the President threatens to say something really mad or dangerous, is to fall back on syntax. They never invoke logic, for the President, they have come to realize, regards coherent sequential thought as another conspiracy of the East Coast intellectual élite.

During the election campaign in 1992, for example, Woodall achieved a legendary success at an overnight stop in Florida, when the travelling press was requesting a statement from the candidate on the hurricane deaths. The candidate, reluctant as ever to delegate, had scribbled his own statement, which began: 'I feel deep sadness that this one among the lives of these Americans should have ended in this tragic way . . .'

Aides had always known that the reincarnation thing was the candidate's private conviction, but this was the first time it had occurred to them that it might become part of his platform. They were used to candidates who instinctively knew what to hide. But Woodall, with the network cameras running up to speed downstairs in the Holiday Inn conference room at Daytona Beach, successfully argued that the construction 'this one among the lives of' was ungrammatical and would open the candidate to ridicule from the educational establishment. He won.

Now, in the Oval Office, on November 15th, 1993, Woodall tries again.

'With that many clauses and sub-clauses, sir, if you use so great a number of personal pronouns as well, it becomes confusing.'

'Yes, sir, too many "I"s can obfuscate the content,' adds Boyd. There is still enough of the wordsmith in him to be pleased by the use of the word 'obfuscate' actually to confuse someone.

'There'll only be one guy at that podium,' the President objects. 'Whose stetson they gonna think it's hanging on the rack?'

He aims his zinger finger at them again. Generally, they know that they have lost him when he goes folksy. Boyd and Woodall decide to leave their cosmetic work on the Union address for another meeting.

'Anyways,' their boss concludes, 'one of the reasons for becoming president is that you get to say "I" a lot. Otherwise, I'd have stayed in business.'

The President hits his desk with a fist in his other televisual gesture of emphasis. It is Richard M. Nixon's desk, which he has, symbolically, reinstalled in the Oval Office, as a screw-you gesture to the Washington political professionals and the media, against whom he ran so energetically and successfully in his 1992 campaign. The papers tried to make an issue of the new president's 'Freudian slip identification' with a leader nearly impeached. 'The business with the desk shows us what is in his own bottom drawer,' said a *Washington Post* editorial.

The President, however, was ready for them. 'I hate Nixon as much as you guys,' he quipped. 'But not as much as I love seeing those power élite people's faces when they eyeball this desk in here!' He gained two percentage points overnight.

That was a fairly typical incident in the administration, now eleven months old, of the man elected president in 1992. Newton 'Newt' Sanders, a sixty-eight-year-old electronics billionaire from Seattle, became America's forty-first president, and the first successful independent candidate, when he beat incumbent Republican president George Bush and the Democratic challenger, Governor Bill Clinton of Arkansas, in an unprecedented three-way contest.

Sanders – who had not held elective office since high school sports clubs – had capitalized on an extraordinary mood of dissatisfaction with established politics in America during that campaign year. The Texan software billionaire and occasional talk-show pundit H. Ross Perot was initially canvassed to run for president as an independent candidate. But, as pressure from the public increased, Perot told the CNN talk-show host Larry King: 'I'm kind of a shy guy, Larry. I wouldn't even have lights in the house if I could see in the dark. These appeals are flattering, but I don't need this. I'll stick to business. Anonymity's my bag.'

So the tribunes transferred their enthusiasm to Newton Sanders. His initially self-published treatise *Oh, Say, Don't You See?*, given to each of his empire's employees on the occasion of his fiftieth anniversary in business, was picked up by an established imprint, because of Seattle word-of-mouth, and became a national bestseller. The book contained Rocky Mountain aphorisms with vague application to politics and economics.

For example, a chapter headed 'Halving The Federal

Deficit' began: 'If you asked these Washington guys to skin a cat, the damn thing would have had kittens by the time they've talked to all their committees and their spin doctors. Where I come from, what these spin doctors do is called lying and cheating. Know how you spot a spin doctor? Because his garage sale has got a sign on the table saying Bloomingdale's.'

Like Caesar, Sanders appeared to reject the crown twice – first on an afternoon talk show, then on a late-night programme – before accepting on the third occasion: during a breakfast with the editors of *USA Today*. Running for president, Sanders emphasized his outsider status, his frontier credentials: from Washington State to Washington, DC. Adapting President Eisenhower's warning about the 'military-industrial complex' which sought to influence American government, Sanders raised the spectre of a new vested interest, which he called the 'media-political complex', a conspiracy of politicians and journalists in the national capital.

As the Sanders bandwagon gathered speed, the press tried to suggest that the public was being spun a less than frank account of the candidate as a Washington novice and people's champion, given that he was a billionaire, a country-club member, and had been on the guest list for every White House event from Tricia Nixon's wedding to the launch of George and Barbara Bush's pet dog's memoirs. But Sanders – assisted by Woodall – knew what to do with that accusation. 'Every goddam thing that East Coast media élite throws at me is another sign of how antsy they're getting about the people's candidate! We got these guys scared!' Sanders told cheering crowds on a swing through the Midwest.

'Run hard against the media, and against spin doctors. That stuff is really registering!' Woodall advised Sanders in the final days of campaigning, after consulting private polling. By now, he was reasonably sure that Sanders was borderline crazy, with the borders being forced back by new invaders every day, and was perhaps even potentially America's first tyrant. This conviction solidified after the 'this one among their lives' incident in Florida. But the possibility of a job in a Sanders White House – with senior posts almost by definition closed off to consultants, allied with the Republicans and Democrats – proved too much for his frail scruples.

Two days before the election, the *New York Times* reported that Sanders had told colleagues at a Seattle business lunch in the seventies of his belief that he had been abducted by aliens for fourteen hours on an evening in 1969, and that samples of his semen and faeces had been removed from him by a midget humanoid with pincer fingers. The article contained for-the-record confirmation by two senior Washington State politicians present at the lunch. But Sanders, addressing a rally in South Carolina on the morning that the piece appeared, sneered: 'Politicians say it. The media prints it. You believe those guys, and I don't *want* your vote!' His positives stayed steady overnight, and, in some polls, rose.

On November 3rd, 1992, the popular vote divided 36 per cent to Sanders, 33 to Clinton, 31 to Bush. The tally of seats in the electoral college produced no overall majority, throwing the election, under the Twelfth Amendment, into the House of Representatives. Marginally more alarmed at the possible reaction of the people if they rejected Sanders than they were frightened for their country if they elected him, legislators broke party ranks and confirmed Newton W. Sanders as forty-first president of the United States of America. Allan S. Woodall was appointed Chief Counsellor to the President and Senior Media Adviser. Robert F. Boyd was summoned from Seattle to be Chief of Staff.

12: The Fifteen Club

The hotel is not the best in Dallas, but it provides a perfect view of Dealey Plaza. From the windows on one side, you can share Lee Harvey Oswald's perspective on November 22nd, 1963.

But sinister forces are at work – entropy beckons – from the minute Crick checks in.

'This is your key card, sir. It's a no smoking room with two queen-sized beds. Will you be needing help with your bags this morning?'

'I'll carry my own.'

He involuntarily winds his right fist tighter around the grip of his attaché case, and moves his left arm from in front of his hanging shoulder bag to halfway back across it.

'OK, Mr Crick. It will be room 1077 on the tenth floor. The elevators are through the lobby and to the left.'

'No, no, no. That room's no good.'

He throws the guest information booklet and the two credit-card pass keys for room 1077 onto the reception desk, where they slither and come to a stop on the keyboard of the clerk's computer check-in terminal.

'I wrote you two months ago,' Crick hisses. 'It is vital to me that I have room 11, 63, or 22.'

'Sir, we are always happy to accommodate superstitions.'

'This is *not* a superstition.'

'Or to reallocate rooms with a particular past association. The difficulty is that our room identification policy involves a four-digit system. Room 11 would be Room 0111, the eleventh room on the first floor.'

'I see. Well, let's try the eleventh floor. Can you give me 1163 or 1122?'

With an expression affecting almost maternal concern, the clerk makes a few clicks with her fingers at the keyboard. The look of a mother gives way to the appearance of a widow.

'Sir, the eleventh is a smoking floor. You said you . . .'

'Yes. Forget the eleventh.'

He did indeed specify non-smoking. And Crick cannot back off on this. After all, for fifteen years, he has been campaigning for a total statewide ban on cigarettes in Oklahoma.

'Well, how about 6311 or 6322?'

'Sir, the hotel has only fifty-two floors.'

A less intense man than Crick, or a European, might be amused by that 'only', but he merely scowls. The clerk says: 'We'd better check out the twenty-second floor, Mr Crick.'

She is looking smug. She has guessed the game, or, anyway, its basic rules.

'That would be good, Janet.' He has read her name-badge. 'If you can do this for me, maybe I could . . . Do you have an Employee of the Month scheme or anything like that?'

'Sir, nomination slips will be in the stationery folder in your room.'

'Good. I'll certainly think about it when I get to my room, Janet.'

Janet, service industry sincerity creasing her face again, makes a few more plays on the keyboard. Bereavement returns to her features.

'Sir, that floor is all suites, which means that there are fewer rooms. So there is no 2263. I can get you into 2211, but the best deal I can do for you on that is $400 a night.'

He trusts it to his American Express card and, though there is a moment's tension as Janet tries the authorization wipe, the deal goes through. Suddenly, Crick is visited by another possibility.

'Janet, you've been more than helpful, and I will attend to the Employee of the Month thing as soon as I'm settled, but a thought has just occurred to me. Do any of your suites have names?'

'I do know there's a Robert E. Lee suite, sir. Because I just checked a gentleman into it.'

'Uh-huh. Are any of them named after presidents, Janet?'

Before he has finished the question, she is clicking.

'Not specifically, sir. There is a Presidential Suite.'

'Ah.'

'But that's 1314 – on the *smoking* suites floor.'

'OK. I'll stick with what you've given me. Janet, thank you.'

'No problem, sir.'

From the window of 2211, he looks out at Dealey Plaza with a proprietorial tremor, and then rings the hotel switchboard to see if any other members of The Fifteen Club have checked in yet.

13: Profiles in Power

'Oh, and *USA Today* wants to know whether or not you have a view about Elvis Presley, for a kind of symposium they're running.'

'What about him, David?'

'Do you, Mr President, believe that Elvis Presley is still alive?'

'Boomer, are we sure this befits the office of a former two-term president of the United States?'

Boomer, looking up, sees the smile that confirms Kennedy is using his teasing tone. It is the hardest one to pick, pitched, as it is, somewhere uncertainly between comedy and self-contempt. But, as he continues, Boomer is on alert for one of his employer's rare but scary bursts of fury at his predicament.

'I thought, Mr President, that you might seem a sport if you participated.'

'Boomer, you should be in politics. Well, yes, I do think Elvis is dead. I believe what I read in the papers. As a matter of fact, with the guts he had on him at the end, it's a miracle he reached forty-two. But don't quote that part. We don't want to offend larger Americans.'

'Sir, I thought that what you might say is: "Yes, the King is dead. But his music is immortal."'

'Yes, I think I just said that. Print it, Boomer!'

In exchanges like this, Boomer can still recognize the president he has seen on newsreel of the White House press conferences in the years before the shooting: mischievous, witty, strong, corralling listeners with the force of his spirit.

Even now, this power of personality can still break through the degradations of the decades.

This mid-November morning, in the suite of ground-floor rooms at the family compound in Hyannis that serves as the former President's official office, Jack and Boomer are holding their monthly administration meeting. Requests, schedules, and speeches are dealt with over a fresh fish lunch. Behind his old presidential desk, Jack sits in his Oval Office rocking chair, now convex to the point of pregnancy with cushions, because of his bad back. On the wall with the ocean view is a gallery of the dead: old Joe the patriarch, Bobby, Ted.

After working through the interview and quote enquiries, Boomer pauses, closing the latest of his labelled and cross-referenced folders (this one is blue and marked 'Media Interest') and laying it beside a plate smeared with a few remaining flakes of Scrod.

'Sir, in the broad area of media interest, I felt I should bring up two other matters. They're not requests for interviews, exactly, not at all, although you may of course be called upon for comment later . . . but . . .'

'Let me help you, David. I sense from the churning of your mouth that we're speaking of another, uh, bimbo eruption.'

'There is a rumour, sir, that one of the trash mags' anniversary issues has come up with a new name.'

'Ah. And do we have the name?'

Boomer says the woman's name, pronouncing it as neutrally as possible, like a bored teacher reading the roll late in the final semester.

'Ah,' Jack says. 'And they, uh, have this woman, do they?'

'It is believed that she has placed her allegations on the record.'

By arrangement, one question remains stubbornly unasked, unanswered: is this story true? The former President moves his chair cautiously backward and forward, like a grandpa in the movies about to offer junior life's lessons.

'Boomer, "Children of Courage" and so on is all very well. My charities and societies. These are worthwhile organizations. But you know the foundation I'd like to head?'

'Something more political, sir?'

'In a way. An institute to study the relationship between ambition and libido – between hunger for power and hunger for cunt.'

Jack sees Boomer trying to hide a smirk beneath his beard. He guesses what his assistant is thinking: *Oh, wouldn't you enjoy the research!*

'It does seem to me', Jack continues, 'a key question. The link between the rise to power and the fall of pants. There evidently is one. And, yes, yes, I'm not pretending to an outsider's interest in this myself. What we as a nation must address is why – physiologically – this should be so. And, if so, why morally it should be regarded as so wrong.'

'Mr President, what people say is, particularly religious people, and I am only reporting this argument, not supporting it, what people say is: if a man would cheat on his wife, he would cheat on his country.'

'But this is baloney, isn't it? Gerry Ford's marriage was about the only goddam thing he *didn't* screw up. I'd guess Pat Nixon knew where Dick was every night. The problem was the American people didn't know where he was during the day! Nixon was faithful to his wife but fucked the country.'

Boomer has never quite become used to the thirty-fifth president saying 'fuck' in front of him, and he is unable to bury a wince.

'And, also, it does seem to me, Boomer . . . I mean, for me personally, now, all that's at risk is my dignity. And my children, maybe, reading this. But, if these are to be the standards of public life, if nothing in a politician's life is to be out of bounds – not the sack, not the trash can, not the drug cabinet – then there does arise the question of just who the fuck we are going to get to run this country, these states, these nations. St Paul couldn't get elected in America today, because they'd drag up all that stuff before Damascus.'

He is breathing so hard now that Boomer begins to see his future publications including an unchallenged eyewitness monograph on a presidential death.

'I'm sorry, Boomer. That question's sort of my hot button.'

'I understand, sir. On the woman thing, I thought I'd

keep you posted. We can discuss damage limitation at the time, should it occur.'

'Should it occur. Now, God help me, but I believe you said there were *two* of these matters.'

'Yes. The new biography, sir.'

'Ah.'

'Published next year. I understand it will deal in some detail with . . . with . . .'

'Go on, Boomer, I'm stronger than you think.'

'A chapter is devoted to the vote-rigging stuff from 1960.'

'I think you're supposed to say the *alleged* vote-rigging.'

'Yes. Yes, of course, sir.'

Boomer is referring to the story that legions of the long dead voted Kennedy–Johnson in key districts in the 1960 election. Many of the corpses reportedly made their democratic choice more than once. In recent years, it has become a key Republican belief that Kennedy's 1960 victory was a fix by his pa's Sicilian friends. This theory – and the allied view that his re-election in 1964 was a shoo-in on a sympathy ticket – is reflected in a popular GOP badge on which JFK's face is overprinted with the words: 1960 – THANKS, DAD – 1964 – THANKS, DALLAS.

'Boomer,' says Jack. 'You're a young man with an interest in politics.'

'Yes, Mr President.'

'Well, let me give you some advice for free. If you like sausage or you like democracy, don't ever go see them being made.'

And this is the first and last time they discuss the vote-rigging allegations about the first election.

The final business of the meeting is the latest editorial session for Jack's new book. An idealistic or opportunistic publisher is planning a reissue of the 1956 book *Profiles In Courage*, studies by the then Senator Kennedy of eight politicians from history who dared to defy the majority opinion on issues of principle.

Boomer has proposed, and the publisher accepted, a follow-up volume, called *Profiles In Power*, in which, from the perspective of political senescence, the former President will anatomize eight political leaders. The daily observance at the word processor will be Boomer's, with Jack annotating the drafts. So far, they have decided on Abraham Lincoln, Franklin Roosevelt, Mahatma Gandhi, Julius Caesar, and Winston Churchill. They need three more.

'Have you thought about Premier Margaret Thatcher at all, sir?'

'Many times. Oh, for the book? There would be a neatness there, with Pa being ambassador to London and all that.'

Jack does not say so in front of Boomer, but his main fascination with Margaret Thatcher – now, he believes, to be referred to under English law as Queen or Dowager or something similar – is for the exception she represents to him. It has been his habit of a lifetime, a contribution to his ruin, to wonder, on encountering almost any woman, what it might be like to fuck her. But meeting Mrs Thatcher, at a White House banquet in the Reagan years, he found himself wondering what it would be like for someone else to fuck her. He at first wondered if this was a sudden manifestation of age, but he was soon having fantasies about the waitress serving their part of the table, so he attributed the phenomenon to the lady herself.

'I wonder if I could really get inside her,' says Jack, daring Boomer to smirk. 'Now, what about Lyndon? I kind of feel it would be good to have a first-hand chapter.'

'Sir, the publishers believe the volume will have more appeal if you confine yourself to, uh, key players. Former Vice-President Johnson, for all his fine qualities . . . well, his . . . his . . .'

'His full potential was never realized? I queered him one way in '63, and, by '68, I'd done it in another. I guess Lyndon died wishing Oswald had been a better shot?'

'I'm sure he didn't, sir.'

But Kennedy is baring his teeth again, in the grin-is-it? that leaves Boomer so confused about whether to join in or to hold his own sober expression. The complication is that Boomer knows very well the Washington gossip about LBJ's emotions in his closing days. It is generally said that he went to his grave howling against fate.

The former vice-president's memoirs, published in 1969, the year after his election defeat by Richard Nixon, were somewhat sourly titled *A Heartbeat Away*, a phrase that officially applied to the vice-presidency, but perhaps subliminally to events at Parkland Hospital in November 1963. A nurse at the hospital has claimed that, when Johnson met Kennedy in Parkland for the first time after the President regained consciousness following his operation, JFK's brave and typical quip – 'So near, Lyndon. Hire a better shot next time' – was met by the Vice-President with a scowl and a hissed: 'That's not fucking funny.'

Johnson's 1968 campaign biography, *The Making of LBJ*, written by a Fort Worth reporter, had originally been subtitled *At JFK's Side*, but this was felt, by the time of publication, to have negative implications and was scratched from the galley. The one academic biography, published just before LBJ's death in 1973, had been called *The Nearly Man*. The newspapers had reported an unfortunate incident in which, at a Dallas ranch party, LBJ had grabbed his biographer, a Texan professor, and yelled: 'Nearly Man? You're the Nearly Man. You nearly got your fucking balls sliced off. And maybe we're not talking nearly . . .' Johnson, who was brandishing a large barbecue fork, had been restrained and hustled away by a Secret Service agent.

But, if LBJ had grown a ghost and it was tuned into contemporary America, it would see some recompense. A Houston professor of history has just begun to raise a cult of unfulfilment around Johnson. A new 1992 biography concluded that he was 'the best president America never had', and that the country had been denied a great leader by fate. The film director Oliver Stone, a Vietnam veteran who made his name in Hollywood with stories from the war, argues that if Johnson had become president in 1963, the tragedy of Vietnam would have been averted. Referring to President Kennedy in interviews as 'that war criminal', Stone is developing the script of an advocatory biopic called *LBJ*.

Boomer tries to edge Jack away from the subject of his dead deputy.

'Sir, the leaders we have chosen so far are, for all their virtues, Dead White Males . . .'

'Gandhi is *white*, Boomer?'

'I mean, in an American campus context. I wondered, sir, about Dr Luther King.'

'Now, that is a good thought.'

'A majority of your speaking engagements, I would say, are from African-American groups. The civil rights legislation is regarded as your most unimpeachable achievement.'

'Never say the word "impeachable" around presidents, Boomer.'

'I'm sorry, Mr President.'

'It was a joke. I'll send up flares in future.'

'But, seriously, sir, a linking theme of these essays – clearly – would be to what extent an individual's life – or death – can affect the destiny of a nation.'

'Ah. Clearly I have an interest in this.'

'The death thing is particularly interesting. It may well be – I am thinking of Gandhi, or perhaps Dr Luther King – that a man's violent death becomes inseparable from his reputation, from his mission.'

'Ah. Hard shit for that man, of course.'

'Ah, sir . . . I wasn't in any way thinking of your own case, Mr President.'

'Of course you weren't, Boomer.'

'No, really, I wasn't.'

'No, really, I didn't think you were.'

But Boomer sees that his employer is again wearing his most unknowable grin. So he changes – or, anyway, broadens – the subject.

'The central underlying question of the book, Mr President, would of course be one that all tribes have considered down time – do leaders direct the tide of history, or do they merely swim in it?'

Jack cannot deny that this question has possessed him throughout his life. *PT 109*, the torpedo-boat he skippered, smashed in half off Vella Gulf in 1943, could so clearly have turned out the other way. Dallas was an inch between two outcomes. Swirling through his bloodstream even as he speaks to Boomer are adrenocortical hormones, keeping at bay the Addison's disease that, earlier in the century, would have been a death sentence.

People presented politicians as men of destiny. But was it destiny or was it chance? Even the stern Catholicism of his youth fudged that one, spinning impenetrable theological riddles around the question of predestination versus choice. Inasmuch as he remembered it, God knew what you were going to do, but it was still your call. Was that it? But, then, surely . . .

14: In His Time

The second assassin – for did we really believe that there would be a single gunman? – is not an Englishman. He is America's own creation. Later, his neighbours in the poxy apartment block in the neglected part of the city will pool their glimpses of him for the network cameras. They will use the word 'loner', the traditional American benediction in these circumstances. The reporters will also ask if he kept a dog or cat, and was obsessively fond of it, but in this they will be disappointed.

'Books,' the Lithuanian cab driver two doors along will tell Channel 2. 'Books. He always carry books. All you see him. We think he student.'

But he is not a student. It is an oddity of American psychopathy that, in a primarily visual culture, its assassins have been bookish. Mark Chapman, who shot John Lennon in 1981, connected this impulse with his close study of J. D. Salinger's *The Catcher in the Rye*. Even before that, it was common for assassins to read every available book and clipping about their famous prey. But perhaps assassination is in part a literary impulse: the wish to be written about.

Subsequently, would-be assassins read every available book and clipping about famous assassins as well. This was another example of the tendency of everything in the late twentieth century to become divorced from its source. It was a third-hand world. If the assassins – busy reading all those books about assassins – had found time to read books about literature as well, they would have realized that they were part of what was called post-modernism.

The second assassin has certainly read everything about

his celebrity victim, and has stalked the mailing lists and book stores for works about celebrity killers. There is, after all, the question of professional tradition. But his serious reading is in a less obvious genre. The volume gloved hands will lift and bag, when his apartment is stormed afterwards, is a tweaked and smeared copy of a book called *A Brief History of Time*. The author – Professor Hawking – holds down Isaac Newton's old job at the University of Cambridge, England, according to the dust jacket.

This book is the second assassin's bible. He is obsessed with the question of time, not in the sense of clocks – the police who bring him in will note that he does not even wear a wrist-watch – but cosmically. For this reason, after he has done what he is planning to do, he will go down in American history – or, for the moment, American journalism – as the Time Bandit. Fraser – the spidery name written beside the dusty numbered button in the rusted grid on the ground floor – will scarcely be recorded at all.

Fraser is reading now, late on this November night, a follow-up volume of essays by the writer of his bible. The chapter currently occupying his time is called: 'Is everything determined?'

What Hawking is talking about here is whether events are meant or accidental. It is an ancient debate, but science has complicated the classical choice between divine order and natural randomness. There is now the further alternative of natural order. If everything is intended, then is it the product of a Creator (divine, white beard optional) or the result of a physical process reducible to a set of scientific equations? The latter is the 'unified theory' or 'grand theory of everything' which is the grail of today's physicists.

The problem, as the professor points out, is why either God or physics would trouble themselves with pre-ordaining banal factors like the results of ball games or the week's number one on the *Billboard* charts. A 'grand unified theory' seemed scientifically attractive but how could this 'presumably compact and elegant' equation account for 'the complexity and trivial detail that we see around us'?

A further complication – for believers in either religious

or scientific predestination – was that human beings behaved as if they had free will, as was proved by the existence of such concepts as risk:

It may be that everything we do is determined by some grand unified theory. If that theory has determined that we shall die by hanging, then we shall not drown. But you would have to be awfully sure that you were destined for the gallows to put to sea in a small boat during a storm.

The professor resolved these paradoxes through the 'uncertainty principle of quantum mechanics'. This was not entirely a surprise to Fraser. Reading the kind of books with which he now passed his days and nights, it was only a matter of time before you came to the uncertainty principle. Inasmuch as Fraser could be sure, this principle – which established the impossibility of measuring both the position and speed of a sub-atomic particle accurately – was important because it rendered questionable the previously rocklike concepts of physics. Hawking, however, applied the principle in a particularly visceral and visual way:

In the very early universe . . . there was quite a lot of uncertainty, and there were a number of possible states for the universe. These different possible states would have evolved into a whole family of different histories for the universe. Most of these histories would be similar in their large-scale features. They would correspond to a universe that was uniform and smooth, and that was expanding. However, they would differ in details like the distribution of their stars and, even more, what was on the cover of their magazines. (That is, if those histories contained magazines.) . . . We just happen to live in a history in which the Allies won the war and Madonna was on the cover of Cosmopolitan.

A cradle Roman Catholic who later dabbled in Marxism, Fraser has believed at different times that it was God who wanted him to kill Kennedy and that the assassination was historically inevitable. But since he became occupied with Time, mind-blowing new possibilities have opened up. What Hawking seems to be saying is that there may be alternative universes of 'very similar intelligent beings' in which Fraser does not kill Kennedy; in which Fraser himself becomes president; in which Kennedy died at Dallas; in which America smashed the Communists in Vietnam; in which Trudi Brewster willingly took it in the mouth, and wouldn't have had to be trashed; in which Fraser would have been Marilyn Monroe's sixth, and final, husband, the only one able to make her come and keep her happy.

Fraser suspects that Hawking may have his own take on this. The professor, he knows from carefully clipped profiles, rides a wheelchair and speaks through an electronic box, because of a genetic disease. But was the gene that dealt him this existence stray or placed? Was there an alternative universe in which the professor played tennis every evening, and sang in the church choir Sundays, certain of God's place in the world? Was Hawking's research, in this sense, autobiographical?

Fraser, too, has a familiarity with the randomness, or punishment, of life: the jobs, the fucks, the fights, the conversations, that could so easily have gone the other way and changed his life.

What Fraser does not entirely comprehend – although he has studied 'Is Everything Determined?' for the last three nights – is whether the professor is saying that these alternative worlds could just as easily have been the way history turned out; or if he is suggesting that such parallel universes physically exist, beyond our visitation or vision. The problem with the former, it seems to Fraser, is that it isn't much consolation for the life story you've got. The difficulty with the latter is that you can't take a trip to the version you'd prefer. The professor writes that he does not believe time travel will ever be feasible.

He could write to Cambridge, England, for elucidation, but he worries about leaving footprints. And, anyway, the solution seems obvious. Robbed of the other possibilities, your only option was to intervene in the time scale, to change the narrative, of the universe in which you found yourself. You just had to be determined.

15:   Sunset

In deep disguise, from fear of those who think they love her, she trudges down Sunset. She hangs a right on Highland, heading for Hollywood Boulevard.

Since the weight thing in the paper, Jean is walking wherever she can, although there is always the risk for pedestrians in modern America of ending up with nature's ultimate slimming cure. At least today – in her shopping costume of shades, hat as big as a dinner table, and billowing raincoat – she is at risk only from those psychotics targeting the rich in general rather than herself in particular.

She is already uncomfortable in the coat. The temperature, which television's numerous sky watchers had predicted would not reach the sixties, is now threatening to leave them. Yet, simultaneously, flood and mud-slide warnings have been entered for tonight.

But this is what they expect, and what they deserve. Los Angeles is a willed city, an arrogant bet by man against the elements. He came across a desert – and one beneath which the earth's crust bubbled and buckled – and built there one of the world's great conurbations. Los Angeles had been a challenge to the planet, and one day it would be taken up, in the earthquake which the city's inhabitants had all been educated to expect but only in the theoretical way that they were prepared for death. With each flood, fire, mud-slide, and riot, it was increasingly clear that the city of Los Angeles was not the story intended for this land. They had imposed their own alternative version on it.

On Hollywood, Jean heads for Mann's Chinese Theater. Four Japanese are aiming a camcorder at Marilyn Monroe's hand and foot prints in the cement. She instinctively touches her hat and shades, to check the barrier between Marilyn and herself. At the booth, she buys a ticket for the 2.30 departure on the Tour of the Stars' Homes.

She pays cash, because a credit card would be suicide for her disguise. Although her plastic money all belongs to someone called Jean Norman, a reversal of her hyphenated childhood first name, this subterfuge is by now well known to readers of celebrity magazines as a quirk of Marilyn's personality. When she rings her agent's office, and says 'It's Mrs Norman,' the receptionist chirrups. 'Oh, hello, Miss Monroe,' as if her alibi were some kind of egotistical desire to be recognized, to test the reflexes of the staff.

It is almost departure time and Jean is the last aboard the air-conditioned van with tinted windows. Inside, up front, are the four Japanese she just watched videoing Hollywood's concrete record of her. At the back is a sullen couple, surely five hundred pounds between them. The woman is flapping at her sweat-wet face with a folded copy of *Variety*. The man takes alternate lunges at a candy bar and a diet soda. Jean takes the empty bench seat in the middle of the van.

She has nerved herself to endure one of these tours for years, since she read a sarcastic paragraph about them in the *Los Angeles Times*. Twice she has made it to the booth at Mann's, and then shuffled away. But it has felt to her recently like a rite she must fulfil, as part of her return to the world.

'Welcome aboard this Tour of the Stars' Homes,' croons their guide through a hand mike, as he heads the van west on Hollywood. 'You all from out of town?'

'Chicago!' yells the sweaty woman, indoctrinated from watching TV quiz shows always to answer loud and first. Her husband, chewing hugely, nods consent. The Japanese, after a shrill conference, are unable to file a reply. 'Texas,' drawls Jean, in an accent she once employed as a homicidal nun in a featured guest star appearance in *Murder She Wrote*.

'My name's Steve, and I'm a native of New York City,' their guide reveals. 'I'm an actor, like all of the Star Cars guides.'

'Would I have seen you in anything, Steve?' demands the perspiring Chicagoan from the rear of the van.

'I had a small part in *New Colombo* last season,' says Steve. 'And I'm auditioning for *Picket Fences* Tuesday.'

Steve is small and balding, with a lazy eye, a flicking lid. Jean guesses that, at best, he would be up for geek parts on TV: the office wimps, computer wonks. Once, he might have got the psychopaths, the neighbourhood stalkers, but those were the leading males roles these days. Jean's antennae – mixed record as they had with men, admittedly – told her that Steve was gay.

'Our tour today will last two hours,' Steve explains, as they battle the traffic on Sunset. 'We'll be showing you the homes of many of the great Hollywood legends of today and yesterday. Some of today's stars, I'm afraid, aren't too keen about letting us know exactly where it is they live, but we'll do our best . . .'

'They don't want us to see their houses, maybe we don't want to see their films,' suggests the woman from Chicago. 'We paid for these houses! We paid for them!'

A hand crashes down on Jean's shoulder, and she wonders if this woman with such certainty about the obligations of celebrities can have penetrated her disguise through some kind of witch's instinct.

'Listen!' the woman says. 'Listen! I'm Molly from Chicago, by the way. If you like this trip, you wanna try the other one they do. You travel in a hearse, OK?, and the guide's dressed like an undertaker. It's kind of the downside of fame, I think, is the idea. They take you by where Fatty Arbuckle flattened that chick. You see where John Belushi took his fatal last cocktail. And River Phoenix, just along from here, in fact, on Sunset. The same drugs in both cases, by the way, did you know? What they call a speedball. The house where that dwarf from *Fantasy Island* shot himself by the pool. Suicides, murders. It's very well done.'

'Wayll, thaynk you,' Jean replies in her *Murder She Wrote* tones.

They are passing a dingy bar on Sunset.

'On the right here is the bar where Marilyn Monroe and Joe Di Maggio had their first date . . .'

'I hear she still likes a drink now,' Molly hollers. Jean feels a current of air behind her head, and assumes that the woman is miming the swing of a lush's arm. For a moment, Jean considers bursting out of disguise and filing suit for defamation, but she would not want Molly as an enemy. And, anyway, Jean would probably just be dragged away, as one more nutty woman who claims she is Marilyn Monroe.

'Marilyn Monroe. Now, there's a life the churches should be using in commercials, as a warning,' Molly adds.

The Japanese are activated by any mention of the name of Marilyn Monroe, which two words seem to be the limits of their English.

In Beverly Hills, they pass a jogger striving up an incline.

'Now, look very closely,' Steve advises. 'We often see Madonna jogging here . . . Oh, oh, but that's just some rich nobody.'

They drive through the estates where people are so rich and so image-conscious that they pay a company to spray-paint their drought-browned lawns green. Outside two of the houses said to belong to current movie stars, Molly from Chicago makes elaborate sniffing sounds and jabs her finger towards her nose, in a cocaine charade. Displaying insider information from his own different perspective, Steve says of the stars: 'He's a nice man,' or 'He's real.'

Jean recognizes the house just before Steve says: 'On the left is the Marilyn Monroe château, where Marilyn and Joe Di Maggio spent their ill-fated nine-month marriage.'

So this is what happens, thinks Marilyn. They turn your dates and divorces – your disasters – into dollars.

'Steve, is Marilyn's current residence featured on this tour?'

'Molly, Marilyn lives out in Brentwood, which is just a little too far for a two-hour tour starting downtown. And, frankly, there's not much else out there. There's only really O. J. Simpson's place. He's an old football hero, by the way, for those of you from other cultures.'

'Uh-huh. I wondered. It wasn't on the hearse tour either,

Steve, even though that was where she tried to kill herself. Also, that's where the Kennedy brothers came to see her. I read in a magazine she was seeing Jack and Bobby just before she took the pills. Of course, Catholics, they say sorry in those boxes of theirs and then they get to do it all again.'

One day, thinks Jean, I will publish, perhaps posthumously, another memoir, in which this scene will feature. And Molly in Chicago will read it. And what? Would she even feel embarrassment? She would probably consult a lawyer, feeling that her rights as a fan had been impeded.

'Now this', says Steve, 'is Barbra Streisand's house. I'm sorry you won't be able to get much with your cameras. She's built high walls all around. Barbra likes her privacy.'

'How dare she! I paid for this house. I paid for it!' Molly complains.

The house's high walls are painted in strawberry shades.

'As you see, Barbra likes pink,' says Steve.

'She also likes green,' growls Molly, making the money sign between finger and thumb.

'Now let's see if any of you folk can guess which house along here is the retirement home of former President Reagan,' Steve teases his passengers. 'You can usually tell by the security . . .'

'Reagan' is another word of English that the Japanese possess, and they uncap their camcorder.

'I read in a magazine that Reagan and Marilyn Monroe had an affair in the early days of Hollywood,' says Molly.

And here the scenery nearly falls down, the microphone intrudes into view, for Jean is on the edge of shouting, 'No, they goddam didn't!' before she remembers who she isn't.

16:   He Stole My Life!

'Go on, have a drink of water. You need another handkerchief? Take this slowly. We know how tough this is for you.'

'I'm sorry. I . . . What have I just said?'

'It would be your very, very special secret. You were not
to tell J. Edgar Hoover, even if he asked you.'

'Yes. *Yes* . . .'

'That's what you told us he said to you.'

'Yup. He always mentioned Hoover. Hoover would still
have been alive then. In power. He was kind of a bogeyman.'

'For you and a lot of other Americans, Diane.'

'And then, after he said that, he took my hand and rested
it on his . . .'

'Whoa! Diane, his zipper is open at this point? He has
dropped his pants? You have not told us that he opened his
zipper or dropped his pants . . .'

'I *told* you.'

'No. We must be very sure about this, Diane. You are
talking about a president of the United States.'

'He . . . People have got to *know* about this. He . . . he
stole my life!'

'We know he did. But, because of who he is, Diane, this
is a very powerful man, because of who he is, there must be
no holes in the story. If we are tough with you, it is for that
reason only. Now, he mentions Hoover, he takes your hand,
how is it that his penis is free?'

'I don't know. He took my hand, my eyes followed, his
hand and my hand, and . . . it was *out*. He must have done it
while I was looking at the book . . .'

'The De Tocqueville?'

'Yes. He had pointed something out on the page, before . . .'

'Now, tell us if you need to rest, Diane. It's your hand on the, er, it's you running the clock here, you understand? Now, what does he do next?'

'He takes my hand and puts it on his . . . I don't know what to call it . . .'

'What did *he* call it, Diane?'

'Uh . . . Ap . . . Apollo 11 . . .'

'Apollo 11?'

'Yes. He was always very big on the space race.'

'This is 1970, June 1970?'

'I told you . . .'

'Diane, his attorneys will be over every date, every detail, like stink on shit. They'll have computer print-outs from NASA to prove how many times, and in which states and in which counties, the words "Apollo 11" were spoken aloud in 1970. This is why we may sometimes ask the same question twice.'

'June 1970. Just after my eleventh birthday.'

'Thank you, Diane. You're doing very well here. A lot of people are going to be very glad you've done this. A lot of people are going to admire your courage. What happens now?'

'He calls his . . . his . . . thing . . . Apollo 11. He also has a name for his . . . his . . . his . . .'

'I need to say for the tape, Diane – it is important there is no suggestion that we are influencing you – I need to say for the tape that you are indicating spheres, circles, with your hands. You are telling us the term the alleged abuser used for his testicles, his scrotum?'

'Yes.'

'What did he call them, Diane?'

'Boosters . . . I don't know why . . . he always called them *boosters* . . .'

'That might fit, Diane. It's NASA terminology.'

'Uh? Really?'

'A rocket has boosters at its base. I just need to say for the tape, Diane, that my remark was tangential, arising spontaneously from an element within your evidence. It was not my intention to intrude that new detail into your account. You see how careful we are being? Now, in your own time, please, take up the story.'

'He put my hand on it. Then, he said . . .

'We can take a break here, Diane.'

'No, I . . . He said, "Let's fly Apollo 11 to the dark side of the moon" . . .'

17: The Tomb of the Unknown Child

In the Oval Office, on November 16th, 1993, Boyd and Woodall are meeting the President to schedule a session with the Republican and Democrat minority leaders in both Houses on the subject of health care reform, which Sanders totally opposes.

But, before they can begin, the President says: 'With you guys here, let's have two hand jobs for the price of one . . .' Although he ran on a platform of 'family values', the President favours physical simile and sexual metaphor in private discourse. 'We seem to have gone into turnaround on the Tomb of the Unknown Child thing.'

The Commander-in-Chief's advisers flinch, because here is a mad and dangerous idea which consists of only five words and can therefore not easily be tackled from the angles of grammar and poetry.

It is the President's desire to construct in the major American cities a Tomb of the Unknown Child, with a curved wall design not unlike the Vietnam Memorial in Washington DC, though in white brick instead of black and with teddy bear motifs. The monuments will commemorate the victims of what President Sanders refers to in private, though to the relief of his aides not yet in public, as 'America's contraceptive Vietnam' – abortion. In front of the wall, there will be a 'Garden of Tears', containing a small white cross for each reported termination.

'There's this really boffo ad on at the moment. You boys seen it?' asks the President, not waiting for an answer. 'There's this dame in a park, and sometimes there's this boy beside her. Now you see him, now you don't. This, you see, is

77

the life of the child she flushed away. Now tell me I don't know Poussin from pussy, but this seems to me a work of art.'

You didn't argue with him when he was in this mood. Actually, you didn't argue with him if he was singing 'Oh what a beautiful morning!' and wearing a 'Disagree With Me' T-shirt.

Sanders continues: 'Joan and I do not like to speak about our own lost children . . .'

In fact, he referred to them on at least five talk-shows in election year.

'But each of them,' he goes on, 'those three miscarried souls, paged by God before they had even left the check-in desk, is, to us, a nightmare of If Onlies and By Nows. How a woman or man could choose to endure those agonies of speculation is a mystery to me.'

'Mr President,' says Woodall, 'I know you have no time for politics.'

'That's why folks voted me in, Al.'

'But the fact is that you were elected by a coalition, an unprecedented coalition, of different interest groups. Indeed, in a sense you are the first true cross-section president. Some of those who voted for you feel exactly as you do about abortion. Many, many others are pro-choice—'

'Pro-*death*, Al.'

'The point being,' says Boyd, providing covering fire, 'that the question of legislation is for you more complicated than for any of your forty predecessors, except, perhaps, Washington and Lincoln.'

If they couldn't use grammar or poetry, there was always flattery.

'What Bob says is very interesting,' Woodall resumed. 'With less than a third of the popular vote—'

'A third of the vote, less than a year after I might as well have been Joe Schmo with a bag over my head,' the President objects.

'Sir, I was not referring to the scale of the achievement,' says Woodall. 'Far from it. I am suggesting that part of your unprecedented responsibility to the American people and to the Constitution . . .'

Boyd nods at these words. Because it was the President's belief that he had in some way triumphed over history by the very fact of his election, they countered his wilder schemes by establishing a sense of America as a continuum, politically, historically, or religiously.

'. . . part of your unprecedented responsibility to the American people and to the Constitution', Woodall is continuing, 'is to establish a separate national consensus for each discrete piece of legislation. I am not convinced that we have yet gone through that process with the Tomb of the Unknown Child . . .'

'They have them in Japan, Al,' says the President.

'With respect, Mr President, you recently said in a National Security Council meeting, in respect of the Japanese, "Would you trust folks who ain't realized yet you cook fish before you eat it?"'

'That was foreign policy. This is domestic,' Sanders answers, giving them his zinger finger.

'I would propose a closed-session commission, perhaps under the Chairmanship of the First Lady, to examine the feasibility of the Tomb of the Unknown Child idea,' says Boyd.

'Well, OK,' the President replies. 'But if that turns out to be your Washington, DC, equivalent of what they do to dogs back home to stop them spreading, then you'll be hearing from me.'

'You've made a wise decision, Mr President,' says Boyd.

'Back home, they say, if you pat a guy on the back, you're checking the angle for the knife,' the President growls, but he lets the matter go, or almost.

'I've been thinking,' he says. 'Is there some kind of medal we can give to the people behind that child-who-mighta-been, the maybe-baby, commercial? Service to the Arts, Valiant for Truth, maybe. I've been thinking a lot about this. I've been thinking a lot of people's lives are like that, anyway. A movie running in their head, like on another channel. Ross Perot, down there in Texas, there must be moments, alone, when the scene on CNN pans out the other way, and he says, "OK, I'll run." Governor Clinton, there must be times in the long cold Arkansas nights when he isn't quite sure whether he's a guy who didn't get it dreaming he did or a guy who did get it dreaming he didn't . . .'

'Do you, sir, sometimes dream you lose?' Boyd wonders.

'No, Bob, I don't. But I guess that's because I never set out for this job. What happened happened. But listen to what I'm saying. Jack Kennedy. Take Jack Kennedy. There must be days. I mean, there must be days . . . Back home, they say fate is just the educated word for failure. But, hell, sometimes you've just got to wonder. It's an interesting business, all this.'

'Yes, Mr President,' says Boyd. 'Alternative history.'

18: Today

'Thanks, Matt. Back at the news desk in an hour. A Tuesday morning on *Today*. Coming up in the next half-hour, the author of a new book on what's really going on inside your dog's head. And how a South Carolina project is adding to our understanding of living with Aids. But first, our very special guest this morning, passing through New York on this November day, is former President John F. Kennedy. Good morning, Mr President.'

'Good morning, Bryant.'

'What brings you to town, sir?'

'Number of years now, I've been involved with what we call the "Children of Courage Awards". These are prizes for young Americans who have come through illness or injury, saved lives, or otherwise been school or community role models. We handed out the 1993 batch of those in New York City yesterday.'

'And we've got some film here of you talking with, uh, Scott Lawrence, from the Bronx, who, I believe, came through a classroom shooting incident to still finish as an honours student.'

'That's right, Bryant. One tough little guy.'

'And you've also been speaking up on this visit for one of your favourite causes?'

'That's right. One of the few really true bits in those biographies of me – you often have the authors through this studio . . .'

'First Amendment, Mr President!'

'I'm sure, Bryant. But the serious point I'm making is that people may know from some of those books of my own

81

life-long struggles with back pain. And in a speech here yesterday to the American Lower Back Pain Society – I've been their president for some time now – I called for more medical research and for recognition in the American workplace of the real scourge this is . . .'

'Right. Now, it's not every day we have a president in the studio—'

'Seemed like it during the election, Bryant.'

'True, sir. But some big political stories in the news at the top of the hour. Be good to have your take here. Republican and Democrat minority leaders on the Hill calling for urgent talks with the President on the direction of his administration. President Sanders coming up to the end of his first year in office. What's the verdict of the thirty-fifth President on the forty-first so far?'

'Well, Bryant, there's kind of a rule that predecessors don't dump on incumbents. But this guy's flaky, isn't he? I mean, this is a man who talked about a Mexican hit squad poisoning his salsa because he rejected the North American Free Trade Agreement.'

'The White House said that was a joke.'

'Do *you* believe it was a joke? What I'd say to the American people is this, Bryant. I understand your pain and anger against quote conventional end quote politicians. I know you think they've let you down. I appreciate there was a mood in '92 of "Let's throw them all out." But the answer isn't to put some rookie with a fistful of nice sound bites in the White House. Particularly if the rookie turns out to be kooky.'

'There are those, Mr President, who would say that you contributed to this disillusionment with conventional politicians. People say there was a great wave of belief behind you in '60, and you'd thrown it away by '68.'

'OK, some people think I crashed the car. Fine, but get a mechanic to fix it. Get someone who's spent their life around cars. Don't get a *vet*.'

'President Sanders being the vet in this analogy?'

'I've said what I'm going to say.'

'OK. Another political story of the day. The sexual

scandals afflicting Senator Bob Packwood. How important is the private conduct of a public servant, Mr President?'

'Oh, look, Bryant, I don't do this one. If I answered this question once, I'd spend the rest of my life answering it.'

'In general terms, Mr President.'

'In general terms, I think there would be a danger, if certain standards of conduct were imposed, and if certain standards of intrusion were permitted, that our countries would end up being run by men who were great at keeping their pants up, but ought by rights to be wearing their jackets back to front.'

'OK. Coming up to the thirtieth anniversary of Dallas. A lot of Americans doubt that you were the victim of a lone gunman, Lee Harvey Oswald. Do you?'

'I accept the report of the Warren Commission, Bryant. So do my family. What happened in Dallas is I had a big piece of bad luck, and then a big piece of good luck.'

'Seventy-fifth birthday last year. You're looking good. Apart from the work you've told us about, how'd you fill the days?'

'I still sail at Hyannis, when I can. And that's a big when. The FBI have got to drain the ocean first. Palm Beach when the East Coast gets too cold for my old bones. I'm writing another book. People shouldn't worry that my days seem long. They don't.'

'Mr President, wish you luck, been a pleasure talking to you.'

'Our chats are one of the highlights of my declining years, Bryant.'

'This is *Today* on NBC. And we'll be back after this station break.'

19: Everything is Subject to Change

During his long fall from the twenty-second level, Crick watches the unforgiving marble floor waiting coldly for his arrival, then rushing to meet him in the final moments like a lover at an airport gate.

Crick likes glass-sided elevators – and the hotel in Dallas has the fully transparent pod design – because they allow the passenger to imagine what it would be like to fall to your death from a skyscraper. Strike that. What is he thinking of? To imagine what it would be like to be *thrown* to your death from a skyscraper.

In the hotel lobby, the conference motif is visible on lapel badges, walls, and notice boards. The logo shows a question mark in the place where the cross-lines would be on a rifle sight imposed over a silhouette of Kennedy's profile.

At a conventional conference, the main throng of delegates forms in the centre of the lobby, radiating away from the table which holds the whispering coffee boilers. At this conference, though, it is the extremities that are packed. There is more or less a waiting list for corners, with the heart of the lobby sparsely populated.

As Crick seeks out the public telephones where he has arranged to meet McShane and Evaristi, fellow members of The Fifteen Club, he listens to the conversations of the other delegates.

'Now, I filed under Freedom of Information for four FBI documents on Oswald,' a woman on crutches is saying. 'And you know what? They arrived in three days. But – this is the thing – they were *totally clean*. No security deletions. Did you ever see a fully cleared FBI document? Who are they trying to kid? What are they trying to pretend they haven't got to hide?'

The conference has a distinct protocol of eye contact. Most of the speakers stand exceptionally close to their listeners, virtually kissing eyes. But if the glance of a passer-by should cross the range of vision of one of those speaking, their eyes will flash with fear or malevolence.

'It seems to me', a yellowed and chesty old guy with white hair is wheeze-whispering to a woman of restricted growth, 'that all we have to do is to find where they buried – or froze, froze is favourite I think – the body of the *real* President Kennedy, and the whole jiminy-riddle will come tumbling down.'

Crick finds the public telephones, but there is no sign of McShane or Evaristi, so he leans against the wall and reads his conference information pack, by the low spooky light of the phone booth bulbs.

The first sheet is a schedule of sessions. It is headed: 'Everything Is Subject To Change'. Although this is merely a legal precaution by the organizers against disgruntled scuffling for refunds, Crick feels it has a ring of wisdom to it. It reminds him of 'There it is . . .' the motto of the stoned in Vietnam. Everything is subject to change. The document continues:

Dealey Plaza Researchers — Fifth Quadrennial
Symposium
20th–22nd November 1993

Saturday 20th November

10 AM "Will the Real JFK Please Stand Up?" In a lecture based on an unpublished book — available in Xeroxed copies from the author's stall in the merchandise hall — James A. Draycott, a researcher from Nebraska, offers startling new evidence that the Dallas assassination attempt was a cover for the replacement of President John F. Kennedy by a lookalike primed to prosecute a ruinous war in Vietnam to the financial advantage of the military-industrial complex. Draycott offers photographic

and documentary proof that the "former president" living out his days in Hyannis is, in fact, a highly trained agent-actor.

11:30 AM "Murder at Chappaquiddick?" With slides, and new recorded interviews with Massachusetts residents, Kim Winstanley, a researcher from Springfield, Illinois, uncovers worrying inconsistencies in the official account of the mysterious death of Senator Edward Kennedy at Chappaquiddick in 1969.

12:30–2 PM LUNCH Special dietary requirements to be given to delegate desk by 10 AM.

2 PM "A Woman Scorned" Hell famously has no fury like a rejected lover. In a provocative new book, *Bring Me the Head of the Man I Once Loved,* Californian author Laura Lee Hauser argues that the assassination of Attorney General Robert Kennedy and the attempted assassination of President John F. Kennedy were initiated by Marilyn Monroe, the spurned mistress of both famous brothers, through Mafia contacts in the movie industry. Ms Hauser will be signing copies of her book (Hauser & Hauser, $23) after the talk.

3.30 PM "Our Days are Numbered" The Fifteen Club is a group of scientifically trained researchers who take their name from the sum of the individual digits in 11-22-63, the date of the Dallas shooting. In recent months, The Fifteen Club has run all the numerical information connected with Dallas—from the date to car licence plates to telephone numbers and the timing of key events—through a high-powered computer. This afternoon Fifteen Club president Professor Richard Crick reveals some of the startling patterns that emerged.

Sunday 21st November

10 AM "The Oxygen of Sympathy" Bestselling non-fiction author Tom Andrews was the first to argue (in his 1981 work *Staging Greatness*) that the Dallas shooting

was a carefully managed attempt to win sympathy for the beleaguered President Kennedy and ensure his re-election. This morning—using new information from Parkland hospital staff, and fresh ballistic evidence—Andrews expands his controversial theories.

11:30 AM "Cathode Ray Codes" Researcher Joanie Tamaro, from Oklahoma, argues that the network television series *Dallas* (CBS, 1978–91) is really a commentary on the November 22nd events in Dallas, and on other aspects of American myth in the late twentieth century. Dr Tamaro argues that a startling number of parallels, codes, clues, and confessions are contained in the serial. Talk illustrated by extracts from the pivotal 1980 edition of *Dallas*: "Who Shot JR?"

Crick meticulously folds the schedule, and stows it in his inside pocket. He is beginning to fear that McShane and Evaristi have played a trick on him, are even now talking about him in one of the hotel's three eating places. Crick has believed for some time that Evaristi covets the presidency of The Fifteen Club. Perhaps he is plotting with McShane a *coup* at the next AGM.

Crick re-opens the symposium information folder, and locates the delegate directory. He sprints through the list of names, checking for further members of The Fifteen Club, of whose attendance he was unaware, but who might be organizing behind Evaristi. He is unable to find any, unless they are using other names, but what he does see, in the M block, is: Malone, Katherine P.

Crick is suddenly alert, his arteries sprung and humming. He is glad of the beta-blockers dissolving in his stomach. Kathy Malone. She was, as he remembers, Katherine something, and plausibly enough Patricia, so it is quite possible that this is her. He feels fate playing games with him.

When Evaristi and McShane arrive, they need to say Crick's name twice to raise him. He has taken a plane to the past. They are both wearing The Fifteen Club's tie, of scattered multi-coloured numbers on black silk. Crick can smell no food or drink on their breath, so he is reasonably sure they have not been meeting secretly.

'I don't think much of the hotel,' Evaristi moans. 'The premium room numbers they don't even have. 1163 maybe, but you die o' nicotine.'

'Oh? They gave me 2211,' says Crick softly.

'*No*. You bastard. You sheer bastard,' chuckles McShane.

20: Double Whammy

Fraternelli was never designed to look friendly, but, waiting at the same table of the exact Manhattan trattoria in which the original meeting was held, he is taking the scowl into areas no previous practitioner has tried. He is in the *avant garde* of disappointment.

As soon as Meredith, who has booked the table under that one among his names, arrives and is seated, Fraternelli says: 'This is irregular. I hope you know this is irregular. A second meeting at this stage of the project . . .'

He fails to complete the sentence but improvises a period with a hard bite of a bread stick.

'I am so sorry to trouble you again,' begins Meredith who, though generally uncomfortable with his Englishness, can still do the manners when it suits him. 'It's just that a question occurred to me. A new dimension.'

'A new dimension? If it's financial, let me just say that the organization is already walking to school without shoes for this one.'

'No, it's not financial, Mr Fraternelli. Look, how would you feel about me doing someone else as well as Kennedy?'

'At the same time?'

'Side by side.'

'A double job?'

'Yes. I know it's . . .'

'Who?'

'Marilyn.'

'Marilyn? Listen – and I mean this nicely – you don't feel there's a chance you're over-reaching yourself here?'

'Mr Fraternelli, I'm a professional.'

'Tell me about it. We hired you.'

'I ask you to look at my record.'

'This we have done, I promise you. We know about things in your past that haven't happened yet.'

Perhaps this tense joke, or joke of tenses, is intended as a threat that the organization might turn on Meredith if necessary. Or maybe the big Italian-American is simply not a words man. Fraternelli meditatively throw-paints all the planes of his glass pale orange with the remains of his Bellini, stabilizes the liquid again in the middle, sucks down the last of the champagne and peach juice, and looks directly at the man he knows as Meredith.

'Why?' he asks. 'Why both?'

'Because, Mr Fraternelli, they belong together. Their stories touch at so many points. They belong – forgive me, if this sounds cruel – they belong in the same box.'

'And you are actually saying that – for some reason – it is not for me to ask – you would do them for the same price.'

'I would. Yes.'

'Because, we would inevitably have to think this, because of some, uh, *agenda* of your own.'

'Agenda is not a word I like. Put it down to my sense of history.'

'Mr Meredith, I have to say to you, that our organization is, by nature, what they call hands-off.'

Here, the half of Fraternelli's face that can still show emotion attempts a smile, and he continues: 'In fact, myself, I am *so* hands-off that, back in the office, they call me Captain Hook.'

Fraternelli uses his right hand to fold his left hand down and under to simulate a stump. He taps the rounded end with his other hand, to underline the joke. Meredith rewards Fraternelli with his chilling giggle.

'But,' Fraternelli goes on. '*But* something like this, an adjustment of this scale to a project already agreed, that would have to be sanctioned at a level higher than myself.'

'I was obviously not expecting an answer today.'

'I will have to talk to the board. And I would have to say

that, for myself, these double jobs have never seemed as neat. They worry me . . . uh . . . *aesthetically* . . .'

The word comes out uncertainly, rough edged. Meredith guesses that he has witnessed its birth in Fraternelli's mouth.

'OK,' the Italian says. 'We order now. And if you go for double portions here too, remember I have kids to feed.'

But Fraternelli seems to warm to the idea, for, later, he raises the residue of his second glass of wine towards whatever obscure light source illuminates the restaurant, and says, 'To Jack and Marilyn, then.'

'Jack and Marilyn,' echoes Meredith, through a bolus of gnocchi, now moistened by wine.

21: Project Apollo

The tapes of the session with Diane – three hours of emotion tightly restrained in three plastic cases – lie on the desk between Thomson and Washington. The tapes are labelled, with a humour typical of the office, but which Diane herself might not necessarily enjoy, *Project Apollo*.

Diane is resting at her hotel. They have booked her into the Plaza, an arrangement half reward and half inducement. A representative from the organization is with her to ensure that she does not make or take telephone calls she might later regret, and to expedite arrangements should she suddenly remember more, and need to talk to Thomson and Washington again. The conversations so far seem to have freed some kind of blockage, and memories are arriving now in floods, some of them in dreams. They have given Diane a micro-cassette recorder to keep beside her hotel bed.

'What kind of guy is it', says Thomson, 'who would call his donger Apollo 11?'

'Donger?' asks Washington.

'Cock,' Thomson translates, with a roll of his eyes. Thomson is an Australian, so three languages of slang are spoken in the office. There is his Sydney vernacular; the cuss-tongue of the mainly American staff, including the Chicagoan Washington; and the pan-lingual, some would say post-lingual, vocabulary employed in the writing of the publication for which they work.

Famously damaging, or commercially miraculous, front covers of *America Now* magazine are framed and hung on one side of the editorial offices, so that it is almost as if the one wall in the room that lacks windows in fact has hundreds of them, each with a face pressed to the glass.

The publication uses two standard cover layouts, which virtually alternate in the trophy editions preserved on the wall.

The first set-up is a wedding picture ripped in half, or, in the regrettable absence of the ceremony negatives themselves, a shot of a couple obviously tolerating each other's company in public, also torn in two.

The second most tried design features two opposed photographs. Smaller, foregrounded, will be an official image of a man: suited, toothy, smooth, the approved iconography. This picture will be taken from a public source: a campaign stop, a photo-op, a shareholders' report, an autographed publicity portrait. Background, larger, the biggest single image on the cover, will be a picture of a woman, generally twenties, not infrequently blonde, eyes that have done some crying but you wouldn't, guys, mind seeing smiling into yours. This picture will have been privately posed for *America Now* at an expensive session in a Manhattan loft.

It is generally the case that the man is famous until the magazine appears, at which point he becomes infamous or, at the very least, his celebrity thins. The woman, by contrast, is usually quite unknown until publication, when she attains something between fame and infamy.

In a few cases, the library picture in the foreground is of a woman, and the bigger commissioned portrait behind it shows a man. On one cover, both featured faces are female, although, in general, the circulation has not been thought ready for such innovative stories.

In all cases, the front page contains sensational phrases in jazzy shades of ink. More than one reporter from the national grandee broadsheets, working up a piece on journalistic ethics, has compared the garishness of the colours to a whore's fingernail paint. On the wall of honour now, these circulation-surging words can be read from several paces.

HERO TO ZERO: HOW JFK BROKE MY HEART, read identical cover lines, though with different pictures,

from 1968, 1972, 1974 and 1978. A BABE TOO FAR –
JACKIE CALLS FOR DIVORCE OVER HOLLYWOOD
ROMPS, pants another, from 1969. KISS ME BEFORE I
BOMB CASTRO – JFK'S AMAZING CUBAN MISSILE
TRYST was a teaser to readers of a 1972 edition, marking, in
the only way the magazine knew, the tenth anniversary of the
White House's avoidance of nuclear war. KENNEDY AT 70:
GREAT LOVER, LOUSY LEADER? wonders a cover from
1987, unusually allowing his picture to be the biggest image,
but compensating by dotting ten insets of sexy young women
around his head and torso in a kind of nymphet necklace.

A second pattern can be discerned among the arranged
frames. MARILYN: A NEW MAN IN HER LIFE? is the
question on separate covers from 1965, 1968, 1970, 1971,
1977, 1981, and 1988. WHAT MARILYN TAUGHT ME is
the wording on three front pages, all with main male picture,
secondary female one, from the 1970s. MM AT 40: THE
PARTY'S OVER? enquires the magazine in 1966, repeating
the cover line, with merely decimal adjustment, in 1976, and
1986. MARILYN FIGHTS DRUG HELL is flagged across
several editions from the seventies.

Displayed separately, behind the editor's desk, are the
three highest-selling covers in the publication's history, each
of which required doubled print runs. They are 1968's JFK
AND MARILYN – THE TRUTH, 1976's JACK AND
MARILYN: MORE SHOCKING REVELATIONS and
1987's JFK AND MARILYN – THE UNTOLD STORY.
On each of these covers, the art department junks house style
to give two portraits equal weight: the teeth and tan of the
president, the tresses and breasts of the actress.

But none of these lucrative exclusives was published
during Thomson's tenure. He was appointed by the new
Australian proprietor two years previously. His main achievement to date has been to add a small amount of journalistic
respectability to the magazine: the equivalent of the literary
short stories in *Playboy*. For example, he has initiated a
competition to discover the kindest, gentlest town in America:
'Nice Town, USA'.

Such features, however, are merely calculated ballast for

the scandals, and it is real H-bomb gossip Thomson needs. He is conscious of the weight of circulation history on the walls above his head, as he faces Washington across the desk, the record of Diane's confession in boxes between them. The wide windows, eighteen floors above Seventh Avenue in the lower 40s, frame, as the light dulls towards dusk, flurries of snow, but they are so far only sketches for a proper fall, like a sudden sneeze from someone eating cream cake.

'They'll need new printing presses for this one,' says Washington, whose voice it is on the cassettes, testing and protecting Diane.

'I've had wet dreams about a child abuse exclusive these last few years,' Thomson admits. 'But *this* one . . .'

'Child abuse? We're gonna call this child abuse? I'm thinking statutory rape.'

'She was eleven. Anyway, child abuse is what people are saying these days, I'll go with the flow. Where are we getting on the other thing?'

The magazine is following up a tip-off that the subject, or object, of Project Apollo pays $1,000 a month into a private bank account in Texas.

'Nothing yet,' Washington reports.

'That's laryngectomy cash, I'm sure of it,' Thomson says. 'A wad to lose your voice. Either it's another kid he fingered, secret baby payments; or maybe some faggot thing from college. Either way, the American people has a right to know.'

They laugh together at the last line. It is in the culture of offices that jokes develop, their humour depending not on freshness but on repetition, and this is Thomson's and Washington's.

22:   Writing Home

This morning began badly for Ford, with the report from his bathroom scales that he has gained a pound over yesterday's weight. He is beginning to fear that if you consume, in compensation, twice as many diabetic pretzels as you would have eaten regular, then reduced-sugar food can be fattening.

This is a setback, because Ford has just begun to see one advantage to losing weight. If he were thinner, then his colleagues, at least the new ones coming in, might just stop calling him 'Gerry'. Abraham R. Ford on his driving licence, he has, since he joined the force just after Watergate, been called 'Gerry', because of a slight resemblance, in poor light, to America's thirty-seventh president: one of the dumbest and slowest, in general opinion, there has been. Perhaps, if he can take off the weight, he could aim for the nickname, because of his ancient but now unusual first name, of 'Lincoln'. He envies his partner. Duke is a cool enough tag and the only hassle he gets is people asking him about his cousin, the movie star Olympia Dukakis.

They turn left from Beacon onto Arlington, past the Public Gardens. On Beacon, there was the usual gaggle of tourists photographing the frontage of a bar. This is supposedly the hostelry featured in the TV series *Cheers*, although, in fact, this Boston building is shown only in a credit sequence photo. The real bar was a studio set in Los Angeles. In effect, an illusion has become a tourist attraction. It is, for Duke, a perfect symbol of the American derangement with fame.

As they cruise in the blue-and-white, Ford is sure, from Duke's air of twitchy mischief, that he is playing the minus game. But he just can't pick the pitching. There have not, for example, been any letters missing in anything Duke said.

'Hey, Duke,' he says. 'Is the chief pissed with you? They been calling you four days about the shifts for the Kennedy thing, and you ain't ever rung them back. What's up? You got some little squeeze keeping you busy nights?'

'They called me?' asks Duke.

'Where were you last night?'

'Home. We ate. I walked round to check today's shifts with Hughie. Did you know he lives near? I wrote my mom. I wrote the kids.'

Walked? Wrote?

'The fucking telephone!' shouts Ford. 'The fucking telephone!'

'What's the matter? You left it off the hook?' says Duke, but he is smiling and Ford has clearly hit another homer.

The radio spits out a call to a firearms incident at the Frankie O'Day Block on Columbus, near Holy Cross.

'I wish this fucking country would play the fucking minus game with guns,' says Duke.

Four police officers have already been shot this year. Now, in Massachusetts, capital of modern American liberalism, there is pressure for the death penalty.

Ford, who would jump to vote for such a measure, hits the siren, activates the flashing tricolour strip on the roof – red, white, and blue – and snarls at Duke. 'Yeah, great. But what'd you fucking liberals do if someone raped your wife?'

23:   Last Things

Boomer doesn't like too many bones, when there is business to be done, and the fish today is grilled red snapper. He has been nervous of this meeting, anyway, because he brings to it a single folder, pink, and labelled: 'Dallas 30th Anniversary – Final Plans'. An emotion cyclone warning is in force throughout the office at Hyannis.

Finding his employer in sombre and elusive mood, Boomer begins on what he guesses is the safest territory: the thanksgiving mass in Boston's Holy Cross Cathedral at noon on November 22nd, 1993. The cardinal will preach a sermon on public duty. All surviving family members will be present, except for the divorced wives and Rose, the matriarch, one hundred and two years old, and too weak to leave the compound. Boomer, at best a holiday Christian, has often wondered how the Kennedys deal with what seems to be one of God's sicker jokes, in which the sons are struck down young, while the mother goes on for ever.

'No cameras inside the church, sir, we have said.'

'Well, this isn't a photo-opportunity.'

'Of course not, sir.'

'Although I spent my political life being abused by Protestants for being a Catholic, and by Catholics for not being a good enough one, I attended mass on the morning of my Inauguration, and I have done so, initially at my mother's prompting, on each anniversary of Dallas. It is a private matter. If there is more fuss this year, it is because of the round number. The fuss has been made by others.'

'I realize that, sir. I'm just giving you the facts. I wasn't putting any spin on them. We can't stop them filming family members going in. The dignitary list is in your folder.'

Doctor Perry, from Parkland Hospital, will be present; now sixty-four, he is a distinguished surgeon on the brink of retirement. Father Huber is long dead.

'A small number of members of the public – mainly from the parish – have applied for tickets. They've been vetted and, well, of course, there'll be metal detectors at every entrance.' ·

'Metal detectors at Holy Cross? Do you ever stop to wonder, Boomer, at the country we have made?'

'It was a Secret Service requirement, Mr President.'

'I'm sure. You're invited, Boomer, of course.'

'The mass I can make, sir. I'll have to skip the dinner in the evening. I have a family date. My folks. Big wedding anniversary.'

'That's good. How many they got on the clock?'

'Sir, my parents married the day after you were shot. They had to clear the church – they couldn't get the guests in – they had to clear the church because of people praying for you.'

'Boomer? Is that a Catholic name? I had you figured as Dutch Protestant.'

'My dad is, sir. My mom's a Catholic. They married in her church.'

'Ah. A "mixed marriage". My mother's biggest fear. She always said they didn't last.'

The subject of his own failed – Catholic – marriage looms.

In the silence that follows – a heavy, almost, churchy mood – Boomer loses himself in the shuffling of sheets within his folder, as if this trifling filing required the concentration of chess. Jack is chewing the last of his snapper with perfectionist attention. Boomer sees the need for an emotional diminuendo, so puts a sort of musical comedy lilt in his voice, and says: 'Those conspiracy nuts have been in contact again. Checking if your no to addressing them was really a no.'

'Oh, it really was.'

'I guessed it might be, sir. Today, they rang from their

hotel, where the whole . . . the whole . . . I'm not sure what the collective noun would be for conspiracy theorists.'

'A bowl . . . a bowl of nuts.'

'Hah hah *hah*. The whole bowl of them are at this hotel in Dallas, and they wondered if you even had a comment for them.'

'Tell them that the phenomenon of grown men and women devoting their lives to the question of what really happened during a few minutes on a day thirty years ago . . . tell them that sounds *incredibly suspicious* to me. I wouldn't want to make them paranoid, but I can't help wondering *who is putting them up to it*.'

During the last few sentences, Jack pantomimes wild staring eyes, edgily checking from left to right. Boomer hoots with laughter and the meeting has been retrieved from the dark thoughts lying underneath it. Boomer turns over the third divider in his pink file.

'The Library ceremony, sir, on the twenty-fifth, is relatively straightforward. Governor Cuomo will give the keynote address, you will say a few words yourself.'

The John F. Kennedy Library and Museum, the official presidential archive, was finally opened in 1978, after a decade in which private investment had proved hard to attract. To mark the eve of the thirtieth anniversary of Dallas, a new exhibit will be opened at the museum, which overlooks the sea at Boston's Columbia Point. The first new room expands the previous scant display on Vietnam. The second, three times the size, is titled 'Other Forms of Duty'. It covers the former President's activities in the seventies and eighties: the charities, government commissions, reports, three volumes of memoirs, goodwill visits to young democratic governments overseas.

'You realize, Boomer, that, unless they bring in an amendment permitting third terms, or I save a hundred children from a burning bus, out walking one morning, this will be the last room in the museum?'

'You should never rule out a future, sir.'

This exchange has hidden edges. There is, in fact, pressure from the museum's trustees for the creation of another room. Two displays already commemorate Robert Kennedy, assassinated in 1968. Now momentum is gathering behind the idea of the museum admitting a shrine to the other Kennedy brother denied by fate a presidential library of his own: Teddy, tragically drowned at Chappaquiddick, a Massachusetts island, in July 1969, while gallantly saving the life of a research assistant trapped when his car overturned in a creek. But Jack is nervous of the growing cult of his youngest brother – and the implication that the family's greatest politician was robbed of his proper life story – and has resisted this initiative.

'The dignitary list for the library ceremony', Boomer continues, 'is in the folder you are holding now.'

'Yes, yes. I know. I've been looking through it. And I want to add a name.'

Boomer's mind switches to girl alert, babe limitation. He is already thinking damage control. But the name, when it comes, is beyond the recourse of whatever media training he has gained.

'I am very keen', says the former President, 'for you to invite Miss Marilyn Monroe. Her address, I believe, has not changed these thirty years.'

Although, during his period of employment at Hyannis Port, that name has often entered Boomer's head, he has never expected to hear it spoken aloud.

But into Jack's mind has come a phrase from his Catholic education more than sixty years before: last things. And he looks directly at Boomer, challenging him to deny this final neatness.

Part Two

A WORLD SAFE
FOR HISTORIANS

24:   The K Brothers

When in disguise, Jean tends to remember her Uncle Marion. He left home on an errand in 1929, and was never seen again. Perhaps – as her aunt had come more than half to hope – he had been murdered. But there was another explanation – dismaying to his closer family, but intoxicating to Jean – which was that he had made a whole other life, unknown to them, lost in America. This evidence of the possibility of invisibility has been a comfort to her at many times in her career.

This evening, Jean has added, to her usual nobody costume, a raven-shade wig, under the floppy summer straw hat, because, on this particular assignment, there must be no risk that her pretence might be penetrated.

As she waits in line outside the tiny movie theatre in Venice Beach, the sun is setting in a blush-wine sky. Jean can hear the gleeful anticipatory conversation of the bronzed beach bleach-blonde boy-girl couple in front of her.

'Brad – you know Brad, who waits at Sushi On Sunset?' the male of the species says. 'He saw this the last time they ran it in a season. He says this is *the* one, man. The turkey di tutti turkeys.'

'Yeah, like, has anyone ever sussed, like, why she done it?' his mate enquires. 'Like, it's kind of a hike from *Some Like It Hot* to this.'

'Oh, bimbo denial, I guess. The story behind half of Hollywood's disasters: *Look at me, I'm really serious*. Apparently, she read the novel when she was with Arthur Miller. He promised to do a script as a love gift. Never did, but she couldn't get the idea out of her system. Until the reviews, I guess.'

Jean is stung by the young man's total recall for what she most hopes to forget. Venice already provokes too many memories for her, anyway. Her mother and grandmother lived here, and she recalls outings with Gladys Monroe Baker on day furloughs from the 'clinic' Jean later realized was an asylum. Mother and daughter would walk St Mark's Square, and the bridges, canals, and lagoons of the doomed attempt by the cigarette millionaire Abbot Kinsey to imitate Italy with a Venice on America's West Coast.

With a ritual childish half-cheer as the door is released, the line begins to file in to the theatre. Inside, there is tiered seating of reduced-blue, ass-battered velvet. The walls of the auditorium are painted with gold and silver planets on a lilac background, dating the most recent decoration to the Beach's psychedelic era. The paint has faded now and the main continuity between epochs is the smell of Indian hemp already floating from the first rows filled at the front.

Jean takes a seat on the left-hand aisle, close to the exit, allowing an easy escape in case the ghosts choke her. On each seat, there is a leaflet, from which the stink of cheap ink rises to combine with the narcotic fog. She reads:

VENICE MOVIE TURKEY ROAST—
Autumn 1993 Season

Welcome to the latest selection of the Venice Movie Turkey Roast Society—every movie guaranteed a loser!

For a reasonable annual subscription fee, you are able to watch the films their makers wish you wouldn't. Studios and agents accuse us of cruelty, but we believe that we are performing an important public service—allowing you to view the careers of the Hollywood greats in the round, and offering the new generation of stars a warning against the temptations of "vanity trash," that moment of creative madness, in which all the lessons learned in a working life are gloriously ignored.

This season, we believe we're serving you the plumpest set of turkeys to be found in the studio fridges. "Attractions" include: Steve McQueen's version of Ibsen's *An*

Enemy of the People; Steven Spielberg's only disaster, *1941*; Dustin Hoffman and Warren Beatty's *Ishtar!*; and— beginning the season—*The K Brothers*, the legendary floperoonie starring Marilyn Monroe.

There is a football-crowd shout as the lights begin to dim. Although Jean has already shaved her shame in preparation for the operation, she is still surprised to find that the giggling begins during the pre-credits sequence which, although she accepts that the picture as a whole has limitations, seems to her no worse than stolid. It shows three horsemen, bearish in their hat-to-ankle furs, swirling across the snowy steppe to the music of Tchaikovsky's 'Symphonie Pathétique'.

'Even the music's pathetic!' cries a camp voice, receiving two appreciative peals from other musicologists present.

On the screen, the riders have arrived at a town, full of buildings with onion domes, where they sweep, through sprays of snow like whitewater waves, into the court yard of a palatial residence, dismount and rush inside. Slapping his thighs in front of a spitting fire, one of the horsemen speaks the film's first line of dialogue.

'It's like Siberia out there! Dearest Mother, I hope you have the samovar boiling.'

'Indeed I have, Aleksey Fyodorovich!' growls a heavily made-up middle-aged afternoon soap actress, whom the camera now locates amid the inky canvas tent that is her dress. Both speakers use unhidden American accents.

Some of the matriarch's subsequent words are lost in the snarls of laughter, as the dialogue in the film, not by intention a comedy, was not paced to allow recovery time to the audience.

But now the grizzled mother trudges round the semicircle of her sons as they warm their backs by the fire and, in gruff sub-eucharistic fashion, serves each a glass of tea from the samovar. Conveniently, for the viewer of the film, she reminds herself, as she pours, of the names of her children, both patronymics and diminutives: 'Here you are, Aleksey Fyodorovich, my Alyosha . . . this'll warm you, Dmitry Fyodorovich, my Mitya . . . And for you, Ivan Fyodorovich . . .'

'Poor Ivan's only got two names!' comes a whisper from the half-dark around Jean.

As the sons sip the warming liquid, the mother unsteadily sloshes a glass for herself, and raises it towards her offspring. 'My sons, you are already a credit to your father, Fyodor Pavlovich.'

'He's got a funny way of showing it sometimes,' grumbles Dmitry Fyodorovich, in the intonations of the Bronx.

'Your father loves you,' the mother reassures Mitya. 'He just has kinda high standards. But I know, as God is in his heaven, that the three of you will take good wives, and bring honour upon the family name, and that you will always be true to Mother Russia and to each other. To my sons!'

They seal their affection in tea. Then Aleksey Fyodorovich, a midwesterner, returns the gesture. 'To our mother!' he cries. 'And to . . .' The camera drags back from medium close-up to wide-shot, as Alyosha and his two brothers share a fraternal smirk: 'And to . . . the Brothers Karamazov!'

After yelling out these words, all four performers drain their glasses in one head-back splash, chink their drinking vessels against each other, and then hurl them into the furnace of the hearth. As the brothers link arms for what looks dangerously likely to be a Cossack dance, and the 'Symphonie Pathétique' swells on the soundtrack, the screen creeps to black and the opening credits begin to spill down.

The audience, already applauding, shouts 'Yo!' and 'Way to go!' when they see the name, in undeniable large white letters: MARILYN MONROE in . . . THE K BROTHERS.

The crowd is subdued throughout the rest of the name-checks, except for a spasmodic yelp of recognition for a performer later mildly famous in *Cagney and Lacey* or *Dallas*. So Jean is able to hear another pedantic archivist lecturing his partner in the seats behind her: 'Of course, the studio called it *The K Brothers* to cash in on the gossip about her and the Kennedys. But this was the Cold War, a year into Reagan's first term, and Mr and Mrs America weren't exactly ready for a lot of Commies rushing round shouting, "God save Mother Russia!" A year after the first flop, the studio tried to repackage it as an adventure yarn. They called it *The*

Three Ruskateers!, and released it in a couple of theatres. *Nyet* again.'

Once more, Jean is shaken by this evidence of the durability of humiliation. One of the ways a performer survived their career was the belief that flops were soon forgotten, but she was surrounded here by people who studied duds.

There is another collective tremor in the audience, when the writing credit comes up: SCREENPLAY BY JACK BERET-TOVICH, BASED UPON THE BROTHERS KARAMAZOV BY FYODOR DOSTOEVSKY.

Here, at least, is one nuance that seems to have escaped the fact-heads in the theatre. The three writers who contrib-uted to the screenplay – a distinguished American novelist, and two once-promising off-Broadway dramatists – all suc-cessfully petitioned the Writers Guild to have their names removed from the film. 'Berettovich' is an invented credit, formed from the pistol brandname 'Beretta' and the Russian suffix '-ovich' to mean, literally, 'son of a gun'. Only Pauline Kael noticed, calling this, in her review, the movie's one good line.

During the opening scenes, the mood is restless, eager for Marilyn's first appearance. There is a buzz of expectation when a character refers to 'that little prostitute, Grushenka', who they obviously know to be the Monroe role.

In a flurry of confessional and confrontational scenes around the seminary where Aleksey Fyodorovich is studying to be a monk, it is established that both Fyodor Pavlovich and his son Dmitry Fyodorovich have – in the script's uneasy transcontinental patois – 'got the hots, as God is my witness' for Grushenka, the 'dirty little former concubine' of a mer-chant in a neighbouring village. Dmitry, little Mitya, is engaged to marry Katerina Ivanovna, but, as someone puts it, plans to 'palm her off, like a second-hand hay-cart' on his brother, Ivan.

Finally Aleksey, little Alyosha, summoned from the mon-astery to mediate in this family crisis, crunches through the snow to Katerina Ivanovna's home on Main Street. In conversation with her, he is surprised when Katerina suddenly shouts out for Grushenka, who he believes to be the other woman's enemy and nemesis, to enter the room. At this point, Marilyn's signature breathy voice is heard for the first time in the film.

'Oh,' she says, 'I was just waiting behind the drape for you to call me . . .'

All around Jean, there is cheering. On screen, the curtain is pulled back, and Grushenka enters. Her blonde hair is twisted into a severe top-knot, but the red silk dress is low-cut, and thrusts the actress's trademark bust forward.

'I figured we could work this whole thing out, girl to girl,' says Katerina Ivanovna.

'You are too good to me,' replies Grushenka. 'Sometimes I think you will live to regret your kindness.'

'Oh, no, how could that ever be?'

For the next two hours, each of Grushenka's lines is met with hysterical squeals. When the lights go up for the interval – they are obviously screening the original 275-minute cut – Jean moves only to let those in the inside seats on her row push past in search of drink or piss. The information magus in the row behind has also chosen to stay and commences another lecture to his girlfriend. Jean sits very still and listens.

'Of course, on screen, the whole idea seems comical,' he begins. 'But Marilyn *had* read the book, and liked it. As early as a press conference to announce *The Prince and the Showgirl*, with Laurence Olivier, in 1956, she was talking about a film of *The Brothers*. Arthur Miller was keen to do the screenplay. And, you know, she wasn't, in principle, a mad idea for Grushenka. Dostoevsky actually describes her as a kind of 'child-woman'. She is "buxom", and he specifically indicates a "sugary" voice, an "artificial" way of speaking. The difficulty is that he also states Grushenka is twenty-two, and the kind of Russian woman whose beauty would have "run to fat past thirty". By the time Marilyn finally got finance, with the money Onassis left her, she was well past fifty. The moral, I guess, is that life-long dreams have a sell-by date.'

Jean cannot deny this insight, and considers leaving before she sees or hears more. But, if the ritual is to have any significance – seeking, through this humiliation, a kind of purification before her return to the public eye – then it must be followed to its end. She must admit this failure, as addicts must declare in public their destructive appetite.

It has often occurred to her, anyway, that fame is like consistently over-hearing comments about yourself from people who didn't realize you were listening next door. She had merely formalized the process.

As her ridiculers come back – and she stands to let them in – she remembers the title of the second book of *The Brothers Karamazov*: 'An Inappropriate Gathering'.

25: Will the Real JFK?

The first session of the symposium begins on the stroke of the time shown in the brochure. In fact, every row of seats was filled twenty minutes before the charted start time. The conspiracy theorists, it seems, are obsessed, among so many other things, with punctuality. Crick suspects that they fear, in some atavistic reaction to their dweeb days as kids, that they have maliciously been given the wrong information, and were allowing time to find the real location if they had been tricked.

Crick's complicated wrist-watch, which subdivides time right down to milliseconds, is showing 10 and then a neat line of zeroes you would dream of seeing on a cheque, when the opening speaker coughs softly at the podium.

'Good morning. I'm Jim Draycott, a researcher from Nebraska, my talk is called "Will the Real JFK Please Stand Up?", and it's my privilege to, as it were, fire the first shot of this conference . . . although at least on this occasion we have it established, in writing we can believe, exactly how many shots there are!'

Draycott waves the symposium brochure to underline his joke about the Warren Commission, and its version, which has no worshippers in this room, of how much ballistic activity there was in Dallas. Even the just woken throats of his audience manage a grunt of approval.

Draycott, who has an aura of mid-forties, wears his hair in ropy tendrils hanging down from a nearly abandoned scalp. Crick noticed a real drama school limp as the man approached the podium. He guesses Vietnam. At each symposium of Dealey Plaza Researchers, Crick has become more sure of the uncomfortable truth that the majority of delegates are in some way dysfunctional.

There are the three-hundred-pounders, going five rounds with the hotel breakfast buffet. Then there are those who take only orange juice from the display, but use it to gulp down an entire bracelet of vividly coloured pills from the table in front of them. Finally there are the people with the weals deeper in, initially unseen, who will suddenly say, late at night, over a second-bottle conversation about the role of Lyndon Johnson in the plot: 'The government lies. I'm a patriotic American, but the government lies. It lied about the way my son died . . .'

Or their wife, or their daughter, or their lover. So many of the delegates seem to have lost someone. Even Evaristi – sitting next to Crick in the Fifteen Club's enclave in the third row from the front – qualifies for that group too. He is convinced that the coroner's verdict – suicide – on his nineteen-year-old daughter, found dead in bed at her sorority house in 1987, is false. He is convinced that she was murdered by the CIA: a warning to her pop that he had got too close to the truth about Dallas.

Sometimes Crick believes himself to be the only delegate who is not compensating. And, this morning, he has been able to examine his colleagues in unusual detail, closely scanning the rows for researcher Malone, Katherine P. Although his photographs are locked away at home, in the concealed filing cabinet within the filing cabinet, he is certain he would recognize his own Kathy Malone, even given the facial recriminations of three decades.

But he must look out front now, and concentrate on what Draycott is saying.

'I voted Kennedy–Johnson in 1960,' the speaker reveals. 'On November 22nd, 1963, in the hour when it seemed that the worst possible catastrophe had happened, I cried so much I had to change my sweatshirt. But, like so many others, I lost my faith during Kennedy's second term. Partly, it was 'Nam. Of course, it was. But it was more. How many times have you heard old Kennedy Democrats say: "He wasn't the same after Dallas"? and: "How could *Jack* have made the mistake of Vietnam?" You will have heard these things said. And you will have thought, as I did until ten years ago, that these were just everyday figures of speech. But . . .'

There was a special style, an agreed way, of saying 'But', which, at the symposium, produced a shiver of anticipation in the crowd, like the moment at a pop concert when the first bars of the performer's fingerprint hit are heard.

'But', Draycott says, 'I will show to you this morning that the Jack Kennedy of the second term, and thus the JFK who wasted an American generation in Vietnam, was indeed *not the same man* who, in 1960, illuminated and enthused his nation. Lights!'

The light skulks from the room, and the first slide is projected on the screen behind the podium. The picture – bleeding onto Draycott's scalp, because of his height – shows Kennedy in a still from the campaign trail in 1960. There is the punctuating click of the projector tumbril and a second photograph ghosts in. This is the Kennedy of 1968, freeze-framed from an Oval Office telecast about the war.

'What you have seen', Draycott says, 'are the faces of two quite different men. Not merely visually, not merely chrono-logically, not merely metaphorically – but actually. It is my contention that the former President John Fitzgerald Ken-nedy, who moves before us now in the shadows of the public stage, who talks to Bryant Gumbel on General Electric's *Today* show . . .'

Draycott clearly understood his audience. Delegates to the symposium traditionally stiffened, or even hissed, at the mention of one of the nation's large corporations. By attrib-uting the breakfast television programme not to the producing network, but to its parent company, Draycott won his lecture vital friends in its early stages.

Two delegates boo when they hear the words General Electric, and Draycott needs to raise his voice to continue: '. . . that man is, I believe, an impostor. An off-Broadway actor, recruited by the CIA in 1962, while appearing in an adaption of *The Wings of the Dove*. Because of his astonishing resemblance to the then President Kennedy, this per-former–agent walked out of Parkland Hospital, Dallas, in early December 1963, and was elected – *re*-elected, the newspapers erroneously said – as president in 1964!'

There is a gasp from half the audience of a sort for which an author of stage thrillers would kill. Crick, however, turns to Evaristi and whispers: 'This is fucking crazy. The only actor there's been in the White House was Reagan.'

'Listen,' growls Evaristi. 'These people can murder my daughter, they're more than capable of this.'

Crick lets it go. Evaristi has just offered a classic conspiracy syllogism, in which a highly arguable contention – here, the nature of Mimi Evaristi's death – is solidified into a fact from which other propositions are logically extended.

'Why', Draycott is asking, 'would such a bizarre and dangerous switch have been attempted? The answer, my friends, is Vietnam.'

A third slide nudges aside the image of the second-term Kennedy on the screen. The new exhibit is a faded piece of cream paper, with the official White House heading, and a classification line: EYES ONLY.

'This is National Security Action Memorandum Number 263,' says Draycott. 'Dated October 11th, 1963. In it, President Kennedy recommends the withdrawal of one thousand US military from South Vietnam by the end of December 1963. The President, my friends, was planning to pull back America from the abyss of Vietnam. But the military-industrial complex – that club of blood- and money-hungry soldiers and arms manufacturers – needed de-escalation in Vietnam like Texaco needs a car that runs on water.'

'There was such a car,' mutters Evaristi to Crick. 'Texaco pay the inventor two million dollars a year to keep quiet about it.'

'You don't *believe* that, do you, Johnny?'

Draycott's reference to Texaco has provoked an even larger reaction than his mention of General Electric. So he is almost shouting when he resumes: 'And so the military-industrial complex concocted a terrible and treasonable plan. They decided to put another Kennedy in the White House. And they *didn't* mean Bobby. President Kennedy was travelling to Dallas – and it was decided to kill him there.

115

Meanwhile, in CIA headquarters in Langley, Virginia, an off-Broadway actor was learning the lines of the last, but greatest, role he would ever play.'

But Crick is no longer listening. Blessed, or cursed, with a hypersensitivity to peripheral movement, which saved him many times in army days but has ruined too many civilian nights, he has sensed a late entrant at the rear-right door of the hall. He turns and looks back, hoping to see Kathy Malone.

26:   The Invitation

Meredith – the 'English assassin' – has to ring three times, and play please-please-please with a secretary who always sounds frightened, before his call is accepted.

'Fraternelli.'

'Ah. Mr Fraternelli, it's Meredith.'

'OK, I've spoken with my colleagues. They make the point you're the only guy this outfit ever employed who volunteered to do more work for the same money. They think you're crazy. But they accept your logic. Well, in fact, the board was split, but you got a majority. What swayed them, by the way, was the publicity angle. They think this *will* make more of a splash, as you said. So, you can do Jack and Marilyn together.'

'Well, separately, but in the same job.'

'The details we leave to you.'

'That's excellent. I don't think you'll regret it. There is one other thing.'

'Don't tell me. You've been thinking maybe you'll do Frank Sinatra while you're about it as well. Three-for-one deal you're offering this month.'

'No. No, nothing like that.'

Meredith manages the chuckle in his voice he feels is called for here, although it always pains him to join in laughter directed at himself.

'No, what it is, Mr Fraternelli, is that for the Kennedy side of things, there's an entry I need.'

'OK. Try me. I have connections.'

'The thirtieth anniversary mass in Boston.'

'Holy Cross Cathedral.'

'You know about it?'

'I read something. You need permission to go to church? Just wear a "League of Mary" T-shirt and remember to kneel at the right time.'

'It's all-ticket. Security.'

'Uh-huh. Well, Kennedy has a lot of enemies.'

Meredith gives his deepest laugh, so that it must sound to Fraternelli as if a dog has seized the mouthpiece of the telephone and started eating it.

'OK,' says Fraternelli. 'This I think I can arrange. There are a lot of Catholics in my family.'

27: Nice Town, USA

Thomson and Washington examine with professional dispassion the pictures from the session with Diane. She was not an easy sitter, rejecting all the dresses the *America Now* fashion editor had selected for her, with their economical fabric-saving bust and hem design. 'I didn't come to you to be a sex symbol,' she kept complaining. 'He stole my life!'

Sifting the products of two hours' photography, Thomson is concerned.

'I don't know,' the editor says. 'I really don't know. Looking at that, would *you* want to cover her in frozen yoghurt and lick it off?'

Uncertain whether this remark reflects Sydney metaphor or an actual Australian sexual practice, Washington tentatively answers: 'I figured different editorial priorities might apply on this one, chief. This is our serious political story. Our, uh, Watergate.'

'Maybe you're right. Big on him – one with the presidential seal in the background, ideally Oval Office – and Diane smaller, bottom left corner. Get Design to mock it. And, hey, I hadn't thought of that. You American hacks and your "gate" gimmick. I dream of one of your pols misfiling to the IRS over some sort of ornamental door at one of his homes. Gategate! It would sound so fucking stupid, the next scandal would just get called a row. What'll they call ours? *Daughter*-gate, if it had been incest, but it isn't. Statutoryrapegate? Too long, oh Lord, too long. Rapegate?'

'Apollogate?' Washington suggests.

'Yeah. That's it. That's it. You're right . . .'

Project Apollo is being prepared, amid air-sealed secrecy,

for the edition of *America Now* dated November 20th, 1993. The name of Diane's abuser has been omitted from all transcripts, layouts, and page-proofs. It has been represented in all pre-publication material by the variations 'Mickey Mouse', 'Mouse', 'Mr Mouse'. There is deliberately no reference to 'President Mouse', which would limit the field too much. Even so, this device has given the descriptions of the physical encounters in the article a kinky surreality – 'And then Mr Mouse placed my hand on his penis . . .' – which Thomson finds disturbingly exciting.

Minutes before press time, a computer word-change program will substitute the real name of the accused. For this reason, a reference in Diane's testimony to a pet mouse she kept as a child – originally, a sly reminder to the reader of her age and innocence at the time of the encounters – has been cut from the copy, to prevent the computer blindly replacing the animal with a man's name. A cautionary story is told in American publishing of a novelist who had used a software revision facility to alter a character's name from 'David' to 'Jeff' throughout a manuscript. Readers of the book were subsequently surprised to find a reference to 'Michelangelo's famous sculpture of Jeff'.

So it is Mickey Mouse, too, who is accused on all the cover mock-ups of involvement in a CHILD ABUSE SCANDAL. And, for this issue, press time has been delayed until minutes before printing, and distribution advanced to minutes after printing.

These precautions are intended to minimize the possibility of a minor employee – runner, secretary, printer – leaking the exclusive scandal to a rival publication for a fee larger than their annual salary. This risk existed because, in Thomson's view, the average person was now far too sophisticated about the media. For the same reason, the picture desk has ordered from the library the files on nearly a hundred prominent Americans, including every president since Roosevelt, heads of corporations, movie stars. The best a bike-boy could guess from that was that they were planning an encyclopaedia edition.

Preparing this issue, Thomson feels ever less cowed as he

sits, swearing into two telephones in American and Australian alternatively, before the glory wall of former editors' triumphs. The child abuse lead is a real creamer, but he is also pleased with the 'Nice Town, USA' survey and spread. Thomson calculates this feature as a mark of journalistic honour if the ponce press should seek to denigrate the magazine in an attempt to discredit Diane's story.

With a brief to discover and photograph an American town in which there had not been a homicide in living memory, and where children still played out at nights, *America Now*'s rarely activated state stringers drove through their patch, visiting those communities which had never showed up in the homicide charts. This was an hour's work for the Detroit and New York bureau chiefs, several days' employment for the New England correspondents. The experiment was delayed by the fact that, in many towns, the children rushed indoors as soon as they saw the reporter, believing him to be a potential molester.

Eventually, however, the town of Newton, Maine, was selected. *America Now* had retained a photographer from outside its usual roster – one experienced in framing bodies with clothes on – to produce a Rockwellian portfolio of the town. In the photo leading the feature, children tumbled and laughed on a rust-and-lime duvet of fallen leaves. In another, a young girl, scarcely bigger than the bag she shouldered, trudged home in the soft dusk light along an empty street of clapboard homes, with flags on most front lawns.

In the accompanying article, Mary E. Robinson, thirty-seven, an assistant teacher in Newton and mother of two, told the reporter that she was 'cool' about Betsey, seven, and Nathaniel, two, playing on the streets near their home between school and dark, and at weekends. Mrs Robinson said: 'Obviously, Betsey knows to keep an eye on Nat, but otherwise I know they're fine. Yeah, it's true that watching CNN, you sometimes think this is the last safe place in America. But Newton *is* safe.' A picture of Mrs Robinson, with her daughters, was one of the three supporting illustrations on the third page. Graphics had roughed up a mock certificate, with lavishly squiggled ink inscription, announcing

Newton, Maine, as inaugural winner of the first *America Now* 'Nice Town, USA' campaign.

The magazine's letters page – 'Forum, USA' – carried every other week a complaint about the 'negativity' of the modern media. The correspondents asked why the 'good news' could not be reported. Well, Thomson was giving them some. It was Newton, Maine.

The editor has never experienced such professional contentment as he feels now. In forty-eight hours, the newsstands will unpack the bundles of an edition of *America Now* destined without doubt for the office glory wall, and perhaps even for a footnote in histories of journalism and politics. And, on Thomson's desk, is a file marked APOLLO 2: the investigation of accusations that Diane's abuser has paid $1,000 a month for fifteen years into the checking account of a Texan man. The national investigation desk is down to a list of four possible recipients of what the magazine believes to be hush money.

'OK,' Thomson says to Washington. 'Apollo is on the launch pad.'

'Yeah. Boosters away . . .'

28: And Was Made Reincarnate of Man

'Guys,' the President scolds, 'the passage on reincarnation seems to have gone. Well, I think that better, uh, *come back . . .*'

The Chief of Staff and the Senior Media Adviser again attempt the diplomatic gymnastics of smiling at Sanders' joke while at the same time exchanging coded glances of alarm. This is an almost daily work-out for them now.

It is November 21st, 1993, and the administration's inner circle is once again discussing the text of the forthcoming State of the Union address. The words about rebirth have been removed from the draft. Calculating that amnesia is sometimes a stage in derangement, Boyd and Woodall hoped that Sanders might not notice. He has.

On this occasion, it is Boyd who voices the objection, while Woodall nods support. To be the voice of sanity in this administration is long and lonely work, and so the two men share the load. They are particularly exposed, in having no vice-president with whom to plot.

This constitutional lacuna results from another of Sanders's protests against political tradition during his campaign. Pressured in the summer of 1992 to announce a vice-presidential nominee, he placed the names of all his registered state supporters in a barrel, and plucked one with his eyes shut. The running mate selected in this way was a soft drinks salesman from Pittsburgh, whose name was duly entered on the buttons, posters, and ballot papers. But after the Sanders victory, Congress refused to confirm the beverage vendor as vice-president, and so the Bible was used only once on inauguration day.

'We felt, sir,' Boyd says, 'that the passage you refer to interrupted the flow of your arguments.'

'Is that right?' Sanders replied. 'Well, back home, we always say, you don't ever want to go with the flow, except when you're in a canoe. And are we in a canoe?'

'No, sir,' smiles the Chief of Staff, although, in fact, an image has arrived in his mind of just such a craft, made of balsa wood, balanced on the brink of a roaring waterfall. There are three people in the doomed canoe: the President, Woodall, and himself. If this were an editorial page cartoon, the name of the boat would be 'Administration', or, from one of the grander satirists, 'Democracy'. Perhaps – yes, yes – there would be a speech bubble coming from the caricature President, containing the words: 'Back home, they say that paddling's what steam-boats do.'

'You seem to find something funny, Bob,' the President says.

'Oh, no, sir, I . . . well, this is going to sound creepy, but I was just thinking how much fun it is to be in government right now, how unlike other politicians you are.'

'How unlike politicians. Not *other* politicians, although I hesitate to pull up you Ivy League guys on grammar and such. Because, see, I am not a politician.'

'No, sir, Mr President.'

Boyd and Woodall think of exchanges like this as Rosencrantz-and-Guildenstern moments. Just as for Hamlet's college friends, the realization that their master was playing games with them – pretending to be crazy – would have been humiliating, but it was still more reassuring than the alternative. When the President speaks again, however, the possibility that Sanders is shamming madness seems to recede from them.

'Jesus Christ was reincarnated.'

'Mr President, I'm not sure that Christian Americans would—'

Now it is Woodall playing defence. Celebrated throughout his career for his softly spoken style, he is virtually mouthing his contributions at the moment, as if trying to prevent his entry on the historical record. But Sanders has already heard enough to disagree.

'No, no, Al. This is the true message of the Resurrection – not that we shall live for ever in some kind of rest-home in the ozone. But that we shall live for ever *cyclically*.'

'Sir, I wonder . . .'

'Let me develop this. What *better* theme for a State of the Union address than this? Death – the final mystery for Americans.' Boyd and Woodall have to admit that Sanders has the trick of putting a patriotic spin on matters. 'What do the voters care about, really care about? Tax? Welfare? Defence? Yes, yes, I know, Al, I see you reaching for your polling folder. Those are the issues that show. But all of your surveys are flawed by the fact that people never mention the single issue they most care about. Death. When people mention health care, when people mention gun control, what are they *really* grousing about? Death! And I am the first American President to tackle this. I am able to say, "My fellow Americans, there is an answer to this greatest of human questions, to the departure of so many of your loved ones, apparently before their time. If only they were still here, you say. They are still here! The clerk at the ticket office. The company vice-president. Perhaps it is one of them. I am one of your family. You are one of my family. This is how it works . . ."'

The canoe is nearly over the waterfall now, the three of them a minute away from being reincarnated as red-stained driftwood, but Boyd has seen the chance of a way back.

'Sir,' he says. 'I would not interrupt, except that I believe I have just heard one of the great political anthems of our age. Listen to what you just said. "I am one of your family. You are one of my family. This is how it works." It is a perfect crystallization of your political message. It is my belief that these words could become your equivalent of Kennedy's "Ask not what your country can do for you, but what you can do for your country." Let us take those words and use them as the basis of the State Address.'

'So you're accepting the reincarnation stuff stays, guys?' Sanders asks.

Boyd looks left for help. Woodall replies so quietly that the President and the Chief of Staff have to lean towards him, as if eavesdropping on their own conversation.

'Mr President,' he whispers, 'I think what Bob is saying is that, yes, indeed, you have convinced us. These words will be the headline item in your speech. "I am one of your family. You are one of my family. This is how it works." But what we are also saying, I think, is that, in those three phrases, you say everything you wish to say on the subject of, uh, reincarnation. The great political slogans – and this, as Bob says, is up there with the greatest – do not need explanation.'

'The Bible has no footnotes, sir,' Boyd adds, and is so astonished at the opportuneness of what has just popped into his mouth that his position on the nonexistence of God is seriously compromised.

'Well,' the President replies, 'back home, they say, if you do ever meet the devil, he may not be holding a toasting fork to tip you off. But I think you guys are on my side. So, OK, we'll try that passage in the next draft. Now, Bob, was it you mentioned that line from Kennedy's inaugural?'

'Yes, sir. I believe that yours will—'

'That wasn't my point, Bob. What I'm saying is, did I ever tell you my Kennedy and Marilyn joke?'

'No, sir.'

'OK. Jack and Marilyn in bed together. He's trying to get it in her, but she tells him to go down on her first. And Jack looks at her, and says: "Ask not what your cunt can do for you, but what your cunt can do for me." Ain't that great?'

Boyd and Woodall laugh to the edge of oxygen deprivation, but, inside, what the President has said seems to Boyd a kind of blasphemy: another indication of the cynicism of their patron. Surely none of the millions of 'Sanderistas' – the media's name for the backers of the independent candidate – would ever guess that such was the soul of their hero.

'My point is this,' the President is saying. 'What else is the American dream but a promise of reincarnation? You can be anything you want to be . . .'

29: Jack's Dream

In Jack's dream, the assassination succeeds. The surrounding detail is the material of his memories and nightmares – the blue limousine, the insouciant pink dress, the unexplained umbrella – but the narrative is altered.

In the dream, his perspective is from outside the car, looking down the route, as if in the Zapruder movie of the shooting. But his subconscious runs the pictures on, beyond the point – the shot or first shot – at which he always turns away when the Dallas footage unexpectedly shows up on television.

In his dream, his nightmare, the bullet connects centrally and his head ejects a spume of tissue, a spray of brain. He knows that he has not survived, and is somehow outside his body, watching, as the car is raced to Parkway.

He is lying on a bald, cold, trauma room table. A nurse is taking off his watch, thick with a crust of clotting blood. A pencil light is shone in his eyes, then dimmed and pocketed with resignation. There is an old man with his collar on back to front. Of course, a priest. Jackie, weeping, red on the pink of her dress, is speaking to him. His name is – Cooper? Hoover? Hoober? The acoustics of a dream are poor. Jackie requests the final sacrament for her husband.

And now the grass and gravel of Arlington cemetery on a chill and glittery DC day. Bobby's grave is there, so this is later, years later, and a dream in which the sleeper is aware of the reality that is being contradicted. But – wait – there is no plot for Teddy. Instead, Jack reads on a slab laid in the earth: PRESIDENT JOHN F. KENNEDY—1917–1963. Fire! And now there is fire. Is he dreaming of his soul in hell?

127

No, there is a small flame rising from the earth of his grave. Children kneel before it, spilling flowers.

Next a classroom, like those from the campaign in '64. But this is later. The kids are mainly black, African-American, wearing baseball caps backwards. They are chanting the presidents: '. . . Hoover, Franklin Roosevelt, Truman, Eisenhower, Kennedy, *Johnson*, Nixon, Ford, Carter, Reagan, Bush, *Clinton* . . .'

His italics. And, as if to answer the dreamer's queries, the narrative screens pseudo-newsreel from these two never-presidencies. The Vietnam protest marches, nothing new to his nightmares, but with one change in the terrible chant: 'Hey, hey, *LBJ*, how many kids did you kill today?' And Lyndon, *President* Johnson, sweaty on television from the Oval Office: 'I will not seek, and would not accept, the nomination of my party . . .' Now Humphrey, Hubert Humphrey, instead of Johnson, making the concession speech after Nixon's victory in 1968. And Bobby shot, as Bobby was, but not in Washington, in Los Angeles, in a kitchen, surrounded by weeping people in 'RFK for President' badges.

Fucking crazy dreams. Next he sees Governor Clinton, on the campaign trail in '92, his sleeping brain's pick-up of real material from CNN, no surprises here. Except that, suddenly, Clinton is talking about 'the Kennedy legacy', which he was certainly never stupid enough to do in the real thing. And there is a television ad campaign, with a clip of Jack shaking hands with the young Bill Clinton, part of a group of Arkansas students, in the White House Rose Garden in 1962.

And a pundit on one of the Sunday shout-shows is saying: 'One of the cleverest things Clinton did – one of the reasons he won – is that he played the JFK thing for all it was worth. He had his hair cut like him, he talked up his youth and energy. The dream of a new Jack Kennedy is a very potent one in American politics—'

But a younger commentator interrupts, saying: 'That's right. We saw off the British – and for what? Belief in an Irish-Catholic monarchy! First, genetically, through Bobby and Ted. And now, would you believe, through some Bubba ventriloquist. America has raised a death cult. The death cult of Jack Kennedy. Let's face it, Bob, if Kennedy had lived, you'd scarcely even have him on this programme now, he'd be so goddam obscure.' Now the two other guests and the moderator round on the young guest, shouting for dominance, until the senior speaker wins with: 'I'm not surprised *he* writes for a small magazine because he isn't going to find many buyers in America for what he just said. If Jack Kennedy had lived, he'd be remembered as one of our greatest presidents *and* America would be a better place.'

Oh, vanity, vanity, all is vanity. Where, though, was Newton Sanders when all this took place? In the question-and-answer method by which this dream seems to proceed, there appears an *Election '92 Special* on television. Clinton 43%, Bush 38%, and Perot 19%. Perot! And now a documentary retrospective, a defeat rewind, on the Bush years. The miraculous survival from the ditched plane, CIA, Reagan, the 1988 election debates. But standing there at the other lectern is . . . get outta here . . . not the big Italian-American Mario Cuomo, but a little Greek-American called Mike Dukakis. And the key moment in the campaign, a reporter is saying, was the question in the debate: 'What would you do if someone raped and murdered Mrs Dukakis?'

And, with the casual geography of dreams, Jack is removed to a bookshop, which looks like the Globe Corner Bookstore on School Street in Boston. He is standing on the sidewalk now, looking at a window display. In the centre, suspended by cotton, is a picture of himself and Jackie, waving to the crowds at Love Field Airport, Dallas, on the day. Hung beside it is a movie poster: *JFK—A Film by Oliver Stone*. Beneath, dark blue velvet laid over blocks creates a range of steps and tiers on which several dozen books rest in a configuration more like a shrine than a stall. *The Death of the President, A Thousand Days, American Hero, Jack and Jackie, Who Shot the President?, Nightmare In Dallas*.

Now, without resort to doors, he is inside the bookshop, able to remove volumes from the shelves, and read them. Here, in Biography, under K, he finds one called *Jackie!* – its cover showing his wife, veiled in black beside a flag-draped coffin – and another called *The Other Brother*, the face on the dust jacket recognizably Ted's, but puffy and grizzled as it never had the chance to be in life. Unexpected phrases jump from the page. He reads of 'Mrs Kennedy's 1968 remarriage to the Greek shipping billionaire, Aristotle Onassis'. And 'the still unexplained mystery of the death of a young woman in the senator's car at Chappaquiddick' . . .

Jack shakes awake. It is 3 a.m. Downstairs, the watch will be swapping: the roster of those who underwrite his life. The bed shows the signs of a nightmare: scattered blankets, rolled-over pillows. He reseals the sheets around him, and lies on his back, screening what he can retrieve of the dream.

That his coma show should so largely have taken the form of news footage is a consequence, presumably, of filling his head with so much of the stuff every day: one theory of dreams being that they are a kind of waste-pipe. Of the rest, the departures from reality, much of that is the usual denial, compensation, rationalization of the subconscious: court of appeal material.

The creations of the Johnson and Clinton presidencies are explicable enough distortions within the logic of dreams, for one reflected a long obsession in himself and the other a deep neurosis in his party. And there is – in the archives of the presidential library – a clip of Jack shaking hands with the young Bill Clinton in the Rose Garden. He knows of its existence because the library agreed not to release the clip to the Republicans in 1992 for hostile commercials.

The Clinton sequence, admittedly, might be accused of arrogance: the idea that Jack's dead legend would have saved the Arkansas governor's skin. We are all egotists in our dreams, but the version of himself Jack saw is so glorified that he feels furtive and guilty, as after a sexual dream in adolescence.

Yet, finally, as often in the matter of dream-reading, it is the trivialities that most irritate. Transferring the 'How many kids did you kill today?' chant to LBJ is clear enough: night denial, the self-protection of his conscience. Seeing Bobby shot while running for president was classic subconscious contrition: a belief that Jack had killed his brother's chances. But what the hell did it mean to dream that George Bush beat some little Greek Boston cop in '88? Officer Mike Dukakis has guarded Jack on a number of occasions, but even so. In fact, what *is* this thing with him and Greeks? For now he remembers marrying off Jackie to Onassis.

Did I eat cheese? he thinks. Did he miscount the steroid tablets? Maybe he should see an analyst. People liked to believe that dreams were the key to your soul, but sometimes they seemed more like a joke against it.

30: Murder at
Chappaquiddick?

In the coffee break between the pre-lunch papers, Crick keeps skimming the talking and listening faces, hoping for the double-take that would identify Kathy Malone. But his quest is restricted by his lapel badge which, its red lettering designating a speaker rather than a mere yellow delegate, encourages disciples.

'Professor Crick?' croaks a man with a mechanical larynx, his jaw also foreshortened by surgery; an absolute shoo-in for Crick's developing theory that it is not uncommon for the delegates to have suffered losses of their own.

'Yes . . .'

'May I say how much I'm hoping to enjoy your address this afternoon?'

Crick notices that the pleasantry is worded like a threat. Also, although he tries to adopt the agreed conversational demeanour, the metallic delivery is distracting. It is as if a coffee-grinder has suddenly joined in a dinner-party.

'America is a picture-led civilization,' the man rattles, 'and I think you are right to redress this by examining the numbers.'

'I hope so,' Crick replies. 'Though unifying theories have a habit of collapsing. At college once, reading some stuff about Julius Caesar doing something in something BC, before *Christ*, I suddenly thought: waydaminnit. Julius Caesar, Jesus Christ. I went big on this thing about significant initials. Was there something special about the letters "JC"?'

'Did anything come of it?'

'After Jimmy Carter, we couldn't get funding.'

The man is cranking up for a supplementary, but Draycott, the morning's first speaker, has limped into the space between Crick and his supplicant.

'Professor Crick? Jim Draycott. I'm – appropriately enough – counting the minutes until "Our days are Numbered". I'd truly be glad of your comments on my own talk this morning.'

Vietnam veterans are not always ready for candour from non-combatants, thinks Crick, and says: 'I really thought you were on to something.'

Though a lie, that sentence contains little dissemblance. Remove only the small word 'to' and it became a proper expression of the listener's sentiments: *I really thought you were on something.*

'There was only one point that occurred to me,' Crick continues. 'If the former President Kennedy among us now—'

'The so-called "former President Kennedy".'

'Yes, indeed. If that man is really a former off-Broadway actor . . .'

'I think I know what—'

'Then has no one ever wondered at the sudden suspension of the career of a man who, by your account this morning, was not an untalented performer? He'd have had an agent, family, wife, well actually more likely boyfriend. Wouldn't one of them have wondered where he's been these thirty years?'

'He's dead.'

'Dead?'

'His loved ones *think* he's dead. Consult back-numbers of *The American Stage* – for 1962 – and you will see an obituary of the performer in question, who I cannot, of course, for ethical reasons, name. The certificate says *leukaemia*. But that was just his *cover*.'

A convincing cover, Crick thinks. A clay and limestone cover; an oaken and brass-handled cover. But all that he risks saying is: 'But wouldn't there have been a body, a funeral, that kind of thing?'

'Richard – can I call you Richard?'

'Sure.'

'Richard, the people behind all this are *professionals*.'

A bell rings to announce the second session, and the majority of the delegates rush towards the ballroom door as if the sound is a fire alarm. Crick guesses that these paranoids fear the capacity of the hall has been reduced in some administrative coup during the interval.

Crick returns to the same seat in the early rows, between McShane and Evaristi. The second speaker is already at the podium. She wears her blonde hair long in irregular spaghetti strands and her face has the rouged moon surface of the serious acne graduate. As she stands at the lectern, her head is hung far back, as if she is trying to see her heels. She jabs fingers at her right eye, and Crick realizes that she is adjusting contact lenses. She snaps her head forward, stares into the strip-lit glare, blinks, and coughs.

'Hi, I'm Kim Winstanley, researcher from Springfield, Illinois. My talk this morning is entitled "Murder at Chappaquiddick?", although I hope that, by the time you've heard me out, you'll wonder why that pesky little query mark was ever there. For more than twenty years, Americans have been led to believe that the tragic drowning of Senator Edward M. Kennedy in his car at Chappaquiddick Bridge in 1969 was a senseless accident, tragically robbing America of a potentially great president. But I have come to believe, my friends, that this was no accident. Lights!'

A slide is projected. An image painfully familiar to Americans older than forty, it is the first press agency photograph taken in the early hours of July 20th, 1969, as Martha's Vineyard police struggled to raise the broken Oldsmobile. Constrained by the available light, and the darkness of the brackish water, the picture is objectively a haze of shapes, but it is an obsession of the age that events deserve a visual record, and the reproduction fees easily funded the photographer's pet project of following the activities of an Indian village through a decade.

'Look closely here,' says Winstanley, hitting the screen with a long white rod, at the left extremity. 'Until now, just a shadow. But with modern image enhancement techniques, as shown in this slide . . .'

She waves the stick towards the rear of the room, and

there appears on the screen a second print, not obviously to Crick more specific than the first.

'Examination of this shape establishes almost without doubt that it is the figure of a frogman, swimming away towards Wasque Point, where, interviews have established, many residents recall seeing a stranger on the morning of July 20th.'

'And this frogman did what?' whispers Crick to Evaristi. 'He stuck his foot out and tripped up the car?'

'So, Dick, we don't know what he did? Why was he there? That's the question.'

But, in turning to speak to his colleague, Crick's primed eyes have seen a shape far more interesting to him than a possible frogman who has had twenty-four years' start on his pursuers. Framed in the rear doorway, her soft bob of hair still hazelnut in the overspill from the projector, is, unmistakably and shakingly, Kathy Malone.

31: Square-Shaped or Pear-Shaped

The University of Texas has scientifically accounted for the appeal to men of Marilyn Monroe. According to a report on the television morning news, the Austin boffins have concluded – in the course of what a representative unsmilingly describes as 'a study of desirable female shape' – that the majority of males are attracted to 'pear-shaped' or 'hour-glass' figures.

This traditional prejudice is also, according to the scientists, an evolutionary one, because such women are more likely to be fertile, thus confirming folk wisdom about hips and tits. The men thought they were just after a good fuck, but their genes were seeking the best mate, until contraception interfered with nature's deal. The data for the survey was pictures and reported physical statistics of Hollywood goddesses, including Ms Monroe; *Playboy* centrefolds since 1955; and Miss America winners since 1923.

Real one-handed research, thinks Jean, waiting for a call in her Winnebago on the Fox lot on the first day of principal photography for *She's Back!* For surely it is not possible that these men in their laboratories were able to be objective about the bodies they were studying. The history of male behaviour – from her own experience, and from history, literature, and anecdote – suggests gruntingly otherwise.

Jean considers her own body, examining its reality with squinting, lowered eyes, and then its reflection in the mirror which fills almost one wall of the trailer. It was assumed in the television report she saw that viewers understood that the survey referred to the Marilyn Monroe of the fifties and sixties. The experiment had been conducted on old photographs. Because, if the criterion for physique were to resemble a pear or an hour-glass, then her shape would never pass the quality control of either fruiterer or jeweller.

It was a shock, when the early call-sheets arrived this week, to see that three hours had been allowed each day for her make-up. This was the kind of bore chore of which actors playing monsters in horror flicks boasted in the publicity profiles. But, in their cases, the time was spent creating sags and wrinkles. Jean, she fully realized, was booked in for the reverse expertise.

'Ms Norman?'

Jenny, her personal assistant and public spokesperson, is at the door of the trailer. She wears her tread-gently-this-dame-has-been-in-therapy expression, so Jean is braced for information far more painful than what is announced.

'Listen, Ms Norman, there's a problem, only a small one, with the lights. Your call's gone back an hour. Now, they can drive you home or you can stay here, if you want. The director says he'll come and explain to you personally, if you need it, but . . .'

'They're worried I'm going to stomp off set, honey?'

A recent Monroe biography has recounted the rows, no-shows and sick-outs, revealed by the papers in the dragged out court case, on the set of *Something's Gotta Give*. It has clearly been read by the team on *She's Back!*, who now fear a repeat.

'I'll wait here, Jenny,' she says. 'You get to my age, you *want* them taking time over the lights.'

'Hey, Marilyn, you heard? Should we have a coffee?'

Jean's hot young co-star, who always calls her Marilyn, speaks from behind Jenny, who moves instinctively aside, in the invisibility sidestep quickly learned by those who serve the stars.

'Yeah, OK,' Jean tells the other actress. Jenny, without apparent movement, has rematerialized in the kitchen area of the trailer, and is fiddling in the fridge.

'Milk?' Jenny asks.

'I didn't mean actually coffee,' the more recent idol replies. 'I'm not permitted stimulants. Evian would be best.'

Jenny fixes the water, and the usual herbal tea for her employer, then soundlessly leaves the trailer.

The younger actress lifts her glass.

'Well, Marilyn, here's to *She's Back!* Let me get this out of the way before shooting begins, but I really can't believe you're in one of my movies.'

'That's, uh, kind . . .' Jean replies, shocked by the confident assumption in the pronouns of the real star hierarchy on this film.

'I mean, when I was in high school, I dreamed of being you when you were younger.'

'You did?'

'Well, yes, until I read the books about you. The really yukky stuff started coming out, I guess, just when I was thinking of being an actress. Then I wanted to be you, when you were young, but with my head straight. No offence.'

'Please, I know what you mean.'

'In fact, as soon as I became famous, after my first film hit, I studied the lives of the old – I don't mean *old* – movie stars. Including you. I learned a lot about how not to fuck up my life.'

Although the younger actress is often said to resemble early Monroe – this is why the studio regards it as a coup to secure both Jean and her for this movie – she represents the image with a modern twist. She may be pear-shaped, but it is unripe pear, and she is not hour-glass, but sun-dial: hardbody beauty. Morning work-outs and evening runs have given her a muscular curvature of a kind that was left to circus ladies when Jean began. The actress is also, Jean knows from a profile in *America Now*, a Buddhist, non-drinker, and macrobiotic dieter.

'Stop me, Marilyn, if you don't want to go into this, but it seems to me your problem was you viewed penetration as an accolade.'

'What you call penetration is what we called sex?'

'Uh-huh.'

'Oh, I've heard it explained so many ways. Analysts for thirty years telling me that all these men were replacements for the father I never knew. It seemed kind of trite, though I kept on paying. I don't rightly know what my problem was, honey. You see, people say sex was my weakness but sex was my strength. My only strength, it seemed to me then. I wasn't an actress. Or, I thought I was, but that wasn't why the studios used me. I was somebody every man wanted in the sack. Which was fine, as it goes, when I was on the screen and the guys were in the movie theatres. They were just Joes with a hope. But I had to have a life as well, and the men in that, they also wanted Marilyn not me . . .'

Jean pauses, and repeats something she said in an interview in the fifties, but which seems appropriate here: 'Men expected so much, and I couldn't live up to it. They expected bells to ring and whistles to whistle, but my anatomy was the same as any other woman's and I couldn't live up to it.'

'I know what you mean. I played this girl once, and, in this bedroom scene, I made her sort of yodel when she came. I don't know why. It just seemed true to the character, she was something of an exhibitionist, although she wasn't Swiss. But the boyfriend I had then, he kept saying, "I want to make you come like you did there." Finally, I yodelled just to please him, and he said: "That sounded phoney." I said, "Baby, it always *was* . . ."'

'That's good. I like that.'

'Well, I haven't had that problem since I gave up penetration.'

'You mean, you don't . . .?'

'No. Massage and external genital stimulation only. It seemed to me there was a contradiction in my life. I was drinking Evian, eating beans, pumping weights, and doing yoga. And, after all that, I was letting a guy put one of his rest-room appendages in me and swish it around. In my view, Aids was nature's way of reminding women they had hands . . .'

As if to tempt her from her pledge, a powerfully built young man appears in the doorway.

'We're gonna have to go,' he tells the co-star. 'There's a rumour he's talked his way on to the lot. We've gotta get you somewhere secure.'

'Shit!' She turns back to Jean. 'Marilyn, there's this guy. You may have read about him. I better do what I'm told.'

The younger woman hurries out, her big-shouldered minder hanging over her like a coat. Jean has heard about the 'stalker', who has sworn in many letters that it is his destiny to bed and wed the actress. He is already the subject of two court orders barring him from a five-mile radius of her Malibu compound. This legal move, however, merely prompted a letter beginning: 'The government would do ANYTHING to keep us apart, but WE know we can BEAT them.' Jean is thankful that her own greatest fame predated what is now an everyday danger for American stars. She would be at risk, she thinks, only from a nostalgic psychotic.

It strikes her that the three above-the-title names on *She's Back!* represent a miniature history of American sexual celebrity. There is Jean, survivor of career-move screws; five marriages; miscarriages and abortions of a number now junked from her memory; the experience of having been, for the ordinary Joes, the number one international wank fantasy, and for the celebrity Jacks, the ultimate prized vagina, phallus-scalp. Now, she is single and celibate, from motives presented to the world as ideological, but not without a practical element. Reflecting on this, she feels the usual mixture of grief and relief at her retirement from the sexual arena.

Then, there is her female co-star, a celibate macrobiotic Buddhist declining to be penetrated, yet able to communicate this decision only to those closest to her. Men in general – and, at the most fearsome extreme, her 'stalker' – viewed her as a public cunt in much the way that Marilyn had once been seen.

Finally, there is the male lead, whose womanizing was minor by the standards of the Hollywood Jean knew, but who had been required by his wife to enlist at a recovery clinic, to be cured of his addiction to sex. Both of her co-stars would have claimed to have arranged their lives better than Marilyn Monroe's, but it seems to Jean that, in both cases, the problem has been acknowledged rather than solved.

The door of the trailer flaps again, and she looks up to see Jenny.

'Ms Norman? Your call's delayed again. There's a security scare on the set.'

'Yes. I know.'

'This time you can't go home. They've sealed the lot. I've got Marcie outside right now. I wondered if we mightn't use the time for correspondence.'

'Sure.'

Marcie is Jean's secretary: a plump grandmother from Colorado, of a generation unlikely to contemplate selling stories to *America Now* or similar magazines, whatever the reported rewards. She pulls up a chair and lays stacks of opened letters on the make-up table. She sees herself in the mirror, and flinches.

'Oh, Ms Norman, those mirrors are cruel, if you haven't got the looks.'

'They're cruel if you had.'

Her post, as usual, divides into four types. One pile is requests for signed photographs. It became clear in the seventies, after letters of complaint from recipients, that what people generally wanted was a photo of the young Marilyn Monroe, so these are now sent, inscribed by her senile hand. The second category is nonspecific fan letters, at their height when *Some Like It Hot* has been reshown on television. These writers also receive signed photographs. The third category consists of enquiries from drug addicts or their families. These receive a government leaflet on substance abuse, details of the Monroe clinic in Colorado Springs, and a signed photograph. The last pile holds enquiries from biographers and conspiracy theorists about how often, and precisely when, she slept with Jack and Bobby Kennedy, or to confirm that her August 1962 hospitalization was a suicide attempt, and/or that she had taken a telephone call from Bobby Kennedy just before. These correspondents receive a standard answer from Marcie that the actress's 1977 autobiography *MM . . . mmm* contains all that she wishes to place on record for the moment about her life.

Now, after the recent conversation with her co-star, Jean is aware of a possible hole in her post.

'Marcie, are there letters from sexual weirdos, nuts and so on, you don't show me?'

'Oh. I wouldn't know, Ms Norman. Remember, your letters come to us from the agency.'

'The CIA?'

'No, why . . . Your *agent*.'

'Right.'

'But, as it happens, there is something a little unusual this morning.'

Marcie picks up a piece of heavy card, the shadow of a fancy logo visible through it. She also raises a letter, on creamy foolscap, which shows the same mark at the top.

'It's from a Mr Boomer, the Chief of Staff for former President Kennedy.'

'*Jack.*'

'You are invited to the opening of new exhibits at the Presidential Library in Boston. Do you want to think about it?'

'Yes, I think I ought to think about it, given that we haven't spoken for nearly thirty years . . .'

So maybe, thinks Jean, I do have my own stalker, after all.

32: A World Safe for Historians

Fraser – the second assassin – is angry. The Time Bandit, as the future will know him, has briefly, this evening, turned against his mentor. For the last two nights, his research reading has been the title essay of Professor Hawking's latest book, *Black Holes and Baby Universes*. The pages show spunk stains of mayonnaise: splashes from the all-night-store half-subs that are his standard study snack.

Fraser is reasonably certain that he understood 'Is Everything Determined?' on his third reading. 'Black Holes And Baby Universes', though, has left him spinning. He was hoping for an answer to the dilemma presented in the previous essay. Are the alternative universes held out by Hawking – in which Fraser became president, in which Kennedy died at Dallas, and Trudi Brewster took it in the mouth – notional rewrites of time or accessible parallel worlds?

In theory, journeys to other worlds were possible through 'black holes', the last stage in the life cycle of a star, before, as it were, it died and went to heaven. Hawking argued:

There are solutions of the equations of general relativity that would allow one to fall into a black hole and come out of a white hole somewhere else. A white hole is the time reverse of a black hole. It is an object that things can come out of but nothing can fall into. The white hole could be in another part of the universe. This would seem to offer the possibility of rapid inter-galactic travel. The trouble is it might be too rapid. If travel through black holes were possible, there would seem nothing to prevent you from arriving before you set off. You could then do something, like kill your mother, that would have prevented you from going in the first place.

Fraser, who has often contemplated killing his mother, does not immediately appreciate the point being made. Eventually, he understands that the reference is to killing your mother before she gives birth to you, thus removing the future from which you have arrived. These are tough messages – both to comprehend and to accept – and Fraser briefly contemplates shooting Hawking, for writing books that make the ordinary Joe feel slow and small. Now, after thousands of words eagerly studied and stored, it seems that the existence options so headily offered are merely theoretical:

> Perhaps fortunately for our survival (and that of our mothers), it seems that the laws of physics do not allow such time travel. There seems to be a Chronology Protection Agency that makes the world safe for historians by preventing travel into the past.

Long ago, Fraser decided that there is no God, but this moment is like discovering that there is no No-God either. He has seen quantum physics described as the new religion. This is clearly true – in that the scientists, rather than the priests, now tried to account for the creation of the universe – but there is a crucial difference. Both Christianity and physics posited the existence of another world, although science promised a better today somewhere else, while religion held out hope of a better tomorrow. Yet here was the key distinction. God's believers were told they had a ticket to the alternative world; quantum's followers were shown a tempting brochure but told there were no flights.

Fraser channels his betrayal into energy for his project. It is now clear to him that only through individual intervention in the existing world can history be rewritten. The only plausible time travellers are assassins. If Kennedy had died at Dallas, America – this bankrupt, racist, dangerous nation – would have been a better place. Perhaps, with his death, time can be tricked back to that trajectory.

144

He opens a notebook, and records this thought in his thin print. When he has finished writing, Fraser reaches for two thick albums, their intended regular edges disfigured by glued-down mounted items. One contains his Kennedy archives, including a recent paragraph from the *Boston Globe* listing events to be attended by the former President around the thirtieth anniversary of Dallas.

In the second are images ripped from magazines and newspapers. Each photograph shows a child of around two years old, or a family group which includes a baby of that age. These children have featured in the media for different reasons: the heroism of themselves or their parents, a lottery victory for their family, a significant promotion or other professional celebrity for the father of the house. Every news angle is represented, except fires, murders, or automobile accidents. The dead are not collected. They are useless for the purposes of the curator.

The album resembles an amateurish handbook for an adoption agency. And, flapping through its pages, Fraser chooses.

33: Kathy Malone

There is a long wait for the buffet lunch: another aspect of the conference which results from the unusual temperament of the delegates.

'You're sure there's *no* meat in this?' a vegetarian researcher is demanding of a server, while beadily inspecting a yellow quiche. 'Because we're talking litigation if one piece of animal gets past my lips . . .' Gazing into the next steaming tureen, a carnivore has a different suspicion. 'Can you *guarantee* this beef contains no hormones?'

Delayed by these investigations, The Fifteen Club discuss the merits of 'Murder at Chappaquiddick?', the morning's second talk, just ended.

'I'll tell you what convinced me,' says Evaristi. 'That garage mechanic in Edgartown – who may very well have worked on Ted Kennedy's car earlier that year – him dying young in 1971. A heart attack, they said.'

'Johnny, it might have *been* a heart attack.'

'Yeah? You think they're gonna take him out with a bazooka? You think they're gonna slip him an exploding ball at Little League? Of course, they're gonna make it look like a heart attack. My daughter, they make it look so much *like* suicide, it fooled one of the best county medical examiners in the USA.'

Crick has heard it said that conspiracy theory is a form of religion and, when he listens to Evaristi, he can understand what people mean by this. Just as the pious made sense of bereavement through God and heaven, so did the suspicious find purpose in chaos through the invocation of the CIA, the FBI, and the military-industrial complex. There was the same comfort in believing that there was an ordering force behind the mess of existence. The more extreme of the delegates at this conference were adherents of the 'Octopus Theory': the belief that all of America's modern horrors – from Vietnam to Dallas to Watergate, Iran-Contra, Iraqgate, and the Persian Gulf War – were directed by a shady group of businessmen and arms dealers who belonged to the same country clubs in Dallas. Crick called it the Four Men from Texas theory of history. What was this invisible committee if not a proxy God?

'Michael?'

The voice is behind him, but Crick has made a positive identification before he turns.

'Kathy Malone,' he exhales as he faces her.

'Yes. I saw your name on the list and wondered . . .'

'So did I.'

'Well, I guess if you come to these things, you're supposed to be good at making connections. We were both right. Listen, I was booked with American. They're on strike.'

'Yeah. CNN. I saw.'

'That's why I'm late.'

'Where are you flying from?'

'San Francisco.'

'You moved a long way from Boston.'

'Yeah. *You* don't still live there?'

'I teach in Tulsa.'

'Look, I want to try to get a flight with someone else for Monday.'

He feels almost adolescent, in his stiff attempts to elongate the conversation, as he advises: 'San Francisco? I'd try United first.'

'Yeah, I'd . . . No, what I'm saying is, I better go and make some calls. But why don't we have a drink later. I'm meeting some folks I know in Dallas tonight. But what about tomorrow?'

'Sure. Maybe dinner?'

In her small hesitation lies the history between them. But she soon says: 'OK. Meet me in the lobby at seven. And I promise to be back to hear you this afternoon.'

Crick taps his briefcase: 'Dynamite . . .'

'Great. See you.'

'See you, Kathy.'

He watches her as she heads for the telephone booths. Evaristi whistles, and says to McShane: 'Now, this, in my view, is how Professor Crick here became the president of our club. He attends to every detail, including pussy for himself.'

'No, no, Johnny. She's an old friend. We grew up together in Boston six or seven presidents ago. We dated for a while when we were, oh, seventeen. I haven't seen her since.'

'So, why'd you invite her here?' says McShane.

'I didn't. It's coincidence.'

'Come on, Michael, this whole fucking conference is dedicated to the proposition that there *are* no coincidences.'

'Well, this is one. I assure you, there's no conspiracy here. Unless it's Cupid's.'

Crick has revealed too much, and his colleagues exchange exaggerated double-takes.

'Hey, isn't it *sweet?*' Evaristi simpers. 'He's still got her name on his bullets after all this time.'

'Well, she's kept herself nice,' adds McShane.

Crick affects an expression of professorial weariness with their teasing, but, in reality, they have not misstated the position. How many of those locked into relationships could honestly claim that they were never visited by other possibilities, if-only romances? Certainly, Crick could not deny such fantasies, and the reason for his failure was Kathy Malone.

'It never happened to me, that,' says Evaristi, in accents almost of tenderness. 'Seeing someone you . . . after, what, *thirty* years . . .'

'All his, he had killed, as soon as they sacked him,' interrupts McShane.

'Hey, I'm being serious,' Evaristi scolds. 'It must feel really weird.'

'Yes,' admits Crick, the mathematician. 'It feels like squaring the circle.'

'Yeah,' growls McShane. 'Like you wanna put your *square* in her *circle* . . .'

34: RSVP

On the morning of November 19th, 1993, in three locations quite unknowing of each other, two important replies are received, a piece of information is passed on, and an urgent purchase made. Separate destinies, random lives, collide.

When his call comes, Meredith is making a lengthy entry about the moral degeneracy of Jack Kennedy in the leather-bound ledger he keeps for each project. He declines to confide his views to a computer, as cut-throat is an understatement for the business he is in.

On this particular subject – of marital chastity – a cross-reference must inevitably be made in the separate volume dedicated to Marilyn Monroe. Later, when Meredith is written about in the newspapers, much will be made of his 'moral agenda'. He would not argue with this interpretation of his work. It is, in his view, what separates him from mere opportunists in the field. It is Meredith's belief that the cesspit America has become in the nineties is the responsibility of sixties libertines like Kennedy and Monroe.

The answering machine is guarding him this morning, but, as soon as he hears the asthmatic identification, 'Uh, Fraternelli,' he pulls up the phone like a hundred-dollar bill on the sidewalk.

'Mr Fraternelli . . .'

'Yeah. How's it with you? Listen, on account of my, uh, social connections, I've swung you an invite to the thank-God-for-Jack mass. You'll be using the name Reilly. He's a Knight of Saint Gregory, friend of Old Joe Kennedy's. Only thing is, he started fibrillating yesterday, and his doctors say unless he wants the congregation to get a requiem for the same price he'd better settle for the highlights on CNN.'

'Wouldn't the ushers know his face?'

'You think of things, Meredith. We like that. No, Reilly's from out of town. The Family mean so much to him, he was flying in. Lucky for you, God didn't want him there.'

'I'm obviously extremely grateful, Mr Fraternelli.'

'I hope so. Well, show your gratitude by using it well. The view of the board, I think I can tell you, is it will be worth it if we get a hit. You need to be in your seat a half-hour before the service starts.'

'I'll be there.'

In the office at Hyannis Port, Boomer delivers the good news first.

'Mr President,' he says, 'we've had a reply from Miss Monroe.'

Boomer deliberately delays details of the response: this is an infrequent opportunity to exercise power over his employer.

Jack, though, will not play the game, or responds with one of his own, because he rocks twice in his White House chair, turns to examine the fierce November sea, like tongues of steel, beyond the private beach, and at last replies, with so-what modulation: 'So quick. How polite.'

'According to her people, sir, she will be happy to attend the Dedication ceremony on the twenty-fifth . . .'

'She used the word "happy"?'

'It was her people. I think the exact word was pleased.'

'Good. That's good.'

Boomer, as an adolescent in the seventies, read many lurid, and doubtless speculative, accounts of this definitive and symbolic sixties pairing: between the power and the glamour, the East and the West of America, politics and Hollywood. Accordingly, he has carried with him all morning a sense of history about the message he was delivering. But the commencement of this coda to the romance lacks the explosive force, the release of long-restrained flames, that he had imagined. It was rather like telling Mark Antony, 'There is a message from Queen Cleopatra,' and his replying, 'Put it over there. I'll read it when I have a moment . . .'

'I'll have to add her name to the list with the police and the Secret Service, sir,' Boomer says. 'But she insists there should be no publicity.'

'Marilyn Monroe wants no publicity! It sounds like one of those goofy cartoon captions, doesn't it?'

'They say she'll be wearing disguise.'

'She will? You know that was always a fantasy of mine as President – dressing up as Joe Schmoe and going down among the people . . . The dream of all leaders, probably. There's a fairytale – isn't there? – about a king—'

'A prince, I believe, sir. But I think, in her case, Mr President, it's security.'

'Make you pretty *in*secure – wouldn't it? – hearing what people really thought . . .'

But one of the skills required by those in Boomer's profession is knowing when not to offer a reply. This morning, he also needs as smooth a transition as possible into the bad news.

'Sir, there's a rumour, quite a firm one, that—'

'Oh God, Boomer, what are they saying about me now?'

'I can't even be sure that it *is* you, sir.'

'What are you saying? Mistaken identity? Blurred photographs? Oh, Lord, they're not saying I'm the Headless Man now, are they?'

Vanity Fair has just published an article about Margaret, Duchess of Argyll, a British society hostess recently dead, reviving the story of her sensational court case, in which evidence of her adultery involved a photograph of her performing fellatio on a male cropped, as photographers say, at the neck: thus, as it were, giving head to a Headless Man.

'No, sir. It's just that there's a tip-off that *America Now*—'

'Wouldn't you know it?'

'That the magazine is running a cover story on a sexual scandal – a *big* sexual scandal.'

'I thought size wasn't everything.'

'A sexual scandal, involving a senior political figure,' continues Boomer, pushing through his employer's deflectionary humour like someone swimming underwater.

'And you really don't know who, or are you saving my feelings?'

'I can't get the name, Mr President. They're being very careful. On all the proofs, and so on, according to my source, the name is Mickey Mouse . . .'

'Oh, my God! Another American icon gone! Do you think Minnie will stand by him? Look, Boomer, I'm seventy-six, my back wakes me up at night as much as Vietnam does. There are times I'd actually quite like to be able to do things the magazines could write about, but there are practical complications. In many ways, Mickey Mouse is a more likely candidate for this story of yours.'

'Mr President, the incident is, I understand, one that occurred in the past, the fairly distant past.'

'Uh-huh. So I come under suspicion, in theory. But they've already splashed pretty well everyone up to and including my high school dates. Take this as the false modesty of the career politician if you will, Boomer, but would they really think me and sex was such a big deal, after all this time?'

'It's a certain kind of sex, sir. A very topical kind.'

'You'll have to spit it out, Boomer. I don't keep track of fashion like I did.'

'It's uh, child abuse, sir . . .'

'Get the *fuck outta here*, Boomer!' screams Kennedy. 'I guess your generation has grown up willing to believe anything of politicians. And I'm told this is our fault for letting you down. Well, maybe we did, but I don't believe we ever gave you cause to think us capable of fucking stuff like that!'

And, as Boomer leaves the room, he realizes that Kennedy was right in the generational phenomenon he identified, for the younger man is genuinely uncertain whether what he just heard was the sincere outrage of innocence or the first step in a politician's damage-limitation strategy.

*

Later the same morning, Meredith allows a second call past the protection of his electronic voice. His recorded message admits only to 'I', contains no names, for uniformity is not possible in his job.

'Hello,' says Meredith.

'Mr Chichester?'

'Yeah?'

'I think I've got something for you.'

Meredith recognizes the always croaky tones – bronchitis or disguise – of his main police informant in Massachusetts.

'The Kennedy thing . . .' begins the voice.

'You mean the Cathedral?'

'Nah. Not the Cathedral. I've told you all I know about Holy Cross. I'm talking about the Library. On the twenty-fifth.'

'Yes. What about it?'

'Marilyn's going to be there.'

'Marilyn *Monroe*?'

'The same baby. Absolutely. She just accepted. They have to tell us. For security.'

Double whammy, Meredith thinks.

'That's very useful, George. I'll get the money to you in the usual way.'

'Pleasure, Mr Chichester, sir.'

The informant chooses to be called 'George' – 'like Washington', he has said – but Meredith assumes that this is not his real name. A cop, as he believes his source to be, has to be careful, selling stuff on.

'George, can you get me a ticket for this?'

'No, sir. The only tickets are for the platform parties. For those, you'd have the FBI taking blood samples. But there's public access, lots of it, all around the platform and in front. Of course, I'd be there early.'

'Oh, I think I will be . . .'

When the telephone is dead, Meredith reflects on strategy. Until now, he has assumed the whole thing would begin in Holy Cross. Even after agreement from Fraternelli to the two-body project, he still assumed that the subjects would be dealt with separately. He has never expected the opportunity now offered: of Jack and Marilyn in the same frame. It is hard not to view the possibility as a little sign from God that he is on the right track.

And in a city hundreds of miles away, the man who calls himself Fraser leaves his dark apartment and walks with his head down, dreading contact, past the hard slaps of the early winter air. He is heading for the corner stall where – among the impenetrable headlines of the frail newspapers jetted in for the numerous expatriate communities – the earliest available copies of *America Now* are for sale. Perhaps there will be something for his albums.

35: American Lives

Jean's life flashes before her in the middle of the night. Sleepless again, desperate to ignore the possibility of chemical escape, but reluctant to resort to the script of *She's Back!* on the night table, she chases across the channels for diversion.

Somewhere in the upper 80s, she finds herself. Her sixty-seven years have been compressed, or crushed, into the 52-minute hour of commercial television, 120 seconds longer than the 50-minute hour of professional psychoanalysis, but sharing many of the same techniques, though with less indulgence to the subject.

The programme is a documentary series called *American Lives*, an epic clip-and-commentary television biography of children of the Union from Lincoln to Madonna which Jean slightly remembers seeing first time out. In the selections from the middle decades of the century, Marilyn Monroe was wedged between Joe Di Maggio and President Kennedy. 'Appropriately enough,' as the television critic of the *Los Angeles Times* tartly remarked.

A Carmelite nun, under whose influence Jean came in her seventies spin through the world's big religions, suggested that the first experience of a soul in heaven, hell, or purgatory was the screening of a movie of their lives. The famous, Jean informed her, would be well prepared.

With the channel-changer raised ready for use, like the gun of a cop making a blind raid on a house, Jean watches herself unfold.

The generic titles of the series – a computer-generated Mount Rushmore, with the chosen icons placed beside the granite presidents – and the sub-Sousa music give way to a photograph album, open at a late page, which then flaps backwards, revealing a new image on every sheet.

The first picture is the sixtieth birthday portrait, shot by Annie Leibowitz for *Vanity Fair* in 1986, in which Marilyn rests her chin on her hands, fingers ridged with diamond rings. Then the face thins and smooths, back through stills from the fifties and sixties movies, and the platinum-pout-and-cleavage pose which sealed Marilyn's face and fate, to her first shots as a model, and finally to a family photograph of Jean, then Norma Jeane, aged two, with her mother on the beach at Santa Monica in 1928. Through these pupations, a melancholy and ominous piano pings.

The beach picture freezes, the music softens, and the commentary begins. It is spoken by Robert Mitchum, in a manner Jean thinks of as presidential gravel.

'Marilyn Monroe', he intones, as other ghostly childhood pictures are shown, 'was born Norma Jeane – with an e – Mortenson on June 1st, 1926. Her mother, married at fourteen and soon divorced, worked as a cutter, preparing processed film, in Hollywood's then new movie industry. Norma Jeane never knew the identity of her father – and would spend her life in search of a replacement.'

The fucking networks have discovered Freud, thinks Jean. The music is either Mendelssohn or an admirer. The screen fills with a rapid succession of family groups. The narrator growls: 'Lacking a father at all, neither could Marilyn rely on any constancy of maternal affection. At two weeks old, her mother, Gladys, fearing that her working and personal life might be encumbered by motherhood, handed the baby over to foster parents.'

Jean sees herself – bald, round, and out of focus – in the lap of a severe woman in steel-rimmed eyeglasses.

'Ida Bolender', the commentary continues, 'kept with her husband, Albert, in Hawthorne, California, a house of strict discipline and religious observance. The Bolenders' foster children were not allowed to visit movie theatres. The young Marilyn was once told that if the world ended when she was watching a movie she would burn with all the bad people.'

A freeze-frame, and then a commercial break. The first images of the second section are still-shots of Norma Jeane ageing through the walking and talking years.

'In 1933,' Mitchum resumes, 'Norma Jeane left the Bolenders, following an incident in which a neighbour shot the child's much-loved pet mongrel dog.'

Hah! thinks Jean, now I have the pet lovers of America on my side. She expects the voiceover to explain that she has spent the rest of her life seeking a surrogate mutt, but in fact it goes on: 'By now, the child's mother, Gladys, had come under the influence of a tough and socially ambitious woman friend, Grace McKee. She and Gladys shared a house at 6812 Arbol Drive, near the Hollywood Bowl, where they installed a gleaming white piano as a status symbol.'

Mendelssohn or his friend are replaced on the soundtrack by Wagner or an acolyte. The camera dramatically moves in to a close-up photo of Gladys.

'But in 1934, Gladys, whose mother had a history of mental disturbance, was admitted to an asylum.'

The documentary's first interviewee, one of Marilyn's early biographers, a Californian with a toffee tan and wire-frame eyeglasses, explains: 'Grace McKee became Marilyn's second foster mother, and really a surrogate mother. She dressed Norma Jeane like Mary Pickford, and told her she would be a movie star.'

A portrait of Grace, woozily grinning beside a handsome dark-haired man.

'But in 1935, Grace McKee married "Doc" Goddard, a salesman and would-be actor. Moving in to the marital home a daughter from an earlier marriage, Goddard decided there was no room for the nine-year-old Norma Jeane.'

The composer of the 'Ring Cycle' or his disciple returns over flickery black-and-white archive film of a big house.

'Norma Jeane was dispatched to the Los Angeles Children's Home.'

The tanned biographer continues: 'The girl was there for two years, visited by Grace at weekends. She was taken out of the orphanage in 1937. But Grace did not return her to the Goddard home. In the next two years, she knew two more foster mothers: first a great-aunt in Greater Los Angeles and then one of *Grace's* aunts in the west of the city . . .'

Yet another family group is seen, a small brown-haired girl its only link with those already shown.

'But Aunt Ana', the commentator explains, 'was a devout Christian Scientist, and the young Norma Jeane attended services twice on every Sunday.'

The biographer comments: 'In her formative years, Marilyn faced a rather bizarre combination of influences. Her mother and surrogate mother – Gladys and then Grace McKee – represented a world of liberated sexuality, material ambition, and the fringes of Hollywood glamour. But her foster mothers – Ida Bolender and Aunt Ana – stood for piety and chastity, and stood out against the moral loosening, as they saw it, of the 1930s.'

A 1941 group picture from Emerson Junior High. Norma Jeane at fifteen: brown ringlets, defiant lipstick, proto pout.

'The confusions that would dominate Marilyn Monroe's life – between allure and discretion, between conventionality and celebrity – were taking root,' concludes the commentary. Jean's adolescent face is frozen in close-up, then covered over by commercials.

This advertising break includes the abortion message, with the rematerializing child, and Jean flees from it to CNN. When she judges it safe to come back, the commentator is saying: 'But in 1944, Jim Dougherty went to fight for his country in the Pacific. The first of Marilyn Monroe's five marriages was effectively over.'

The biographer picks up the story: 'She was now living with Jim's mother, and, to the horror of her, and, at a distance, her husband, Marilyn signed with the Blue Book model agency.'

Jean at eighteen, brown haired, on the covers of *Parade*, *Personal Romance*, and *Peek And See*.

'In the winter of 1946, her brown hair was bleached blonde at Frank and Joseph's salon in Hollywood. This merely increased her desirability to photographers, who also comforted her in the absence of her husband.'

Jean can smell lawyers behind this line. She mentally

releases the safety-catch on the channel changer and aims it directly at the screen, where she lines up a smirking Darryl F. Zanuck.

'On July 19th, 1946, the model Norma Jeane Dougherty was screen-tested by Twentieth Century Fox and signed by its legendary production chief, Darryl Zanuck. But this contract brought little financial reward and, at this period of her life, she frequently had to rely for food and cash on male acquaintances, many of whom she barely knew. Few who gave her money expected it back.'

Here, Jean nearly presses the trigger, imagining the grin of the television company lawyer as he approved this libel-proof description of the financing arrangements of her early years.

'In the same year, the young actress's agent, Ben Lyon, decreed that Norma Jeane Dougherty was not a name to write above marquees. Somewhat reluctantly, Norma Jeane added her mother's married name of Monroe to the first name of Marilyn Miller, an actress Lyon felt his protége resembled. From now on, she would be known for ever, to one and all, as Marilyn Monroe.'

Jean kills the film, for she is aware that this is the point at which biographies of her become hostile; the rigours of her childhood usually win sympathy. She waits until she has seen the clip of her first line of movie dialogue – 'Hi, Rad!' in 1947's *Scudda-Hoo! Scudda-Hay!* – before abandoning her past again for the present tense, and tense present, of CNN.

She finds it hard, however, to leave her life entirely. After little more than ten minutes, she switches back to the documentary, though ready to recoil from any especially unpleasant memory.

'Square-shaped or pear-shaped/They never lose their shape,' she sees herself singing when she rejoins the biography.

'Marilyn's rendition of "Diamonds Are A Girl's Best Friend" from *Gentlemen Prefer Blondes* made her the preferred blonde of most of the world's gentlemen in 1953,' the commentary explains, 'and for one in particular.'

And now here she is, in January 1954, in San Francisco,

marrying Joe Di Maggio. Then, a month later, Marilyn in a lavender dress, singing 'Do It Again' in Korea, in front of cooped-up troops, as if innocent of the lyric's import, and the effect it was having.

'For a man whose fame is past to live happily with a woman whose adulation is current is a hard task,' the analysis resumes. 'It was one of the few challenges Joe Di Maggio ducked in his career. In September 1954, Marilyn filed for divorce.'

From here, Jean finds it easy to predict the scenes, which seem calculated to develop the twin themes of marital instability and artistic ambition.

Marilyn and Arthur Miller at their wedding in 1956, preceded by an extract from the McCarthy hearings, the accusation scene from Miller's *The Crucible*, and a piece from Walter Winchell's J. Edgar Hoover-inspired broadcast: 'America's best-known blonde moving-picture star is now the darling of the left-wing intelligentsia, several of whom are listed as Red Fronters.'

The Plaza Hotel press conference, with Laurence Olivier, to announce *The Sleeping Prince*. 'Is it true you want to play *The Brothers Karamazov*?' taunts a reporter. 'Do you think you can handle it?' And Marilyn frostily ripostes: 'I don't want to play the brothers. I want to play Grushenka. She's a girl . . .'

A montage of scenes from *The Sleeping Prince*, *Some Like It Hot*, *Bus Stop*, and *The Misfits*. The commentary says: 'Though still watched, and often employed, because of her body, Marilyn was developing as an accomplished movie comedienne. But *The Misfits* – written as a love gift from Miller but filmed when the relationship was already turning sour – was an ill-fitting part for her. Heavily dependent on barbiturates, Marilyn was admitted to hospital during filming.'

Jean switches to CNN for the sequences which she guesses will deal with the turmoil of *Something's Gotta Give*, the involvement with Jack and Bobby Kennedy, and the 1962 hospitalization, which, she assumes, will be presented as a suicide attempt, as is the current biographical orthodoxy.

But still she cannot stay away, and is back for the pictures of her honeymoon cruise in 1968. The brutal blue of the

Aegean shocks her, until she realizes that this is the first colour news footage in the film.

'In 1968', Mitchum growls, 'Marilyn married for the fourth time: to the Greek shipping tycoon, Aristotle Onassis, the richest man in the world. It was a stormy union, but, in 1975 she would be his widow, and inheritor.'

The toffee-tanned biographer is back, and says: 'For the first time in her life, Marilyn is rich, seriously rich. This allows her to pursue the three great projects of her life after the recovery from the 1962 drugs overdose, which I think we must see as a turning point in her life. One, she is able to keep her legal dispute with Fox over *Something's Gotta Give* going for nearly twenty years. Two, when that is over, she can afford, in 1982, to film *The Brothers Karamazov*, although most of her fans probably wish she hadn't. Three, she can afford to become a United Nations Goodwill Ambassador, and help children around the world, which was always one of her great wishes.'

Under the biographer's last remarks run pictures of Marilyn in Africa during the 1984 famine, cradling a fly-blown bone-bag little black child in her arms.

'Apart from the catastrophe of *The K Brothers* and infrequent guest appearances in TV series like *Murder She Wrote*,' the commentator says, 'Marilyn's main artistic activity was as a singer. A series of best-selling albums and sell-out concerts gave her a whole new star career, until, after the assassination of John Lennon in 1980, she became nervous of public stage appearances.'

The last honeymoon footage: Marilyn and her fifth husband outside their Laguna Beach retreat in 1985.

'Ten years after the death of Onassis, Marilyn wed the former astronaut Buzz Aldrin, the second man to walk on the moon, behind Neil Armstrong, on the celebrated Apollo 11 lunar landing.'

A set of newspaper headlines. A MARRIAGE MADE IN THE HEAVENS and MRS STAR AND MR MOON.

A scene of Marilyn showing off her fifth wedding ring – its gem a speck of moon rock scooped from the Sea of Tranquillity – fades into the face of Jean's least favourite female biographer, framed in the bottom corner of the shot, to expose apparently thousands of acres of the Hamptons behind her, purchased from the proceeds of her knives-out Lives.

'Look at Marilyn's five husbands,' she purrs. 'The ordinary Joe, the sports star, the great writer, the tycoon, the astronaut. Marilyn has cast her married life like you might cast a White House dinner or the ultimate talk show. In a sense, Marilyn's body has been a repository for twentieth-century American history. It's as if she was consciously choosing representatives from all the great fields of endeavour. It's not quite a perfect set. It lacks a single emblematic American man: a president. But that's because one got away. There's no doubt that, after Di Maggio and Miller, Marilyn dreamed of bagging a top politician, even of becoming First Lady. And Jack Kennedy was her target. But it could not be. The risk of scandal during the 1964 re-election race was too great – too many people were talking – and so Marilyn was dropped.'

And here again comes Mendelssohn or friend, as the pages of the photograph album flap again, this time in a chronological succession.

The voice concludes: 'And so the extraordinary American life of Norma Jeane Dougherty, later Marilyn Monroe, enters what one may call without lack of gallantry its final phase.'

But it is Jean's least favourite female biographer who is granted the epitaph: 'I think her tragedy is, essentially, that she possessed a perishable talent, a sell-by celebrity. Look at it this way. Someone famous young for their acting or their writing, well, there is a recognized phenomenon of late, mature work, to which age brings grace notes. Even a great sports star, who retires young, their athletic decline is private. You don't get to see them not being able to hit or bounce the ball. But someone famous for beauty and sex – as Marilyn was – the people see the talent go in public. There really ain't no retirement counselling for folks like that.'

The biographer throws up her arms to dramatize her epigram. The frame is frozen, then fades into the annotated Mount Rushmore seen at the start. Over this, the credits roll.

And Ms Jean Norman, aged sixty-seven, lies flat on her bed and tries to pretend to herself that she is not crying.

36:   A Life They Never Knew They Had

If there are – as Boyd and Woodall frequently suspect – secret tape-recorders in White House offices, then the spools, voice-activated when Woodall greeted Boyd, will have stalled again for almost a minute before the next sound is picked up. But, finally, it is Boyd who breaks the silence.

'Frankly,' he says, 'right now, I would rather be reincarnated as a tape worm than be White House Chief of Staff.'

'Me too,' whispers Woodall, his naturally low volume turned down further by stress. 'Maybe we'd get to work the same intestine. I mean, who else could match our experience in handling shit?'

The two senior aides in the Sanders administration are holding a pre-meeting meeting in Boyd's messy den along the corridor from the Oval Office.

On the desk is a copy of the issue of *America Now* dated November 20th, 1993. The main face on the cover is that of President Newton Sanders, pompous and glossy at his Oval Office desk, Old Glory proud behind him. Bottom left, nuzzling his lapel, is one of the session photos of Diane; a strangely disjunctive image, as if the sitter had been instructed to appear both distressed and sexy. Beneath the magazine title runs a headline in high yellow letters on two lines: WHITE HOUSE SEX SCANDAL. At the base of the page, beside the portrait of the confused and alluring Diane, white type within large curly speech marks quotes her as saying: 'He promised he'd change the lives of Americans. He ruined mine!' In a small box in the bottom right-hand corner is a sunny snap of children playing in the shadow of a gleaming, creamy clapboard house. Above it, a caption reads: *Nice Town, USA.*

Boyd and Woodall have read the text of the lead story twice, as if hoping for a time-slip in which, at the second inspection, history would be reversed and America's forty-first president might not stand accused of sexually abusing – in the guise of 'Uncle Newt', a family friend assisting her with a homework assignment on the Constitution – an eleven-year-old girl called Diane, in Seattle, in June 1970.

'Tell me how I spin *this*!' pleads Boyd at the end of the next silence. 'A senior White House official stressed that this criminal perversion occurred long before the President entered political life? I mean, Al, a gay in San Francisco has a better long-term future than we do . . .'

Woodall files that line for a future memoir of these days, as a bigoted utterance that will help to establish Boyd in the reader's mind as the less sympathetic of the two men.

'We seem', points out Woodall in his most feathery voice, 'to be assuming that it's true.'

'I too have clutched at the other possibility,' Boyd acknowledges. 'I admit that, in usual circumstances, if *America Now* announces the start of a new ice age, one instructs one's broker to buy stocks in sun-loungers. But, here . . . what frightens me here is the detail. That Apollo thing, calling his cock Apollo, it's too weird not to be real. If she made that up, she's due the Pulitzer Prize for fiction.'

On one wall of Boyd's office, eight competing television screens give the effect of a technicolour chess board. Frequently drawing and shooting the channel changer he holds in one sweaty hand like a weapon, Boyd keeps checking the networks for breaking news.

So far there is nothing, but both men can imagine the windy ethical discussion taking place inside news bureaux. Should we follow the news agenda of a supermarket magazine? Adultery is a private matter – but to abuse a child is to break the law and therefore a public issue! But we are talking about unsubstantiated claims against the President of the United States!

Boyd and Woodall know that the decision of the news division presidents will largely depend on the first reaction from the White House. The switchboards in the executive wing are, they know, already lighting up like the sky on the 4th of July. So far, however, they have issued only a holding statement that the President is seeking legal counsel, a formula which has the advantage of revealing nothing – guilt and innocence would both require legal action – while sounding somewhat threatening.

Behind the left shoulder of the CNN presenter, there appears a photograph of the magazine cover. Boyd punches up the sound.

'We interrupt this bulletin with a breaking story,' says the black woman anchor in the fast-heartbeat way approved for such occasions. 'The magazine *America Now* has published this morning very serious sexual allegations against President Newton Sanders – made by a Seattle woman. The woman, now in her early thirties, has made allegations about incidents twenty years ago.'

Boyd finds himself crazily grateful that the report is for the moment avoiding the hand-grenade phrase 'child abuse', leaving the viewer to deduce the details from the time-scale given.

'In reporting this story,' the presenter continues, 'we stress that the claims are so far wholly unsubstantiated.'

'Isn't that fucking typical of the mainstream media these days?' yells Boyd. 'Go to the bath-house but wave a fucking condom round for show!'

Although agreeing with the sentiment – that the serious media have become increasingly willing to pass on tabloid gossip with a vague disclaimer – Woodall also stores away this phrase towards a portrait, in his self-exonerating memoirs, of Boyd as a foul-mouthed maverick, with a disturbing line in homophobic metaphor.

'The White House', reports the excited-looking anchor, 'has so far said only that the President is taking legal counsel ahead of an announcement.'

Woodall is staunching a big slick of sweat from his forehead with a handkerchief of show-off silk.

'You'd get a sense from that sentence, wouldn't you, if you didn't actually know,' he says, 'of people in control here?'

'In New York at this time', the television presenter

concludes, '*America Now* magazine is holding a press conference with the woman who has made these allegations, which, we underline again, are completely unsubstantiated. And so we go over live to the Carlyle Hotel in New York where that event is getting under way.'

Emperors and kings, thinks Boyd, had soothsayers to show them how things might play out. Modern leaders had the media.

In the hot trough of light in which they sit, Thomson leans across and whispers to Washington: 'We couldn't have got more press if the story had been about Princess Diana doing it with dingos.'

Washington thinks that this is a reference to some kind of Australian dog, but he can see what Thomson means without translation. The room is so full of reporters and television crews, that through the shimmering slits in the wall of camera lights and flash bulbs, the scene resembles a mediaeval depiction of hell: bodies writhing and pushing for dominance, amid spasmodic yelps of pain.

Squinting out at this tableau, from a long white-clothed table, Thomson and Washington flank Diane, with seats at the left and right ends occupied by the magazine's chief legal counsel and Diane's analyst. These two men seem to reflect some kind of equal opportunities policy, as the guardian of the law is abnormally small and the interpreter of the mind irregularly tall. The latter banged his knee painfully on the table as soon as he sat down.

The early questions at the press conference were the expected ones.

'How much are you being paid?'

'We never discuss contracts with contributors,' said *America Now*'s lawyer, to a cynical low hiss from the crowd.

'Did penetration occur?'

'No,' Diane sobbingly susurrated. 'Only touching . . .'

She glanced over at her analyst, who used the words 'masturbation, manual and oral', and explained that violation was not only a physical event.

'Were you in contact with President Sanders either subsequently or, recently, before speaking to the magazine?'

'Uh. No.'

Across the Nixon desk, America's forty-first president faces Boyd and Woodall.

'So you guys are my advisers. Advise!'

'Well, sir, we've been working on this,' says Boyd. 'I would summarize the obvious strategies as, one, character attack, and, two, legal intimidation. In the first case, the aim would be to identify, and spread, negative material on your accuser. Al has specifics on that one.'

'Thanks, Bob,' says Woodall, but his face as he takes over is that of the relay runner who suddenly discovers that shit has replaced aluminium in the manufacture of batons.

'Mr President, the best news', he explains, 'would be that Diane has been a Communist, a felon, a prostitute, or, ideally, all three as different vacation jobs one summer. We need to paint her as flaky, outside the mainstream of American life. We're working on these lines of enquiry. Bob?'

'Al,' acknowledges Boyd. These curt name-exchanges – like handovers on the news shows – seem to have evolved during their contributions this morning as an intended symbol of competence and organization.

'Mr President,' he continues. 'Legally, there are two routes open to us. Short term, we get on to the papers and the networks and let it be known we'll sue their ass if they don't start hanging a big cloud around the details of these things, and that we're on the point of playing court-room hard-ball with this Diane. Or we play the long game and appoint a Special Prosecutor, hands off, squeaky clean, to investigate these things she's said. A good investigation buys you a year, maybe two.'

Throughout these speeches, Sanders stares back at them with the bleakly superior expression of the investor who wants the banker to know he reads the money pages. The meeting has concentrated only on options. When it began, Boyd and Woodall discovered they dare not ask Sanders whether the

167

details in the magazine were true. They address the question as an abstract presentational matter.

'Recent media research has shown', Boyd tells the other two men, 'that the time may soon be ripe for what we call the Truth Strategy. By this, we mean that cynicism and distrust towards politicians are now so well established that the traditional damage-limitation methods of lying and denial may no longer be advisable. It's currently projected that a politician who came straight out and admitted wrong-doing – the Truth Strategy – might benefit greatly from the shock value of their candour.'

'Only problem with reading the game that way, is I'm not a politician,' says the President.

'That's true,' Boyd lies, 'but the general principle remains. Admittedly, the complication is that these predictions have been for financial or marital-sexual misdemeanours. With a different kind of sexual, er, error—'

'Hey, now, set that horse down there to drink,' Sanders snarls. 'You guys are talking as if I'm guilty. Back home we say, if the cat's always sniffing at the trash can, you know the *house* ain't got no mice.'

It occurred to Boyd and Woodall early in the administration that, if all the expressions Sanders claims are used back home were genuinely in circulation there, then locals would need to pass round glossaries before attempting conversation. They try to look as if they have understood the latest saying.

'And what those media élite guys can't stand', the President elaborates, 'is that there are no mice in this house. So they sniff around the trash can of those who want to bring me down. We sure as hell are going to use the Truth Strategy, Bob. We're going out there and we're going to tell the truth, which is that there are people in this town who would do anything to kill this administration. Let's go out and nail these lies about me!'

And Woodall and Boyd find, to their surprise, that they do not, at this moment, entirely disbelieve him.

*

The next exchanges at the press conference will be quoted and replayed in the days ahead so often that it will be as if time has stopped while this tape was playing.

'Diane,' shouts a balding reporter from the *Washington Post*. 'Did you inform your parents or any other person of these incidents at the time?'

'My, uh, mother died when I was young,' Diane mewls. 'I was raised by an aunt and uncle. But, you see . . .'

Here, the woman is seen to consult her analyst with her eyes. Different newspaper columnists will subsequently invoke the images of an actress glancing at her director and a daughter gazing at her father. Some viewers of the tape insist that the shrink begins to telegraph alarm before the woman says: 'I didn't know these things had happened until quite recently . . .'

Thomson and Washington swap eyes-only oaths, and the editor nervously refills the hotel crystal beakers of his deputy and himself with spring water.

'What do you mean you didn't *know*?' the *Washington Post* follows up, with a vocal double-take that brings Thomson unwanted visions of libel lawyers.

'I, uh, was not aware that I had suffered child abuse, until my consultations with Dr Patullo . . .'

Here again, Diane steals the actress–director/daughter–father peep with her analyst, who unwinds some of his height and leans towards the sun-burst of flash-guns.

'Diane', explains Dr Patullo, in the deep steady voice from which the media likes to hear its expertise, 'is a perfect example of a phenomenon we call Recovered Memory Syndrome. What happens is that the victim of a terrible event – frequently, child sexual abuse – experiences trauma so severe that the memory declines – for, you might say, the sake of the mind – to record any trace of it. Classically, the victim is aware only of an unidentified source of fear or pain, is convinced that something happened to them sometime to cause the psychological discomfort they now experience. *Something Happened*, as Joseph Heller put it. The mind, you see, is unable to cover over the scars completely. But it may be ten or twenty years – the latter, as you know, in Diane's case – before the events are recalled.'

'How are they recalled?' shouts a reporter from the *New York Times*.

'Well, uh, in discussion with their analyst – and, in many cases, with therapy involving an element of, uh, hypnosis – the victim becomes aware of a life they didn't even know they had.'

Hearing this, Thomson does not quite lose sight of the other life he has fantasized for himself – of journalistic celebrity – but one doleful lobe of his brain begins to contemplate different alternatives: of opprobrium and demotion.

As the press conference ends, and the bright lights converge into a blazing halo for Diane, Thomson leans across her empty chair and quietly frets to his deputy: 'Reassure me this Recovered Memory thing is kosher.'

'You'd have to say there is controversy. It's not the therapy of choice for every analyst.'

'Great!'

'But the tendency in America at this time, in cases of sexual abuse, is to believe the children.'

This analysis increases Thomson's confidence. He is glad, however, of the insurance of the Apollo 2 project. Reporters from *America Now* have found the Houston man into whose bank account Newton Sanders has paid the inflation-adjusted equivalent of $1,000 a month for fifteen years. The recipient of the cash has agreed to speak for the record.

37: Lucky Numbers

To her obvious facial irritation, Laura Lee Hauser is the first speaker of the weekend not to claim the full attention of the conference.

This is not the fault of her hypothesis, which – suggesting that Marilyn Monroe organized the shootings of Jack and Bobby Kennedy in a bad case of mistress's syndrome – is properly preposterous. The problem is that early East Coast copies of the *America Now* article on President Sanders have been faxed to Dallas by friends of the Dealey Plaza Researchers. This enticing new lead, the aniseed of possible conspiracy, leads to whispering and fidgeting as the waxy pages are passed down rows.

'And so, to those of you who have been following my arguments,' Ms Hauser testily perorates, 'I would conclude by saying this. We are asked to accept that Robert Kennedy, Attorney-General in his brother's administration, was shot in 1968 by an assassin protesting against the war in Vietnam, unable to reach President Kennedy himself because of improved security after Dallas. We are informed that the Dallas shooting was the work of a lone fanatic, Lee Harvey Oswald. These are motives of a kind. But they are motives attributed by *men*.'

The speaker is a small, taut woman in her middle forties, who wears her hair high and dyed, like an orange-coloured mushroom cloud exploding from her skull. Before starting her lecture, she hung four separate wrist-watches over the prow of the lectern.

'Women', she continues, 'will, I think, understand that Marilyn Monroe had a far stronger motive. The attacks on the Kennedy brothers were, however one may personally disapprove of violence, unequivocally *feminist* acts. Lorena Bobbitt – who, as men in the audience will not need reminding, shortly goes on trial in Virginia for severing her husband's penis – turns out not to have been the pioneer in the field of sexual revenge that she may have believed herself to be. Marilyn Monroe did what many spurned or badly treated mistresses in the past and the present have only dreamed of doing. It was to reclaim this piece of history from male misinterpretation that I wrote *Bring Me the Head of the Man I Once Loved*, and I will now be happy to sign copies of it, while discussing my theories with you. Thank you very much.'

The applause is guiltily intense, and a satisfying line of buyers forms at Hauser's book-heavy desk in front of the stage. Crick, however, heads for the refreshment tables, hoping for a last glance at his notes before his own lecture.

The squinting oldster from Rhode Island, who monopolized Crick during the morning coffee break, falls into step with him again as they approach the exit.

'If you ask me, Professor,' he says, 'it's more than a little suspicious that one of the biggest political stories in history breaks in Washington while all the goddam people most qualified to interpret it are stranded in Dallas.'

'Yes. I hadn't really looked at it that way,' Crick admits. 'What do you think? Do you think Sanders did it?'

'Listen, I have a view on this. Remember once, during the campaign, the story that Sanders had told some guys at lunch he'd been abducted by aliens during the night?'

'That's right. He got away with it, though.'

'Didn't he? Point is, that one of the things he apparently said was that these Venusians or whoever had put instruments in his bottom and cock, extracted fluids. Now that sounds to me like classic transference memory for child abuse – penetration by an alien body, right? – and, in more than somewhat of cases, those abused as children become abusers in adult life. I'd say he did it.'

It is Crick's luck that a conspiracy theorist with a new line will usually seek many hearers rather than one, and so he is soon left alone with his lecture. He believes that he wants no interruption, but, when a specific one arrives, he realizes that this was not true.

'Good luck.'

'Oh. Kathy. Hi.'

'I'll be paying close attention.'

'You better. There'll be a quiz at dinner tomorrow.'

'Oh. What's the prize?'

Like much of the evidence with which a researcher deals, Kathy's smile as she walks away is open to rational or hysterical interpretation. And Crick, who is about to lecture on fate and chance, has far more of a personal investment in the question than when he prepared his address.

On the screens behind Crick are rivers of digits, avalanches of calculations, lines of numbers wide and deep.

He has photographed on to slides some of the torrents of computer printout produced by multiplying and dividing numerical data related to the Kennedy mysteries, testing the figures against each other and against unconnected numbers. The numerals originally input included the date of the shooting (221163 or 112263), the time of the first shots (1230), the number plate of the presidential Lincoln (300), Jack Kennedy's position among presidents of America (35), and among presidents since the Union (19). Other computer runs started from the dates for the creation of the nation (1776), the writing of the US Constitution (1787), the start (1861) and the end (1865) of the American Civil War.

'My fellow researchers, good afternoon,' Crick begins. 'It is my intention in this lecture, which I have called "Our Days are Numbered", to introduce to our deliberations the discipline of number theory.

'In one sense, we are all familiar with number theory. It is not uncommon for a human being to have what he or she refers to as a lucky number: for houses, seats on airplanes, hotel rooms, lottery tickets, and so on. There is, of course, the complication that a number which wins the lottery becomes, by definition, a lucky one, so that backwards rationalization cannot be ruled out.

173

'At a more apocalyptic level, the belief that God – or whatever force or organization lies behind the universe – operates in round numbers is very well documented. The year AD 1000 seemed to those alive at the time a likely termination date for the world, and thousands gathered on hills and mountains with their belongings, waiting for their flight to be called. But they had no more luck than some of you, I understand, experienced this weekend, waiting for yours . . .'

This is a personal reference inserted for Kathy, and he is gratified to catch her smile as he continues: 'Yet our ancestors' assumption was understandable. As human beings, we are seeking shape or meaning in the mystery of being here. One thousand years was a tempting neatness. Nearly a millennium later, the idea still appeals. Perhaps we will not haul our Louis Vuitton cases to the summit of Mount Rushmore when the year 2000 comes around, but the perceived significance of that date, that round number, recognizably lies heavy in the culture at this time.'

'Number theory, as myself and other mathematicians study it, is merely an intellectual extension of this concept of luck or mystique or significance attaching to certain numbers. We divide integers – that's our jargon word for a number – into two groups: prime and composite. A prime integer, or number, is divisible only by the numbers 1 and itself. The first few examples are 2, 3, 5, 7, and 11. A composite number, by contrast, is divisible by more, often many more, than those two numbers. With 3 and 6, for example, you can work out this difference on your fingers: the first prime, the second composite. But, for those who do this for a living, the interest begins with numbers of five, ten, twenty, or more digits, and for which software, rather than fingers, is necessary to discover whether they are prime or composite . . .'

Pausing to sip water, and to allow his eyes what seems to be a general sweep around the room, but which has Kathy as its target, Crick is pleased to see that he is holding the concentration of the delegates. His talks are pitched to flatter a general audience, but there is still the risk of alienation. Accordingly, he throws a softer punch.

'I apologize,' Crick smiles, 'if, hearing all this, your worst memories of Friday afternoon math in school are coming back to you. But I will not be asking you to do calculations. All you need to know is that prime numbers, particularly in their larger forms, hold for many mathematicians an almost mystical quality, resulting from their rarity. They are, you might say, gold to the copper of composites.

'Take, then, the proposition of a world organized and ordered by an outside force, whether we call it God or nature. It would be reasonable to assume that the coherent structure of this universe would show itself in numbers: either in what one might call anniversary composites – as the misguided millennialists of AD 1000 believed – or in prime numbers.

'Such analysis is tempting. As a young student, for example, I was taught math by a Jesuit, who liked to point out that the generally presented age of Christ at death – 33 – consists of the earliest uneven prime number – 3 – repeated twice. The number 3 figures, as it were, heavily in Christian doctrine. Divinity resides in a Holy *Trinity*. Christ rises from the dead on the *third* day. To those who objected that, logically, Our Lord should therefore have died at 3, this priest would reply that even the son of God would have struggled to complete His earthly mission in that time! But we can see a stronger objection. Why should God have shown his hand through what is the second plausible prime number rather than the first – and, by the way, the only even prime – which is 2. Why, in short, did Christ not die at 22?

'The history of our own country, though, does offer one startling example. Each American citizen, and resident alien, pledges to build "one nation *indivisible* under God", and the date of the agreement of our Constitution – 1787 – does indeed prove to be a prime number, in numerical terms *indivisible* . . .'

Crick has calculated that an audible reaction to this revelation will demonstrate that the delegates have ingested the basic information, and he is rewarded with a gasp.

'Thus', he continues, 'there is some mathematical support for the mystical qualities with which the Constitution has traditionally been endowed. Significant modern dates, however, are more or less uniformly composite. This is true of

1939, the date on which the Second World War began, and of all the various dates which may be taken as the commencement of American involvement in Vietnam. The date – 1968 – of the assassinations of Bobby Kennedy and Martin Luther King is a composite; indeed, one which offers many options. I must also tell you that both 221163 and 112263 – the two forms, European and American, in which the date of the Kennedy shooting in Dallas may be presented – are very far from being prime numbers. Indeed, each divides neatly by merely the second available integer: the number 3.'

Dejection or confusion settles on the faces of the delegates. Crick savours their dismay, before saying: 'I see that what I have just said has come as a disappointment to many of you. You wanted 221163 or 112263 to be prime numbers. But to want this is to miss the point. If the key dates of modern history were indeed prime numbers, then the logical conclusion would be that the events of our century were being mystically directed by an outside force: by God or nature. But the fact that our history turns out to pivot on composites is evidence that these events are the work not of God but of man, that they are the product not of fate but of *conspiracy* . . .'

Crick's congregation rewards this proposition with the loud out-breath which is its hallelujah. It is, though, only the reaction of Kathy Malone that really matters to him.

38:   Jean's Dream

In Jean's dream, her body is perfect, but dead. She is naked, face down, on her bed at Fifth Helena, a telephone held in her heavy right hand. Another telephone is ringing down the hall. There is a voice – which sounds like the housekeeper, Mrs Murray's – saying: 'She's fine. She's fine. I checked on her.'

On the clock on the bedside table, hours whirl past, fast as the hands of an aeroplane propeller, like a special effect. Now, Greenson, the analyst, crashes into the room, the housekeeper behind him. Kneeling over her, he hauls her torpid body round.

The front page of the *Los Angeles Times*, dated Monday August 6th, 1962. She is able to read the headlines:

MARILYN MONROE FOUND DEAD
Sleeping Pill Overdose Blamed
Unclad body of star
discovered on bed;
empty bottle near

And then, as her dream's director goes in really close with the rostrum camera, she can make out the text: *Marilyn Monroe, a troubled beauty who failed to find happiness as Hollywood's brightest star, was discovered dead in her Brentwood home of an apparent drug overdose Sunday . . .*

Even in her dream, Jean knows that this is wrong, although in the tapestry fashion of sleep stories, the other items on the page are events that she is almost sure actually happened around about that time. Richard Nixon – defeated by Kennedy in 1960 – has raised a new power base by seizing control of the California Republicans, and Russia has carried out a nuclear test in Sweden.

A jump-cut, now, to the beach at Santa Monica, the early morning sun-worshippers anachronistically shivering and wrapping their arms around them as if cold. From a radio, a disc jockey dramatically laments: 'Marilyn Monroe, dead at thirty-six. We grasp at straws as if knowing how she died will bring her back. Not since Jean Harlow have the standards of feminine beauty been embodied in one woman. Marilyn Monroe, dead at thirty-six.'

And now another new location. In her habitual nineties disguise – scarf, dark shades, billowing coat – Jean is peering into a bookshop window: varnished wood and dark green awnings, which she thinks she recognizes as Brentano's at Century City. Arrayed on crumpled velvet are a set of gleaming books. Half show her own, but unaged, face, the standard Marilyn wank picture; the rest Jack Kennedy's, frozen in his forties. Above the display hang two portraits: one of Marilyn, one of Jack, each decades out of date. On a twist of silk is printed: 'American History Week'.

She recognizes some of her biographies, although the volumes look significantly thinner. But many of the other titles frighten her: *The Life and Curious Death of Marilyn Monroe*, *Who Killed Marilyn Monroe?*, *The Marilyn Scandal*, *Goddess*, *Tragic Venus*. With the stack of books on Jack, she looks only at one – *The Death of the President* – then turns away, guilty about what she fears, even from inside the fiction, is an ill wish.

Now she is inside the shop; able, in the biography section, to remove books from the shelves. Every account of her life is truncated in the same way, listing *Something's Gotta Give* as her last, unfinished movie, and Miller as her third and final husband. On the last page of one exposé, Jean reads the final lines: 'Although Marilyn's early death was undoubtedly a tragedy, many of her friends admitted that it was hard, in honesty, to imagine for her maturity as an actress or, indeed, to see this legend of youthful beauty in old age at all. Perhaps in Hollywood, as in astronomy, the brightest stars are not intended to shine for long.'

*

Coming up suddenly from this other life, Jean experiences the thumping pulse and temporary identity crisis that is the sleeper's equivalent of a diver's decompression sickness. Even the bedside clock seems briefly to be racing like the one in her dream.

On settled inspection, the bedside clock, which moves with proper stealth, shows 2 a.m. Her first reflex is for the quick eclipse of sleeping pills, more likely to be dreamless, or at least muzzy. Her second impulse is for therapy, wondering which friend might recommend a decent dream analyst.

After a long fight, she resists both wishes. Around such victories of willpower this last phase of her life revolves.

Turning on the light, and sitting up, she sees the impression of her features in the pulpy pillow, like a death mask. She flattens it out with her hands, then spins round, flops down on her back, and tries to recover the details of her dream.

Much of it, she guesses, follows from the television documentary she viewed two nights before. The prospect of meeting Jack again may also have contributed.

Jean tries to imagine what Greenson would have said, if he were still alive, and confronted with these images: 'My dear Marilyn, to dream of death is not in itself, ah, conclusive. The dreamer may, indeed, be suicidal. But the dream may speak of a fear of death, and thus lust for life. Or, subconsciously, the dreamer may fear that others wish them dead. Let us begin, then, with the more, ah, transparent symbols. You imagine a career that ends before *The K Brothers*. You try out, in your hidden mind, a life in which your youthful beauty never fades. All of this is classic cathartic denial . . .'

39: Milk Carton

It is late Sunday morning in Newton, Maine, so recently voted 'Nice Town, USA' in *America Now*'s inaugural civic gentility poll. The bright white wooden church in the main square is deserted. Its bells, though diligently polished by a roster of local Christian women, are certain to gather a little dust before they are required again next week.

This morning, during service, the Reverend Auger, by ordination an Episcopalian, though serving here many Christ-fearing creeds in what he likes to refer to as a broad Church, told his congregation: 'It cannot be denied that *America Now* magazine does not always print the kind of material which one would quote from a pulpit.'

At this, the rich New England company executives, seated with their wives and children in the front few pews of well-wiped pine, gave the dutiful whinny of laughter they would bestow on the corporate president in his address at the AGM.

'Although I suppose', the Reverend Auger carried on, 'many of its articles might be taken as a kind of lurid illustration of the parable of the talents.'

Here, the businessmen and their wives looked grave, and meshed their hands in a half-clasp, as they generally did when the pastor spoke of religion.

'But', their celebrant continued, 'this, let us perhaps say, *mercurial* publication has this week preached Good News. At the risk of partially contradicting our Lord, seed does sometimes sprout on stony ground, and we should feel no shame about the declaration of our community as "Nice Town, USA" by this particular source. A town, we are told, which the Homicide Squad has never visited. Well, yes, we knew that.

A town in which neighbours look out for neighbours, in which the old keep an eye on the young, and contrariwise too. Well, this is not news to us. A town in which children play happily outside, without fear and without threat. Well, yes, that we also knew. It would, my brothers and sisters, be too much to expect the magazine to use the language that we ourselves would have chosen. But we know that Newton was, in fact, this week selected as God's town, USA . . .'

Now, however, the worshippers of Newton, having boomed Amens to that and other propositions, have gone home. At 12.15 a.m., on this Sunday – November 21st, 1993 – Main Street is empty. The trees are nakedly admitting of summer's end, but the sun cussedly perseveres, with light if not heat, its rays trying to break the glass in the frontages of those pastel-painted storefronts that cross its path. A silver-haired couple, in well-cut sheeny overcoats and frothy scarves, are reading the display in the window of the Historical Society. The only other figure in the scene is a middle-aged man with careless hair, wearing a padded jacket with enough pockets to satisfy an octopus. He is lining up a picture in a camera with a long round black snout.

A professional, thinks Fraser, as he drives his hired Oldsmobile through Newton. He quickly guesses that the announcement of the prize won by the town has drawn writers and photographers to record its decency. At first, this realization frightens him, for what he plans to do is not usually carried out in proximity to the press. But then he relaxes, recognizing that the media presence, as long as it avoids the specific street he seeks, solidifies his alibi. The cover of other in-town strangers may be of use to him.

Fraser is driving with a soft foot, because New England is notorious for the enforcement of traffic laws. He spent the previous night at a motel near Boston Logan airport, where he tried to divert himself from a room service hamburger with a new work on his subject. Called *Wrinkles In Time* it is written by an American professor, George Smoot. He is clearly a brilliant guy – a member of the Center for Particle Astrophysics and the Space Sciences Laboratory, the book flap boasts – but he does not replace Hawking in Fraser's cosmology of idols. Smoot merely accounts for the existence of the world that turns. He does not explore what Fraser finds most exciting about Hawking's view of the universe: the conditionality of existence, the possibility, however theoretical, of alternative versions.

At the end of Main Street, and beyond a pond, Fraser turns into the residential roads, mainly named, according to his map, for presidents and flowers. Two Robinsons were shown in the New England Bell listings for Newton: a Patrick, on Van Buren Avenue, and an R. J., on McKinley Drive. Irritatingly, the article in *America Now* made no mention of the father of the children – Betsey, seven, and Nathaniel, two – of Mary E. Robinson, the mother vouching for the safety of the town.

Fraser reaches McKinley first, cruising as slowly as he can as he looks for 1124, the number given for R. J. Robinson. A house in which children live generally bears certain signs: most simply, bicycles or toys, but, more subtly, the backs of jazzy posters or the swish of mobiles in upstairs windows. No such help is given by the outside view of 1124 McKinley. Nor does the flag flapping on the front lawn argue either way. Flamboyant patriotism is not, reflects Fraser, a generational indicator in America.

Turning at the top of McKinley and reversing his journey, he reduces his speed as low as he dares, grateful that such inching progress is thought responsible rather than odd in this state. On his second inspection of 1124, Fraser is hoping for the definitive disqualifier of a snowy-haired oldster emerging on to the path, but this is not granted to him. Hanging a left on McKinley, he drives, via Monroe and Rosebush, to Van Buren. The residences here are big frame houses, some of them three-storeyed, most ringed with springy lawns. It is not impossible that his Robinsons live here. The profession attributed to the mother – 'assistant teacher' – might identify either serious bread-winning or the hobby job of a rich man's under-occupied wife.

Fraser has chosen his moment with care. Relying on a stereotype, but one which is not untenable in a community like Newton, he imagines the mothers cooking, while the fathers slouch in front of the Sunday shout-shows – this week, discussing the Sanders scandal or President Kennedy's legacy, thirty years after Dallas – with a token sliver from the slab of the Sunday *New York Times* draped on their knees.

Approaching number 28, the address of the Van Buren Robinsons, Fraser experiences one of his life's few perfect chimes between his plan for an event and its reality. On the grass outside, a group of young children – Fraser guesses them to be in the sevens and eights – are playing a game involving a baseball, a catching mitt, and much running and shouting. They wear track-suit tops or brightly coloured zip-up coats. Rich kids, thinks Fraser, with reflex contempt.

He stops the car, most of the vehicle concealed by a heavy sculpted hedge which separates 28 from the neighbouring property, and watches. Away from the ball-game, near the hedge, at the centre of a rusty whorl of fallen leaves, sit three much younger children; one, Fraser calculates, of around four years old, the others under three. He spreads across the bottom of the steering wheel the photograph of the Robinson family from *America Now*, and tries to judge whether one of the trio of tinies is Nathaniel, aged two, but the baggy woollen hats, worn like a uniform by the babies, make a match impossible.

Taking with him his stolen shoulder-bag and Pentax – originally the props of a tourist, but now of a journalist – Fraser approaches the Robinson home. Before he has even reached the grass, a girl with brown hair in yellow Alice bands skips towards him.

'Not *more* journalists!' she challenges him, her arms melodramatically rounded to her hips, in what Fraser guesses is a copy of a parent's body language and complaint.

'Im afraid so,' he shrugs. 'My editor's really keen I follow this up. I guess Americans really want to hear some good news for a change. Are you Betsey?'

'No-ooh!' the girl operatically objects. 'I don't look anything like her!'

But she turns and yells 'Betsey!' and a bubble blonde he recognizes from the magazine sprints towards them.

'Another of your boyfriends,' says the first girl, and chases back to the sport.

'If you need a picture, I'll give you two minutes, then I'm getting back to the game,' Betsey Robinson, aged seven, informs him, a media sophisticate already, apparently, three days after her introduction to publicity.

'What I'd really like,' says Fraser, 'is to take some stuff from here, of the game. You just play on, I won't get in the way.'

'Oh. You mean *all* the kids will be in the picture?'

Her disappointment is vivid. Fraser, though, has made a study of American celebrity.

'I'll be taking close-ups of you, Betsey, with the others in the background.'

'That's OK. You'd better not show Judy Summers's face. Her dad's a spy.'

'Oh, really? No, it's you I want. And, after, I'd like to take some of your brother. Nathaniel, is it?'

'Nat. Fat Nat. What do you want pictures of him for? He's really stupid.'

She jerks a thumb towards the babies, chuckling and wrestling, in their lagged and puffy outdoor suits.

'Our moms make us bring them to play. But they just keep falling over and ruining the game.'

'Yeah. I remember. Which one's Nat?'

'The dumb one in the yellow hat. Now, can you get on with this, please? You're the tenth since yesterday.'

Betsey skips back to her friends. Fraser takes a few token frames of the ball game, preceded by elaborate narrowing of eyes and angling of the camera, in gestures largely adapted from television golfers.

Under cover of lining up his shots, he has walked backwards, closer to the throng of toddlers. At last, he is able to say, 'Nat?' The child in the yellow hat directs a look of some perplexity at Fraser. On an instinct, Fraser raises the camera, and the boy squeals and poses. A pampered child, a trophy kid, well used to photos, Fraser guesses.

'Nat,' he says, after taking two pictures in this set-up, 'I'm just going to take you over here. The light's better.'

And Nat Robinson, aged two, takes two proud, firm steps across the grass of crimeless, Christ-fearing Nice Town, USA.

40: Cathode Ray Codes

Crick had expected that the reunion with Kathy Malone would introduce an interlude of serenity to his life. In the storyboards the mind draws for the future, he saw himself moving smoothly through the day, his regular demons silenced by the pleasurable event ahead. In the way he pictured today, there would be the occasional knowing look across the room between himself and Kathy.

History, though, has turned out differently. In the coffee break between the Sunday morning sessions, he finds himself tailing her around the lounge with his eyes. If he sees Kathy speaking to another man – and the count is so far three – he fears a potential crack in the pact he believes to be between them.

Crick tries to converge his nervous energy on the male researcher with whom he is huddled: an ex-ophthalmic septuagenarian from Kansas City, who wishes to discuss the first talk of the morning: 'The Oxygen of Sympathy' by Tom Andrews. This speaker is a top-selling non-fiction author, and the resentment of the many delegates with peddled and rejected manuscripts was clearly a piece of the atmosphere in the room when he began to speak.

This hostility was soon, however, diluted by the enthusiasm of the conference for the grandeur of his allegations. Andrews was, as the brochure had promised, expanding on the thesis of his book *Staging Greatness*: that the events in Dallas in November 1963 were a fake, 'a piece of biographical theatre, a coronation through a symbolic survival of violence, after argument and policy had failed to convince the American people of the merits of a narrowly elected president'. This stunt, Andrews argued, had secured Kennedy his 1964 landslide.

'Andrews sure convinced me,' says the Kansas delegate. 'He's absolutely right about one thing. Who, in the short term, gained most from the attempted assassination? Jack Kennedy. Why did he go to Dallas? Because he's sinking in the polls. What happens afterwards? He's a hero. Goldwater, in '64, suddenly finds he's running against the Risen Christ. Few stories about Oswald's Russian connections, and JFK has even got the Republicans pulling for him. And Oswald, of course, is conveniently dead.'

'I guess,' replies Crick, willing himself not even to look towards the left, where he knows that Kathy is. 'But the thing I don't get is, Kennedy recovered but he *was* injured. You can see it on the Zapruder footage. I mean, even for a politician who wants to win the next election, it's a hell of a gamble. Trusting a guy to hit you at the right angle, so he wounds but doesn't kill you, when you're in a moving car. It's like the cosmic apotheosis of the circus knife-throwing trick. Oswald would have to be a perfect shot.'

'Richard, Oswald *was* a perfect shot. Phi Beta Kappa at the CIA rifle agency.'

'Now wait a minute, I read somewhere, in one of these goddam books, that Oswald couldn't hit a buffalo at spitting distance.'

'Well, of course, you read that, Richard. They needed you to read it. You're telling me you're unfamiliar with the concept of disinformation?'

On the last word, he flipped out his hands towards Crick, and gave a tell-me-about-it grin, like Johnny Carson at the end of one of his gags.

'Also,' the Kansas monologist continues, 'I make a point of judging a theory by its supporting detail. Part of what convinces me of Andrews' line is the hospital evidence.'

'You mean the nurse?'

'Absolutely. You're telling me that a surgeon who has just carried out life-saving neurosurgery – as the White House insisted at the time it was – is going to be cracking jokes, is going to be doing a riff about not needing the priest any more? This, Richard, is a guy who knows that a priest was never needed.'

'The point is,' says Crick, rising to the challenge, and happy at the distraction from Kathy, 'Reagan gets shot in '81, and that rockets up his positives too, at a time when he needs it, but nobody tells us that the whole thing was some kind of Hollywood mock-up.'

'That's true, Richard. But you know why? Because there are no loose ends in the Reagan story, no suggestions that John Hinckley was linked to anything except his own strange brain. Dallas and Oswald and Kennedy – there are more questions than on *Jeopardy!*'

The argument is ended by the bells and yells to summon delegates to the final session of the conference. In the crowd at the door, Crick feels a touch on his arm.

'Conversation looked pretty intense.'

'Oh, Kathy. Hi. Yeah, I didn't really buy into the assassination attempt as movie of the week the way he did.'

Crick is thinking: She was watching me, *she* was watching *me*.

'Oh, well,' says Kathy. 'I'll tell you my theory on that one over dinner.'

As a result of this exchange, Crick experiences some trouble in returning his preoccupations to the subject of the conference by the time the next lecture begins. The speaker has cropped, nearly shaven, coppery hair. Lesbian bells at once ring in Crick.

'President of the symposium, fellow delegates,' she begins. 'My name is Joanie Tamaro – I'm a researcher from Oklahoma – and I'm delighted, if a little awestruck, to be addressing you this weekend among such distinguished researchers of what Professor Draycott so rightly called . . . excuse me while I take a drink of water, my mouth is a little dry . . . of what Professor Draycott so rightly called yesterday morning "the lie that keeps us all awake at nights".

'Tom Andrews – in his fascinating talk in the first session this morning – described the shooting in Dallas on November 22nd, 1963, as "a carefully staged drama". Mr Andrews meant this in the sense of pretence. What I aim to demonstrate here is how a carefully staged drama – or, anyway, the CBS soap opera *Dallas*, which ran from 1978 to 1991 in the United States and around the world – may contain less pretence than you previously suspected. I hope to show that what we may previously have dismissed as a soap opera in fact makes a number of connections with the mystery that concerns us all.

'By the way, popular culture often tells us more about the world than it is academically respectable to think. Mr Andrews, it seems to me, might like to reflect on the fact that the 1977 movie *Capricorn One* – in which NASA fakes a mission to Mars for the benefit of television – is almost certainly a giggling and knowing reference by the media establishment to the faking of the Kennedy assassination. One critic, incidentally, described the plot of *Capricorn One* as, and I quote, "entertaining but far fetched". I think we would say to him: get a life!

'Similarly, a surprising number of American cultural commentators have been willing to accept as mere coincidence that CBS should begin, in 1978, a series called *Dallas*, a soap opera with a title that employs one of the most resonant words in American culture: shorthand for the end of political innocence, the end of the credibility of the establishment version of events, the turning point in the Kennedy administration.

'Consider the parallels between the television fiction and a key narrative of American reality. The central family in *Dallas* are the Ewings, a poor family made rich by oil. One son, a handsome charmer, is christened John but known by his initials: JR. He has a younger brother – more solemn and more scrupulous – called Bobby. The family patriarch is a grizzled old souser and womanizer called Jock. The matriarch, Miss Ellie, is a strong, good woman who comes to know many tragedies in her life, and is uncritically devoted to the family men. The son with initials is seriously wounded in a shooting and rushed to Dallas Parkland Hospital. Bobby, the younger son, is killed.

'Compare the Ewings now with another family: the Kennedys. For Jock, read Joe: a harsh patriarch, fond of women and drink, made hugely wealthy by bootlegging, the historical precursor, in the American economy, of oil as a financial life changer. In name, Ellie Ewing and Rose Kennedy are less of a match – Rose being alive, perhaps this was attributable to libel worries – but, in character, the fit is uncanny. For JR, the dashing and ambitious son identified by the letters of his names, read, of course, JFK, taken, after a shooting, as I need hardly tell you, to Dallas Parkland Hospital. For Bobby, the younger brother, read Bobby, the younger brother.

'Such deliberate parallels suggest intended messages. Let me, if I may, spell them out for you. In a moment, I'm going to show you the first clip from the pivotal episode of the series, *Who Shot JR?*, in which the mystery of who attempted to assassinate the sexy and energetic initialled favourite son in Dallas is finally resolved. But, first, I want to reveal to you the most dramatic piece of evidence that CBS, the great American corporate monolith headed by William Paley, was nodding and winking at the American public over the codes hidden within its top-rating show. For let me tell you the date on which the *Who Shot JR?* episode of *Dallas* was screened. It was, my friends, November 21st, 1980 . . .'

The silent room was suddenly filled with a hiss of recognition and the scratching of pens on notepads.

'The very eve', says Joanie Tamaro, 'of the anniversary of the other Dallas . . .'

41: She's Back!

The celibate vegetarian non-drinking Buddhist co-star of *She's Back!* is putting on her make-up at the table of her trailer, when Jean, without knock or announcement, walks in.

The younger actress turns with an intemperate expression: she has given instructions against interruptions. Seeing Jean, her face performs contortions which, in a game of charades, would hand the other players the word 'Astonishment' from a single clue.

'You!' she shrieks. 'How the . . . look, is this some kind of joke?'

'If it is, honey, then it's not on you . . .' Jean replies, in a voice marinaded in pain and loss.

'But, I thought . . . Come here . . . can I touch you?'

'I guess . . .'

Jean spreads her arms like someone just busted for drugs, and her co-star rubs her hands slowly over the time-altered contours of the famous body of Marilyn Monroe.

'Scandal sheets ever get pictures of this, they'd be in heaven,' says Jean.

'I was coming to that. Oughtn't you to *be* in heaven?'

'Honey, thank you for thinking that's where I belong. Actually, that was where I ended up. Any of those critics who said I couldn't act should have seen me at the Pearly Gates. I know this must be kind of hard for you to get your head round, but the big director in the sky wanted to see me in a sequel. Heaven's the opposite of Hollywood.'

'Well, it would have to be, really, wouldn't it?'

'Oh, in those ways too. But what I mean is, in heaven you only get a sequel if you *didn't* do very good business first time round . . . and, I'm sorry, I've completely blocked the next line.'

The director – a veteran light-comedy hand who suffers from irritable bowel syndrome – jumps up into the trailer through its missing wall.

'That's OK, Marilyn, I was going to break it, anyway. The pace was better there, but you were still too downbeat at the top of the scene. This is your big entrance. Everything before this has been the funeral and obituaries. You gotta come on hot.'

Jean looks out through the circle of light, to find the eyes of Susan Strasberg, Lee's daughter, her personal acting coach, with whom she worked on this scene for several hours the night before. Her mentor's brisk nod encourages Jean to challenge the director.

'I have to say I see this scene differently,' Jean argues. 'This woman's dead. It's her first day back on earth. This is a bewildering experience for her. I'm playing confusion, poignancy . . .'

'Marilyn, this is a mainstream movie. The audience we're aiming for thinks poignant is what they say in the Bronx for a woman who's going to have a baby . . .'

'But this has got to be a trauma for her. She's the first person ever to come back from the undiscovered country.'

'No, she ain't. This has happened in a whole lot of movies.'

'I mean, she's the first to do it for real.'

'Baby, let me tell you something. This isn't for real. It's a movie. Marilyn, you're playing a dead woman. You want to method act, it solves a lot of my problems, but otherwise just pretend. OK, let's break for lunch. We'll shoot this first thing back.'

Turning his back on Jean, he simpers at the younger actress: 'Great reaction shot, baby. You just give me that again, and we'll print it.'

Jean steps out of the imitation trailer with the cut-through side and roof, and drags angrily across the sound stage back towards her real, and complete, version of the same vehicle. Her co-star runs to catch up with her.

'Listen, Marilyn, I'll tell him I want the scene the way you're playing it.'

Jean can see that this support is meant to be comforting, but, by underlining the power structure on the set, it depresses her further.

'Well, thanks,' she says, flatly.

'Oh, shit, I know it sounded patronizing. Look, let's get something to eat, and we'll talk about what we're going to do about that asshole.'

As the two actresses walk together towards Jean's trailer, she becomes aware of the four muscular black-clad men, walking in formation, two ahead of the women, and two behind, like photographic hinges framing a square of safe space. Her companion follows the direction of her eyes.

'Oh, excuse my goons,' she says. 'Real small-craft warning in force today. My, uh, unwanted friend has sent me a new bunch of letters. Sort of change of tone. Red-hot pokers up my snatch. That kind of thing. Not very nice.'

'Shit. I'm sorry . . .'

'Well, you know what they say. Why is life like a Sam Peckinpah movie?'

'Why?'

'Just when you think it can't get any worse, it does.'

And – flanked by the four men protecting the younger woman against the darker consequences of the emotions she is paid millions of dollars to provoke – they reach the trailer.

'OK, Marilyn, let's sort out what to do about Louis B. De Nil, Alfred Smallcock.'

'He's going to be even more down on me when he finds I need Thursday off.'

'Problem?'

'Not really, I've got to go to Boston.'

'Business?'

'In a way. Unfinished business.'

42: Statements

In a statement released to the White House press corps at 15:34 p.m. on Saturday November 20th, 1993, President Newton Sanders says: 'I am completely innocent of these monstrous allegations, and have never met Diane Yapullo, at any time during her or my life. The White House will shortly begin proceedings for libel against Ms Yapullo, *America Now* magazine, its editors, publishers, and distributors. I regard the publication of this story as evidence of the fervent desire of the American media-political complex to bring to an end the first modern presidency that they did not themselves engineer.'

One alert White House correspondent spots that the printed text of the statement was, in one place, irregularly presented. Between the words 'my' and 'life', at the end of the first sentence, there is a space considerably greater than that which the lay-out elsewhere allocates. It looks as if a word has been speedily deleted, and then the gap not properly customized. One of the network bureau chiefs jokes, though not on screen, that the word has almost certainly been 'miraculous' – 'my *miraculous* life' – thus twitting the egotism of Sanders.

Only Robert F. Boyd, the administration's Chief of Staff, knows the truth, which is that the phrase originally read: 'during her or my present life'. The President confided that, as a believer in reincarnation, he cannot entirely rule out having committed child abuse in an earlier incarnation, and that any statement must be scrupulous about this.

At a briefing for the White House corps, following distribution of the statement, Boyd insists to reporters that the accusations were part of an 'attempted coup' against 'a man who changed history in a way a lot of people in this town didn't want it to be changed'. This is a translation for public consumption of the last remark that Sanders made before Boyd went down to the briefing room with the text: 'Tell 'em that back home we always say, if there's shit in your yard, sniff your own dog's ass before you go next door.'

However, in a statement timed at 17:15 p.m. on the same day, James L. Thomson, editor of *America Now* magazine, declares: 'We remain convinced of the accuracy of the story, and of the reliability of our source. Attempts by abusers to silence those they abused, with threats and bullying, are well documented in these cases.'

Half an hour later, in a joint statement co-ordinated from their separate weekend retreats, Democrat and Republican minority leaders in House and Senate demand the appointment of a White House special prosecutor to investigate the allegations. 'President Sanders has a long history of failing to respond adequately to allegations about his past,' the statement says. 'But on this matter, there must be full disclosure.'

Next morning, Sunday November 21st, 1993, a *Washington Post* media reporter – quoting sources at the magazine speaking on condition of anonymity – reports that there were worries among editors about the revelation that the source was an example of 'the controversial psychoanalytical procedure, Recovered Memory Syndrome'. However, the magazine believes that it has the 'fireproof insurance' of a second story about Sanders, which it is following up, and which will demonstrate 'a pattern of behavior'.

In the first opinion polls conducted since the breaking of the 'Apollogate' affair, 63% of respondents say that they believe Diane, but 54% express faith in the version of events given by the White House, and 57% answer positively to the statement: 'The allegations were manufactured or exaggerated by the media.' Analysts are unsure about how to interpret these figures.

On Sunday evening news bulletins in New England, the crisis at the White House is relegated to second story, behind the news that Nathaniel Robinson, a two-year-old child, has been abducted in Newton, Maine, apparently by a man posing as a journalist. The abduction, it is reported, comes only a day after the town received a prize as the safest place in America. The local police chief says that he cannot rule out a connection. 'What is happening to America?' demands the Reverend Robert Auger, the local Episcopalian minister, in a tearful interview with the local CBS affiliate.

Issuing his second statement of the day, this one timed at 20:40 p.m., the editor of *America Now* magazine, James L. Thomson, expresses 'horror' at the story of the abduction in Maine.

Dozens of daytime television shows put the Newton kidnapping and the Sanders allegations alongside similar current stories about the singer Michael Jackson. They bill as their topic for Monday November 22nd, 1993: 'Can we trust anyone with our children?' On at least two stations, this item replaces a planned segment marking the thirtieth anniversary of what is called 'the day that Dallas held its breath'.

43: Time Travel

It is an inevitable side-effect of being a conspiracy theorist that life regularly delivers little shivers of unease. The restaurant unsettles Crick even before he and Kathy have been seated.

It stands at a height of four hundred feet, a bowl-shaped pod at the top of a broad concrete stem. The pod completes a revolution every hour; a novelty – of changing scenery at window tables – which the restaurant advertises enthusiastically. But Crick's response is to reflect on what a marvellous target for terrorism the tower represents. Paranoiacs are seldom off-duty.

But even those not burdened with the enthusiasms common to many of tonight's diners might be disturbed by the atmosphere. The illumination in the restaurant is so minimal – presumably in calculation of a romantic ambience – that the waiters carry pencil torches, which they direct at the menus to assist clients wishing to read them.

Down below Crick and Kathy, to their left, is Stemmons Freeway. Crick has left his eyeglasses in his hotel room – from vanity in Kathy's presence – and is aware only of blotches of red, which he takes for brake lights in the stilled and angry traffic. The skyscrapers – the stretched temples of the military-industrial and media-political complexes of America – he is able to look in the eye. Glaring through their insolent windows, he imagines code-protected and trip-wired halls, stacked with murderous secrets and destructive data, to be released or restricted as moves in the power game.

The dimness denies them the usual nervous alternative to conversation of consulting menus. Crick looks busily around for a waiter, but is unable to see one. So, filling the moment, he says: 'Is the conference what you expected?'

'It's confirmed my prejudices.'

'Ah. About which particular aspect of . . .?'

'Oh, not the events. The *people*. I have this, well, theory about conspiracy theorists. They divide into three groups. There are the bug-eyed twitchers, the ones who almost certainly believe that this conference has really been organized by the CIA, to ensure that the keepers of America's conscience are all out of the way while a Martian delegation lands at Newark. Then there are what I would call the realistic cynics. They know that a lot of what happens in democracies doesn't add up, but they accept that some of it does, and it's pointless to query the check every time. Finally, there are the crossword compilers, people whose interest in conspiracy is essentially artistic: if this goes here, then what happens to that? I guess I'm a crossword compiler . . .'

'Yes,' Crick lies. 'I'd put myself in that category too.'

'I guessed that. During your number stuff, that you were turned on by the patterns rather than the politics.'

'Absolutely,' Crick lies for the second time.

Raised voices interrupt them. On the other side of the room, or module, in the inside ring of tables, Draycott, the Vietnam veteran whose lecture argued that the present John F. Kennedy is an agent-actor, is raging at a waiter: 'This beef tastes strange. You're sure there are no fucking growth hormones in it? Because I'm going to take a sample soon as I get back to my bathroom, and if a *trace* of anything shows up, I'll sue your ass.'

'This must be the catering nightmare,' says Kathy to Crick. 'A conference of people on twenty-four-hour patrol for discrepancy, who don't admit the concept of mistakes.'

'Yeah. I had a long conversation with that guy. He probably thinks the chef is in league with the agricultural-industrial complex,' chuckles Crick.

'And when he says he'll take a sample, he really does mean . . .'

'Yeah. Stool, not food.'

A waiter arrives and stands behind Kathy in the shadows,

pointing his torch at the choices. She selects a thick bean soup, followed by pan-fried salmon. Crick opts for a lentil broth and – because he has always been suspicious of fish served inland and of modern meat in any form – the vegetable crêpes. The waiter lights up the wine list.

'Oh, er, Kathy, white OK?'

'Sure.'

Crick opts for a four-year-old Chimney Rock Chardonnay, from the price range between house and sell-your-house, and between the different embarrassments that such vintages might cause to Kathy.

'You're a vegetarian?' asks Kathy, as the waiter leaves.

'No. Just careful.'

'Oh. You think the fish might . . .?'

'No, really, I didn't mean . . .'

Although Crick is not admitting to ambitions for the evening, he has ordered no dish involving garlic, and is pleased by Kathy's matching abstinence.

'It's just that I remember you eating meat.'

'Yeah. But when we were young, Kathy, you had a bit more idea of what a cow had eaten with its cookies . . .'

There is nothing dark in the past that Crick and Kathy share, though perhaps there is something missed and wistful.

They grew up together during the Truman and Eisenhower administrations in Brookline, one of the commuter zones of Boston that became known, during the first phenomenon of a mobile workforce, as streetcar suburbs.

The Cricks and the Malones, both Catholic families of Irish descent, aimed to raise their children frugal but honest and full of God. They attended the local Catholic public school attending to their gender: more or less sibling institutions, dedicated to St Anthony and Our Lady of Lourdes respectively, and run by co-operating orders of missionary monks and nuns.

Kathy was a friend of Michael's sister, Marie, both girls two years his junior. She was therefore a recognized presence at school proms, youth masses, Way of the Cross marches, and, most tantalizingly, around the Crick home. The restrictions that epoch, Catholicism, and temperament – for both were shy – placed on sexual expression created a premiss for intimacy between them; legitimized, for all that they dismissed it, by Marie's teasing about such a link.

In 1959 – Michael's eighteenth year, Kathy's sixteenth – they were more or less formally courting: partners at dances and on walks, guests at each other's birthday parties, delegates to Catholic youth conferences. At one such event in that year – held in a Boston convent, with an overnight stay – Kathy did not prevent Crick from rubbing his trousered crotch against her dress-protected pubic bump, until he ejaculated and she quite promisingly gasped. But what Kathy heard – or claimed to hear – as the footsteps of a patrolling abbess ended the excitement for that night, and, following the girl's next visit to confession, for some weeks afterwards.

Crick was trapped in the classic paradox of the Catholic male of that time. His religion, and church attendance, gave him a clear advantage in winning the confidence of Catholic girls, but part of that confidence was the conviction that a boy of such a background would not require to be offered sex. So when Crick left for Caltech – on a mathematics scholarship – both he and Kathy were still virgins, the closest thing to loss of it his cloistered orgasm in the Boston convent. Despite their frenzied protestations that his departure for college would not have the effect on them that it traditionally had on home romances, Crick was involved in another, and consummated, relationship within six weeks. He felt mature rather than cruel when he gave the news to Kathy on a weekend visit home.

Crick and Kathy did not meet again until January, 1964. Both were volunteers in the re-election campaign of John F. Kennedy, the first president to represent both their religion and their home town. Crick was twenty-two, a teaching assistant at MIT, doing research on prime numbers. Kathy was twenty, training to be a teacher. The campaign office in Manchester, New Hampshire, was something of a hormone zone, the liberation of the sixties in the area of sex combining with the sense of miracle and destiny that attached itself to

Kennedy in the period after his recovery from Oswald's bullets.

Despite the pain – at least for Kathy – in their past, both seemed, on meeting again, to wish to demonstrate their sophistication by being easy in each other's presence. By now, Crick's Catholic faith was fading; undermined, his family believed, by science, by which they meant his work in mathematics. Crick disputed this view. It was, he believed, not numeracy but logic and observation which had caused him to question the reasoning behind the formula of Catholicism: of a God in the sky directing America and himself.

Kathy's universe-view was intact. She referred, on more than one occasion, to 'God sparing Mr Kennedy in Dallas for a purpose'. Privately, Crick regarded this as inanely pagan: his own belief in Kennedy was nearly purely political. But when Kathy asked him, in New Hampshire, if he was still 'active in the Church', he instinctively perjured himself, from a surviving wish to please and reassure her.

One night, after a late evening of leafleting two days before the vote, Kathy agreed to come back to the rooming house in Manchester that Crick had been allocated. Kathy, as a junior and poorer volunteer, was staying in a makeshift dormitory organized by the local Catholic church.

Drinking cheap beer, they talked about their past, and were nudged closer on the lumpy bed.

'Was I a shit to you?' asked Crick.

'No,' Kathy lied, this seeming the proper, adult response.

'I can honestly say that one of the regrets of my life is that I never fucked you . . .' said Crick, intending it as a rakish compliment rather than a proposition.

'I wish you could fuck me now,' replied Kathy, stammering slightly on what he guessed was an unfamiliar expletive, spoken as bravado.

'But you're a Catholic . . .' he managed to say.

'So? Things are changing. People say the Pope will end the ban on birth control in the next few years. There'll be women priests before we're very old. Jesus didn't want people to hang up on sex . . .'

'So you're not a virgin?' Crick asked, feeling a tremor of

jealousy at a subsequent successful assault on defences he had accepted as impenetrable.

'Yes, I am. But I want to stop.'

'Oh, Kathy . . .'

'But, Mike, there's . . .'

'Oh? I'm sure I've got some rubbers somewhere.'

'No. You can't . . .'

'But you've just said. I bet even the Pope uses birth control now.'

'No, Mike. What I'm saying is that it's my period.'

'Oh, fuck, fuck, fuck . . .'

'Oh, Mike, did you really want to do it so much? Come here, let's have a cuddle . . .'

In a desperate last piece of optimism, he discreetly enquired – by saying, 'Poor you. You've been feeling lousy for days?' – what stage of her menstruation she had reached, hoping, perhaps, for better weather next night. But she replied that her period had started that day, so he was forced to accept she would still be bleeding, and out of reach, until after they left Manchester.

Two days later, President Kennedy won the Democrat primary in New Hampshire by a landslide. The volunteers were redirected to distant field offices. Saying goodbye with a lip kiss – and eyes that spoke of a new, and more equal, history to replace their youthful split – Michael Crick and Kathy Malone left for separate lives, and marriages and states.

Michael heard once, through his sister, that Kathy had wed, and reflected for a moment on the sexual luck of another, but he had by then achieved what was supposed to be happiness of his own. Soon, however, there set in the familiar, and generally endless, radio silence between youthful friends in middle age; particularly in America, which swallows lives.

But many people, whatever their contemporary arrangements, harbour an if-only romance in their hearts, and Kathy Malone remained Crick's, the question at its loudest, inevitably, during times of anger or dissatisfaction with his life as it ran.

*

In the revolving pod above Dallas, over the pan-fried salmon and the vegetarian crêpes, and a glass and a half each of the Chimney Rock Chardonnay, Kathy has accounted for her years between twenty and forty-nine. She lives in San Francisco, with her husband – 'Jeff' – who is a corporate attorney. There are two children, grown and gone. Kathy has not taught in schools since she was pregnant, but works with 'learning disadvantaged' children, on what Crick guesses to be a charitable basis.

In response, Crick has spoken about his college in Tulsa, his surviving son (he does not mention the dead one), his Little League coaching, and his wife.

'The marriage works?' Kathy asks.

He likes her for not using the facile 'happy' word.

'We're together,' he responds. 'We – I know people say this, but – we don't share any interests . . .'

'She's not a conspiracy theorist?'

'Well, only inasmuch as she sometimes says I'm so involved in this stuff so as not to be with her.'

'And is she right?'

'Sometimes, maybe, yes . . . You and Jeff?'

'We're together too. I can't really ever imagine we wouldn't be. Jeff's a good man.'

So they have had the conversation, without unsubtle innuendo, without cruelty to others. It is Crick's prejudice – though informed more by television and radio than by experience – that the description of a husband as a good man translates as rich, placid, but quick and dull in bed.

When they have both refused the dessert menu, and are finishing the wine, Crick asks: 'And are you still a loyal daughter of the Church?'

'Well, Jeff wasn't a Catholic, although he went along with the nuptial mass, but that was the first step to hell, the nuns would have said. The Pill was the next, as for many, I guess. Then, keeping my own name when I married. We had the girls baptized RC, I took them to mass when they were carry-on size, and nagged them when they weren't. But, in San Francisco, I got in with a liberal Catholic group. And I mean liberal. Pro-abortion, pro-women priests, questioning dogma, until, finally, there's no real reason why Barbra Streisand shouldn't be Pope, because there's nothing specifically in scripture against female Jewish priests. And, then, why go to mass, because the guy taking it is a century away from Pope Barbra . . . And then you wake up one day and you're not a Catholic any more, which is how I wake up now. I lost my faith, much as I lost it in Kennedy.'

'I know. Me too. Stopping believing in Jack was much worse, though, because those were my own beliefs, Kath, not my parents' and teachers'.'

'Right. The reason I got involved in this stuff, come to these events, is the sense, I suppose, that something happened back then, something must have happened to change him, that he couldn't just have let us down.'

'I know. Vietnam could never have been Jack's. Do you know I voted for Sanders?'

'Mike, you didn't . . .'

'Yeah. Oh, I didn't buy into his platform, particularly not the America-for-Americans stuff. He just seemed to offer the best chance of anarchy, to bring it all down: Washington and the lot of it . . .'

'I know what you mean. I voted for Clinton. I still think he might have been a great president. He'd have done radical stuff. Gays in the military, universal health care and so on . . .'

The conversation stops, but this silence does not have the awkwardness, or desperation to be filled, of those at the beginning of the meal.

Crick feels intimate enough to share with her his pet hypothesis.

'I have this theory – the Four As Theory of World Population, I call it,' he says. 'Armageddon, Antibiotics, Abortion, Aids. Listen. Global over-crowding is a purely modern problem. It's not until the nineteenth century that Malthus predicts the world will run out of food during the twentieth. And is nearly proved right. Except that vast wars in 1914 and '39 put the cork in the bottle. Then antibiotics come along, blow it out. Fifty years since then – I'm talking about the West – of no big wars and penicillin, and we'd be standing on top of each other and eating shit for dinner. If Abortion – you'd have to include contraception generally – and, now, Aids hadn't come along. My thing's number theory, not letter theory, but you have to see a spooky beauty in it. Antibiotics, for example, without Abortion and we'd be drowning in our neighbours' sweat.'

'And who arranges this? God?'

'Oh, my thing's finding patterns, not explaining them.'

Crick is already regretting mentioning Aids on a date.

'Do you know,' says Kathy, 'you once said when I was a naïve and impressionable young girl, that one of the greatest regrets of your life was not to have fucked me.'

She uses the dirty verb with confidence now.

'It was true,' Crick answers.

'It's funny,' Kathy says. 'How things work out. Have you seen *Groundhog Day*?'

'No. It's a movie, I know, but . . .'

'It's a time idea, kind of terrifying if you really think about it, but they play it cute. This pig of a guy keeps getting the same day over and over again, but he can make little changes to his behaviour . . .'

'I hope you're not saying I'm a pig of a guy . . .'

'Oh, *no* . . .'

'Well, I know the general feeling,' says Crick. 'If I got Manchester again, I'd have fucked you, never mind the blood.'

'Michael,' she says, with sudden emphasis, and he thinks he has miscalculated the conversation, but then she grins, and whispers: 'Whatever would the nuns have said?'

It is in Crick's suite, number 2211, that their scenes are replayed.

'Why'd you buy a suite? There must be more money in math than . . .'

'I didn't,' Crick lies. 'They upgraded me. Mix-up over rooms.'

They kiss, but this, though stirring, is a resumption of a known sensation, and Crick is keen, at the third chance history has offered him, to experience the next. He snakes his hand between her thighs. 'Grassy knoll,' he murmurs; a private joke, which she does not seem to hear.

This encounter has dented an aspect of Crick's devoted scepticism. The romance industries, the love corporations – Hollywood, pop music, greeting cards – promoted the fiction of romantic inevitability. I was meant for you, ooh hoo, and you were meant for me, diddlee-dee. Crick saw why people wanted to believe this. He could appreciate that there was no future in a crooner going on the road with the torch song: 'Of all the potential stories for my life/I chose the one with you.' That has, however, been his inner lyric, through a marriage and three campus affairs; one, at risk of ruin, with a student. But, tonight, he feels a different back-beat. This reunion is spooky, and he wants it to be meant.

Soon, he sees Kathy naked for the first time, thirty-four years after he burst in his pants, chafing against her clothes, and twenty-nine years after nature denied him the sight in New Hampshire. Halfway through their first embrace on the bed, she reaches up and kills the lights, so their bodies are outlined only in the seepage from the still-lit living room next door. Exhilarated as he is by this redress, *un*dress, he cannot prevent himself wondering how she might have looked three decades earlier. It does not occur to him that the same time factor might apply to his own physique.

'Kathy, I don't have any . . .' he says, at a point when he is certain that the admission will not result in cancellation.

'I'm through the change,' she says. 'But I do need to use the bathroom.'

The antennae of his secondary profession are activated by this apparent inconsistency. For reasons of both romance and paranoia, he does not want to think of Kathy just pissing or shitting in there. And, as she passes the swirl of her fallen clothing, of which her dropped purse forms a centrepiece, Kathy stoops and, joyously decoyed as he is by this new angle on her lower body, Crick sees her lift a trinket from the purse.

When the bathroom door is closed – he notes with interest that she slides the bolt – he hangs over the left edge of the bed, supporting himself with one arm on the carpet and reaching with his free hand towards where Kathy's dropped purse lies. He cracks open the bag, and inspects its contents. Looking for what? Tampons? Contraception of some kind? Anything at all that trips up her story of the menopause. He does not want, at his age, to put another kid through college.

Lying on his back, with his arms behind his head, he is working on the puzzle so intensely that his recently desperate erection begins to subside, until Kathy's return confirms it.

'Don't worry,' she says. 'The bathroom . . . I realize it might seem . . . I have to use a little cream. Dryness, after . . .'

'Really?' he asks, resentful that he has not drenched her there.

'Believe me,' she says, gently, but with an edge of irritation.

'I do. I'm sorry. Never go to bed with a conspiracy theorist.'

If there is a God, thinks Crick, then He is a squalid one, annotating their embraces across the decades with these commentaries on blood and moisture. He makes a mental note not to go down on her.

The sex is good, but not so shattering that Crick feels he has thrown his life away. Kathy seems, from her breathing and clenching, to come, although, in his many projections of this moment over thirty years, he had her yelling, which she does not.

Crick, when he comes, is thinking something muddled about time, and redemption and the circle being squared, fucks redux. Finally, his mind more coherent in repose, he starts to think of what has happened as a kind of time travel.

Kathy, covering herself discreetly with a sheet almost as soon as they have slithered apart, is the first to speak.

'I read in the paper,' she says. 'This woman, a divorcee, hired a private detective . . . to trace her childhood sweetheart. They'd lost touch.'

'Really? Did she find him?'

'Yeah. They got married.'

For a moment, Crick suspects, in arrogant alarm, that

Kathy intends this anecdote as a template for themselves. But then he guesses, from her quizzical expression, that her thoughts are similar to his: why would someone make that almost mystical gamble?

It is clear already to Crick that what has happened between them has been an act of dousing rather than ignition. But he feels the need for an expression of tenderness, and so he says: 'If only you hadn't had the curse that time in Manchester, things might have turned out who knows how different.'

'Yes . . .' She is looking away from him. 'Michael, there's something I have to say.'

'Yeah . . .'

His neuroses have already written her speech: *I may be pregnant. I was lying about the change. I just like to feel the heat of new sperm in me.*

But what she says is: 'In Manchester that time, it wasn't my period . . .'

'Yes, it was.'

'No. I just wasn't sure I wanted to take that step.'

'But when I tried to finger-fuck you, I felt the pad.'

'Oh, I wore one. Plausible denial, as they say in government. But I wasn't bleeding underneath . . .'

So his life's great romantic if-only had been a fake. But, in his depression, Crick is soon blessing the psychic instinct in his youthful self that made him a conspiracy theorist: a decision now clearly vindicated.

44:   A Good Night Out

Duke and Ford are on foot patrol today. Turning off West
Dedham onto Washington at ten thirty in the morning,
circling the church, they pass the lines on the sidewalk outside
Holy Cross: men with boiled-ham Irish faces, and matchstick-
limbed Hispanic women in fussy veils.

'There's a buzz,' says Ford. 'You have to admit that.
Being involved in these events.'

'Involved?' snorts Duke. 'We're not involved. We're just
observers. A sort of half-Greek chorus.'

Across the heads of the early worshippers, they nod at
their colleagues, blocking the still-sealed doors of the
cathedral. Many of the force – including Officers Ford and
Dukakis – are veterans of student riots and drug busts, so
policing a mass is a breeze. The only worry is that there
might be some nut in the crowd.

'What'd you do last night?' asks Ford. The pleasantry is
partly a manoeuvre to take his mind off food – he is down
only a pound with weighing day less than four weeks away –
and partly because Duke has not tried the Minus Game for a
while now, and a query about his movements off-duty is often
a promising opener.

'I'm glad you asked,' says Duke. 'I guess you'd say I had
an evening of culture.'

'Culture means fun, right?'

'Yeah, theoretically. And last night was. What talent we
have around us! I saw Nureyev dance, I read the new book
by Bruce Chatwin, listened to the new Freddie Mercury
album, went to the Robert Mapplethorpe exhibition, saw the
new Tony Richardson movie, starring Tony Perkins . . .'

Only three of these names – Nureyev, Perkins, Mercury – does Ford recognize, but he knows that they were all faggots, and he read about their deaths, so he says: 'Aids, fucking Aids.'

'You got it,' Duke agrees.

'I fucking hope I haven't,' growls Ford.

'Gerry, it's not funny.'

'Well . . . that's not as good as the others,' Ford objects. 'It's supposed to be inventions and stuff, what it would be like without them. Aids isn't that. If those guys had kept away from other guys' fudge tunnels, they'd still be around.'

'Gerry, you don't really mean that.'

'Sure I do. Hey, do you know this one? How does a spell in gaol affect your football game?'

'Gerry . . .'

'You go in as a tight end and you come out as a wide receiver.'

'Gerry, you don't really mean this stuff. The Minus Game is about the pivots of history. Penicillin, the telephone, the gun. For example, there was a guy in the *Globe* this morning, asking what if Kennedy had *died* at Dallas.'

'Oh, yeah. And what?'

'He'd have been a hero, this guy reckons . . .'

'Jack Kennedy a hero? Come on. And you think that guy's clever?'

'What I'm saying, Gerry, is that Aids is a minus worth considering. All the extra books, films, music, paintings, performances there might have been. A whole generation lost. It's like imagining the later poems of Wilfred Owen . . .'

'Say again?'

'First World War poet. English. Killed at twenty-five, a week before the Armistice. A week. History's pivots. An interview with Wilfred Owen on his seventy-fifth birthday! Owen's *Collected Poems 1918–1968*. That's what I'm saying.'

'Yeah, well, maybe. What I'm saying is, it's different with Aids. I don't suppose your guy went cruising every night, looking for a war.'

'Gerry . . .'

'Duke, we won't agree on this, so let's leave it. All this

arguing's making me even more hungry. I tell you what I'd like to uninvent. Hamburgers, pretzels, bagels, cheesecake, meatloaf, salami . . . give me an America minus those.'

To Ford's considerable digestive distress, it is more than an hour before the service, at least two hours until lunch.

45: Imagine

On the morning of November 22nd, 1993, Jack comes down-stairs at 7 a.m., although he has been lying sleepless for three hours. The agents have placed the first edition of the *Boston Globe* on the breakfast table. Over coffee, Granola and cortico-steroids, Jack reads the comment pages. The fears that lost him a night's sleep prove justified.

In the *Globe*, a grizzled syndicated columnist, veteran reporter of every election since 1948, has written:

Today, at Boston's Holy Cross Cathedral, former President John F. Kennedy will attend a thanksgiving Mass, on the thirtieth anniversary of his survival of assassination in Dallas.

Private as a person's relationship with their God is, and ought to be, many will wonder exactly what he has to give thanks for. In this year's annual polling exercise to rank the standing of modern presidents with the public, by asking them to award points from a hundred to previous White House occupants, the 1993 scores came out Reagan 71, Sanders (before the current scandal) 68, Bush 53, Carter 40, Kennedy 37.5, Nixon 37.

Who, during the "Camelot" first administration, and the triumphant "Jack is Back" re-election tour of the country in 1964, could have believed that Jack Kennedy would eventu-ally finish up only half a mark more popular than the single American president to be forced to resign from office?

There is another angle to this, which is the effect that the wreckage of JFK's promise and promises has had on the electability of the conventional politician. Good Baptist though he is, Governor Bill Clinton of Arkansas, working on his memoir of his failed 1992 presidential campaign, could be excused if he has wished Jack Kennedy dead in Dallas. The exaggerated respect with which the dead are remembered – and more so the young who die tragically – would almost certainly have ensured that Clinton's many perceived similarities to JFK – of age, message, and character – would have been an advantage rather than the destructive factor they in fact proved to be.

I would go further. If the reputation of Jack Kennedy had been, for whatever reason, higher, Bill Clinton would now be President.

By the way, . . .

Jack braces himself. It has been his experience of journalism that sentences introduced with the dampener phrases 'By the way . . .' or 'Incidentally . . .' are invariably more wounding than those which begin with the flamethrower claims 'Crucially . . .' or 'Most importantly . . .' This perception is confirmed again:

By the way, the music for today's sung eucharist heavily features the ·mass composed by Mozart in March 1779. Known to musicologists by the number "K317," it bears the alternative title of "The Coronation Mass." There will also be excerpts from the 1971 mass composed by Leonard Bernstein, a long-time Kennedy family buddy recently dead. "The Coronation Mass" and Lenny Bernstein: dynastic empire and twentieth-century American celebrity. How very Kennedy! This is not religion. It is spin-doctoring.

To some extent, Jack has become desensitized to attacks on his reputation, but it has never before occurred to him, among all the inadequacies alleged, that he might be vulnerable to musicological assault. He distantly remembers initialling a memorandum which listed the readings and music for the service, and Boomer explaining that, for practical reasons, the music combined those parts of the Mozart which did not call for a large choir with those sections which were least atonal in the Bernstein.

Grinding his teeth into his Granola with far more force than is needed merely for eating. Jack looks up at the swing and the click of the kitchen door to see Boomer, a copy of the same paper on top of a stack of folders and packages in his arms.

'Ah, good morning, Mr President. I see I'm too late to distract you from that waste of good wood.'

'All the speeches I've given about the unemployment problem in America. I read that guy and I worry about the *employment* problem . . .'

'I always forget how resilient you politicians are.'

'Good at showing resilience.'

'Sir, we're leaving at 1015 hours for the drive to the service. There's no urgent correspondence. But I thought I'd give you these.'

From his array of papers and parcels Boomer untangles two oblong boxes of black shiny plastic, and places them on the table.

'Sir, these have just come through. They're the final edited versions of the films to be screened in the two new halls at the Library. You might want to check them through before the dedication ceremony.'

'Later, later. Just in case I discover I don't have anything to give thanks for . . .'

Boomer sees that Jack has again thrown him the bright smile used to confuse perception of his mood.

46: Holy Cross

With Reilly's invite in his jacket pocket, Meredith walks south on Dartmouth, crossing Tremont, past the houses and shops built in the tomato-tone stone common to Boston.

The matter of attire for the mass delayed him for some time. He first set aside a dark blue suit and navy tie, before appreciating that he was internally regarding the service as a requiem, rather than the thanksgiving it ostensibly is. His clothes now, he hopes, suggest a proper balance between reverence and celebration: a dark grey suit and red-and-white-striped tie, with a charcoal top-coat. From his right shoulder hangs a black leather shoulder-bag, full enough to force a belly-swell on either side.

Soon, the Gothic pomposity of Holy Cross Cathedral bulks before him. The outside of the building offers a mosaic effect of different stone: grey, sand, and nearly black. Some of the walls have the look of burnt wood, but they are only grimed by time. An imposing oval stained-glass window sits above the central entrance, and, to the right of it, a bell tower rises high and wide. The building has survived weather and pollution well, but its grandeur is made anachronistic by its surrounds, most severely by the gloomy food store directly opposite its arched and burnished doors.

Meredith surveys the scene from the corner of Washington and Monsignor Reynolds; the naming of the latter road, presumably, a small immortality for a dead priest of the parish.

Outside the church, Bostonians are penned behind crash barriers. Most of those waiting are old, and with the ruddy-chubby genes of Ireland in their features. There is, however,

214

a group of six younger men who look to be in their middle forties. Three are densely bearded, and one, who rides a wheelchair, is clumsily strumming a guitar. The others are singing, in fragmented harmony:

> I got a letter from JFK
> It said today's your lucky day
> Time to put your khaki trousers on
> Though it isn't really war
> We're sending fifty thousand more
> To save Vietnam from the Vietnamese . . .

Two of the singers hold aloft a banner, black paint on bed sheet, reading WAR CRIMINAL. Two others fly a similar makeshift standard with the message: THANKSGIVING? NO THANKS.

A pair of cops – one fat, one Greek – is circling the church. Others scowl singly from corners. Meredith crosses the street, and joins a line – consisting generally of people in more costly clothes than the throng beside the road – which stretches from in front of the entrance steps and round to the left side of the building.

Ten minutes pass before Meredith reaches the east door. Inside the cool and echoey vestibule, two walk-through metal detectors have been set up, with a long table parallel to each of them, like in an airport. The steps leading down to the crypt are blocked by two cops. Meredith enjoys the incongruity of these images: the armoured temple.

Now he feels the first drench of adrenalin as he hands over the hard white cardboard invitation. There is a small smudge of blood where its machine-cut edge wounded him that morning.

'That's fine, Mr Reilly. Give your bag to the officer at the table.'

The *Boston Globe* and empty notebook in the front zip-pouch pass without comment. But, examining the innards of the hold-all, and seeing the equipment there, the policeman gives a little whistle.

'Kind of loaded, aren't ya?'

'I'm from out of town. Taking in a little tourism as well.'

Growing up in England, Meredith watched enough American cop shows to be able to ape the accent in short exchanges.

'OK. You're gonna have to show me a picture in this.'

The cop lifts out the video camera, with a big-fisted try at neatness, and places it on the table. Meredith is ready for this test. In a magazine article about the 1992 election, he read that the Secret Service agents guarding the candidates required the television crews to work the playback facility on their cameras each morning, to demonstrate that they were operational, and not weapons. A TV producer was quoted in the article as suggesting that a modified video camera – with its playback facility intact – was probably now the only plausible method of getting guns or explosives close to a modern politician.

With studiedly casual actions, Meredith operates the playback for the cop: scenes recorded that morning at the Kennedy Presidential Library on Columbia Point, at the edge of Boston Harbour.

'OK. That's good.'

The video camera is placed to one side. The cop's large hands dip inside the bag again, and come up with a voice-activated micro-tape recorder. He looks quizzically at Meredith.

'Oh, I keep a kind of journal on it, when I'm travelling. Writing's sort of a chore.'

'Play it.'

Meredith punches the playback button, and his own American-accented voice emerges, maundering about the service on a flight. This second alibi accepted, the policeman searches briskly through the books and papers at the bottom of the bag, and then begins to repack it, saying: 'OK. Pick it up on the other side. And go through the scanner now.'

The magnomometer finds nothing to trouble it in Meredith's pockets or body. Recovering his shoulder-bag, he collects an order of service from one of two teenage girls in white lace blouses, and a mauled missal from the other, then walks through into the church.

The east door gives admittance to the right side of the

altar, facing the body of the church. The majority of the thickly varnished pews are now occupied. There is a flutter of low-voiced conversation under the music of a small orchestra, arranged in a side chapel on the left-hand side. An usher – a stooped man in a tight suit, wearing on his lapel what is presumably some kind of papal medal – reaches for Meredith's invitation.

'I'm from out of town,' says the counterfeit Mr Reilly. 'Could I look around? Some church this is!'

'Well, OK, sir. But you'll need to be in your seat by a quarter of twelve.'

'Sure.'

Ten minutes. Careful to obey the Roman protocol of bowing his head towards the altar, Meredith walks to the rear of the church, turns and looks back up the nave. In front of the traditional recessed altar, with its stone-carved saints and angels, and the aureate and star-shaped monstrance, a shamrock-coloured carpet establishes a kind of large apron-stage. There is a simple wooden altar table, white clothed and candle laden, halfway down this area, and to the left, and even closer to the congregation, a chiselled timber lectern. In the back wall of the church, pill-box slits invite contributions for causes identified as 'God's Poor' and 'Organ Restoration Fund'. Against one side wall rests a hand-carved padded kneeler, where, a plaque reveals, Pope John Paul II prayed on his visit to Boston in 1979.

Meredith takes the video camera out of his bag, and raises it to his eye, lining up the altar, and then the lectern, in the cross-hairs. He feels a hand on his shoulder, and tries to turn round calmly and equably.

'Excuse me, sir.'

It is a priest, in the grey robes and hood of a Franciscan. In thriller films which feature an ecclesiastical element, Meredith reflects, the Franciscans are frequently used. Their habit best accommodates concealment plots.

'Oh, should I not be filming, Father?'

'Well, we usually ask those who do for a donation.'

'That's fair.'

Meredith gives five dollars to God's Poor, and the same

amount to the Organ Restoration Fund. The priest glides away, and Meredith lines up the altar again. Satisfied, he hands Reilly's invite to an usher and is led to a right-side centre pew, ten rows behind the empty benches, which await the arrival of the Kennedy family.

The middle pews in Holy Cross are accessible only from the central aisle, shut off at the far end. The only gap in the pew to which Reilly was allocated is next to the partition. This does not fit Meredith's plans.

'I'm sorry,' he says, with soft politeness, to the congregants abutting the aisle. 'I wonder if I might take this end. I have a slight knee problem, and some baggage.'

There follows the is-this-a-trick hesitation, inevitable in such circumstances in the properly suspicious modern world, before the worshippers warily slide sideways, daintily lifting the tails or hems of expensive coats and dresses clear of the bench. Meredith settles into the end seat, resting his bag on the nearly threadbare, wish-worn kneeler at his feet.

The music now is lush and merry, topped by the balmy, ardent voice of a soprano. Consulting his service sheet, Meredith sees that this is the 'Exsultate! Jubilate!' – helpfully translated into American, in parenthesis, as 'Exult! Rejoice!' – by Mozart. From the Latin of the libretto, and the ornamental enunciation of its performance, Meredith can extract only the title words 'Exsultate! Jubilate!', and, he thinks, 'dulcia'. But, flicking through the pamphlet, he finds the full text perkily interpreted:

> The friendly daylight shines, both clouds
> And storms have now fled; for the righteous
> And unexpected calm has come. Everywhere,
> Dark night reigned; rise up at last in
> Gladness, ye that were afraid till now . . .

Meredith enjoys the irony of this. Just before noon, the soprano stops singing, and sits down, and a contemplative silence spreads across the benches. Soon, cheering and applause is heard outside. Then, deeper male voices, amplified through klaxons:

Hey, hey, JFK,
How many kids
Did you kill today?

And a four-part chant, with three repetitions, building in intensity towards a final kick:

Lee Harvey Oswald
Lee Harvey Oswald
Lee Harvey Oswald
How could you *miss*?

A minute later, the congregation is allowed its first sight of the Kennedys. Wearing mainly greys and dark blues, apparently making the same sartorial calculation as Meredith, they enter in regular procession from the east door; the widows, the children, the grandchildren, and, finally, the former President himself. They bow or genuflect, according to age and agility, towards the altar, and then fill the front rows.

The President, as he turns, pauses, as if to size up the crowd; a politician's reflex. He smiles at what are presumably family friends, and then, for a moment, he catches Meredith's eye. A fast flash of fear and concern passes over the old man's face, and Meredith realizes that he has been recognized. He expects uncovering and expulsion, but the old man merely looks stiffly away, and takes his place, in the seat by the aisle at the end of the right-side pew.

The orchestra begins to play a solemn, unsung, introit, and another procession enters from the east door. First come the altar-servers, wearing bright white surplices, and carrying gold candlesticks in front of them, like little soldiers with blunt and ornate swords. Next are the priests, in shuffling, eyes-bowed formation, including the Franciscan who interrupted Meredith earlier. Finally, the Cardinal, the red of his office at breast and crown.

Leaning forward in his pew, Meredith eases back the zipper on the bag at his feet, and reaches for the video camera.

47:   Child Care

It pleases Fraser that the child he abducted gives his project another unique selling-point in the supermarket of American cruelties.

It is not unusual in this nation for a child to get his name in the papers by being kidnapped. But, in a quirky reverse, Nat Robinson, aged two, of Newton, Maine, was kidnapped because he got his name in the papers; or at least in *America Now*'s feature on the sweetest place in the States. Therefore, what Fraser is attempting involves three levels of celebrity: of the target, of Fraser himself in the future, and of the stolen child.

It is late morning now in Boston – on the thirtieth anniversary of the botched work of one of Fraser's predecessors, Lee Harvey Oswald – and the assassin-in-waiting is once more reading about Time. Today's text is another article about contingency: the possibility of rival versions of the world. As Fraser understands it, the writer argues that the world in which Mr X misses his flight in 1989, and thus becomes jobless or divorced, exists alongside the one in which he makes the plane, hence winning promotion for a successful presentation or fathering another child in a rapturous reunion with his wife. And another in which the plane crashes. And, indeed, a fourth in which aviation remains mere engineering theory. But, again, it is unclear whether this is metaphor or hard science.

The baby is sleeping in the two-room apartment rented by Fraser under yet one more false name. Resting beside the child on a mattress – sterilized bottles and packages of diapers stacked neatly between her bed and the cot – is Consuela, a

Chilean maid, hired by Fraser for a week at a fee of $2,000. Perhaps she is not using her birth name either, for Consuela also has a secret, though one more common than her employer's. She has no Social Security number and no tax record. She melted into America without trace in the early seventies.

This is, for Fraser's purposes, the perfect background in a nanny. In someone who is not a citizen there can be no possibility of civic duty, public spirit. As an additional precaution, Fraser told her – sounding as much like an empowered white American as he could – that if she spoke to any other person of her work for him he would turn her over to the authorities.

Consuela speaks little English, so Fraser sticks mainly to initials with polyglot recognition: such as IRS and FBI. He has told her the boy is his son, returned from the custody of his former wife, an irresponsible mother, in the course of a stormy divorce. This is the trick of such an alibi. Though not true of you, it must apply to many others, and Fraser's tale is a standard of the afternoon talk shows. She accepted the contract between them without protest, entering only one clause of her own: 'You come near me, I cut off your cock.' Fraser smiled and replied: 'If it wanted to fuck you, I'd cut it off first.'

The boy has given Fraser no trouble. Children are fickle, particularly if still too young to understand their family ties. On the drive from Maine, the child cried, until Fraser injected him with a sedative. But he has adapted rapidly to his new home, any tantrums quickly quelled by Consuela.

And, two days from now, his, and Fraser's, time will come.

48:   The Pages of History

In Holy Cross, the choir is singing Bernstein's 'In Nomine Patris'. Jack looks around the cathedral, up to the curved wooden roof beams, like the underside of a vast upturned boat, and then left and right to the walls, where saints and stations of the cross alternate in stained glass.

The history of this church is a chronicle of modern Boston. First serving Irish immigrants, it now divides its masses and confessions between the languages of English and Spanish, in response to the gathering Hispanic community. Yet, historically, it stands because of the Irish, their faith unshaken by the potato plague which had chased them from home.

How was it that Irish Catholicism and Judaism – faiths tested by historical catastrophe – still attracted such solidity of belief? His own family – which had suffered so much, including the ultimate test of multiple early deaths – had never abandoned God or Catholicism. It seemed to be confirmation that the religious expected, or accepted, from God terrible questions rather than reassuring answers.

Unless, that was, you thought, as nonbelievers did, that people were drawn to worship only by the solving promise of heaven, where the inequalities of human biography would somehow be worked out. This, he assumed, had been his mother's comfort, the source of her faith, until senility took from her even such simple, trusting reason. For himself, he cannot hope to understand the paradoxes of providence: the happy accident of being one of only thirty-five men (still only forty-one) to lead his nation, the ill luck of his administration's failure and Vietnam, the harsh chance of his brothers' deaths.

Jack's belief, such as it endures, is partly a result of family inculcation, and otherwise an acknowledgement that the alternative proposition – that all of human history, art, invention, and politics could follow from a collision of rocks and gasses – requires no less a leap of faith, and suppression of questions, than does God. But this compromise cannot be called faith. He comes to church now not to worship but to wonder.

Turning as far in his seat as his sore and corseted vertebrae permit, Jack sees four brawny Boston cops standing against the railing of the organ loft, like a parody of the angelic stereotype of a choir. If they were to sing the mass, thinks Jack, it would be all bass notes. Turning back, he again sees Meredith, his nemesis, smugly occupying an aisle seat on the other side. He knows that he might call for a cop or an usher, but, ultimately, he is powerless to stop whatever Meredith may choose to do to him. He must take his chances. He pauses at this thought, too distant now from theology to know whether it is Catholic orthodoxy or heresy.

The setting of the Roman liturgy by the Jewish Bernstein – another example of religious confusion – tinkles down to silence. Preceded by great clouds of incense, like an old Hollywood mogul photographed through cigar smoke, the Cardinal rises from his gold-leafed seat at the side of the altar and processes to the lectern.

'My brothers and sisters in Jesus Christ,' he begins. 'We are here today to give thanks for the survival and the life of one man. A man who rose to become the only Catholic president of his country. In giving thanks, we express our love of God. But thanksgiving is not a simple thing, and that is what I want to talk about today. The question which we all find hardest in our lives in Jesus Christ – cardinal or priest or congregant – is: "How can a loving God permit this?" This pain, this death, this injustice, this evil. But if it were impossible for people to believe in a God who allowed bad or unhappy things to happen, then there would be no churches. And there are churches! Many churches! So we must see thanksgiving in this context. The average life which allows God into it will include as much anger as gratitude . . .'

Tell me about it, thinks Jack.

*

As the Cardinal begins speaking, Meredith eases the sleek black video camera out of the bag and rests it on the shelf, for hymnals and gloves, which juts from the rear of the pew in front. He can hear the reproachful whispers of the congregants beside him, but, ignoring them, he leans forward, and squints through the view-finder. Kennedy's head is in the lower right-hand corner of the frame. The Cardinal is caught in the cross-hairs.

'Excuse me, sir.'

Meredith straightens and twists round. He sees the elderly usher with the papal medal. Beyond, he is conscious of a cop, hovering at the end of the nave, under the organ loft, ready to move.

'I really don't think so,' says the usher. 'Not during the mass.'

'I just wanted a record of this.'

'Please. I'll have to ask you to put that away.'

Shrugging, Meredith begins to replace the camera. At the edge of his vision, he can see the usher muttering to the policeman, who retreats to the back of the church. Still doubled over, using as a shield the overcoat that is folded at his feet, Meredith reaches for the small tape recorder, and brings it up to his lap, holding it there under the coat, which he now repositions across his knees.

This is going to be more difficult than he hoped, but it is still possible. Fumbling under the thick cloth, he tries to find the recording keys. And, robbed now of a visual record of the event, he wills himself to memorize the details of the scene. For Peter Meredith, the 'English assassin', is increasingly certain that he has found the beginning for his latest biography. He begins to write it in his head:

They came – the star-struck and the friends of the family – to give thanks. But many among the majority of Americans who had not been invited to Boston's Holy Cross Cathedral on November 22nd, 1993, wondered what precisely they were expected to give thanks for.

Certainly, the Vietnam veterans singing sixties protest songs outside the church felt no cause for gratitude. Nor, it might be assumed, did the dozens of women who had gone public in recent years with stories of their mistreatment by this Catholic politician, even now being fulsomely praised in a sermon by the Cardinal of Massachusetts. And what thanks had been shown to this epitome of the modern career machine politician by those millions of disillusioned Americans who had just voted into the White House Newton Sanders? A man who had reluctantly become president through public pressure; not, like Jack Kennedy, through the spending of millions of dollars, the calling in of family favours, and, in his 1960 presidential victory, outright vote-rigging.

No. Very many Americans, in thinking of the Kennedy presidency, would have been tempted to echo, from their particular perspective, the sentiment of a banner held outside Holy Cross Cathedral on that bright and cold November day by two of the Vietnam veterans.

"Thanks? No thanks!"

As a result of this inspiration, Meredith experiences, during the rest of the mass, a feeling like he imagines grace to be.

In the limousine, leaving the service, Jack is angry. The hand that has been waving at the crowd – in which the cheers of the veteran Irish compete with the jeers of the Vietnam veterans – crashes down on Boomer's shoulder, as soon as they are out of view of the church.

'Boomer, how the fuck did Meredith get in that church?'

'I don't know who you mean, sir. Who is Meredith?'

'He's a dangerous maniac.'

The Secret Service agent in the front seat looks over his shoulder with alarm.

'Is this someone who has threatened you, sir? An assassin . . .'

'Oh, no, no. A *character* assassin only. And he's threatened me merely in *Publisher's Monthly*. In fact, I believe he is known in literary, to use the word loosely, circles as "the English assassin". He's a biographer. He's done Frank Sinatra, John Lennon, Elvis Presley, Barbra Streisand. Whatever these people may have had in common when he started with them, they were closely related by the end: cruel, deluded, addicted, sick, egotistical, according to his researches. Prose style by Sigmund Freud, with additional material from William Burroughs. Now he's moving on to politicians. Starting guess where.'

'Yes, I know the name, sir,' says Boomer. 'In fact, there was something in one of the cuttings this week. It's now a joint biography of you and Marilyn Monroe, I think the publishers just announced.'

'Oh, wonderful, Boomer. He's obviously moving upmarket.'

'But Meredith was in the *church*, sir?'

'Yeah. A few pews behind me. I imagine this will mean some really toney prologue to the biography in which I go down on my knees, stooped beneath my many sins . . .'

'I'll order a full investigation into how this man obtained an invitation,' says Boomer. In reality, this means that he will telephone the local police chief, but he is speaking, as usual, in mock White House style.

For the next half-hour of the drive to Hyannis Port, the car is silent. Jack is reading a new biography of Truman, which seeks, at least from the tone of its first two hundred pages, to move its subject a couple of places up the table of presidential reputations. Boomer is importantly under-scoring with a Shaeffer pen certain passages in thick typed texts. But, as they speed away from Boston on Route 6, Boomer says: 'Mr President, may I interrupt you for a moment?'

'Please do. I'm getting seriously envious of the hero of this book.'

Jack waves the heavy volume of the Truman biography.

'Sir, as you know, I'm off to my folks late afternoon. Their wedding anniversary.'

'That's right. In fact, I have a small gift for them. Come and find me before you leave.'

Boomer notes – against the appearance of this scene in some future memoir of his life in politics – that Kennedy mentioned this, admittedly impressive, kindness in front of two witnesses: an agent and a driver.

'Tomorrow, Mr President, when I get back, we'll work on your speech for the library opening.'

'Ah. I need to say something, don't I, about each of my *uncles*?'

'That was the idea, sir. I've sketched out something for each of them.'

The agent in the passenger seat laughs. 'We'll look after those *uncles* for you, Mr President.'

After the shared amusement about these presidential relatives, there is silence again, until Jack says: 'Boomer?'

'Sir?'

'About the twenty-fifth. I'd like you to put something else to Miss Monroe.'

'Well, sir, I . . .'

'Or to her people. I'd like to invite her to lunch at Hyannis, before the ceremony. Even though I quite appreciate that a walk on a beach with a Kennedy male may not be every woman's dream date right now . . .'

This is a reference to the rape trial, in West Palm Beach two years previously, of the ex-President's nephew, William Kennedy Smith, accused, though found not guilty, of assaulting a girl on a beach.

'Even so,' Jack finishes, 'I'd like the proposition put to her.'

'I'll call this afternoon, sir, before I leave,' says Boomer. Now, at last, the legend is developing as he expected. He feels as if Mark Antony has asked him to send a messenger to Egypt.

Crumpled leaflets distributed by the Vietnam protesters – headed GO TO CONFESSION, JACK – flutter in the gutters of the now empty streets outside Holy Cross. Duke and Ford stand on the steps of the cathedral.

'Home safe,' says Duke. 'I have to admit I expected a different ending. I was convinced someone would try to kill him today.'

'There you are,' replies Ford. 'Maybe America's getting less crazy.'

'Hey, Gerry, foul ball. Foul ball. It's me that always throws first pitch in the Minus Game.'

49:   A Nice New Coat

It is early afternoon on November 22nd, 1993, three days before the date chosen for the assassination, when the stolen child wakes after his first morning rest in the Boston apartment. Biologically, he is crying for his mother, but in practice Consuela suffices, lifting him from the cot, clamping a bottle to his mouth, and setting out some books and toys, while boiling a kettle to heat up a jar of mush.

Hearing the sounds next door, Fraser puts down his book on Time, and crosses to a cupboard in the corner of the room. He unlocks it, and removes a chunky paper bag. Treading gently to the doorway of the bedroom, he watches Consuela, supervising while the child messily attempts to feed himself. The boy's eyes shine with false security.

'How you doing?'

Consuela shudders at his undetected entrance.

'Oh, Mr Kendy. I din see ya.'

'If junior could interrupt his lunch for a minute, I've something for him.'

Fraser crouches down, and beckons to the child.

'Here, Nat.'

The boy, responding to his name, glances back for approval at Consuela, a bond already forming with this new provider of food and comfort.

'Go Papa.'

With delicate, satisfied steps, the child walks towards Fraser, who, as he approaches, pulls from the bag a small jacket, in pale canary-coloured canvas fabric. The child, coming from a family background in which such offerings are probably not uncommon, giggles with appreciation as Fraser dresses him in the garment.

'Oh, Nad!' trills Conseula. 'A nide noo code!'

'A nice new coat,' echoes Fraser, 'for when you go outside.'

50:   My Fellow Americans

At 8 p.m. Eastern Standard Time on November 22nd, 1993 –
and, subsequently, with a tape delay, at the same relative
point in other American time zones – President Newton W.
Sanders addresses the nation.

'My fellow Americans,' he begins, 'I speak to you tonight
as so many of my predecessors have done from this Oval
Office. But there is a difference. Alone among the modern
presidents of these United States I was placed here by you –
by you, the people – and by you the people alone.'

'That's certainly an interesting gloss on American democracy,' murmurs Boyd, as they watch in the Chief of Staff's
quarters. They were squeezed out from the Oval Office by
the personnel and paraphernalia of the television crew.

'Sound not sense,' whispers Woodall. 'Sound not sense.
What the American people want from a president is low
taxation and stuff that sounds like poetry.'

They are tense, as Sanders, his paranoia about Washington intensified by the allegations of child abuse, locked the
door of the Oval Office that afternoon, refused to speak to
aides, and wrote his television address on his own. Boyd and
Woodall are hearing their employer's words for the first time.

'You may say, as the *Washington Post* and the *New York Times*
will certainly say,' continues the President, 'that you voted
for me in the usual way – by pulling a lever, by making a
cross. But that is not true. The process for choosing a

president of the United States in recent years has been that the newspaper editors and the network presidents get together in New York, sift through the candidates, and choose the one who most suits them, who is most likely to pursue their corporate agenda. The American public is then instructed – subtly, almost subliminally – through the news media to choose that candidate . . .'

'I mean, yeah, just look back in history and see how right that is,' says Boyd with telegraphed sarcasm, making the sign of the winding finger at his temple. 'Dick Nixon would never have made it if he hadn't been the darling of the media élite.'

'The American public has no memory,' whispers Woodall. 'No politician should ever forget that.'

Boyd memorizes this line, in case it should be necessary in *My White House Years* to cast Woodall as a Beltway cynic, contemptuous of the average American.

'In a sense, each recent American president has been a reincarnation of the one before,' Sanders reads, from his big green motorized text, oozing down the autocue.

'Oh, fuck,' gasps Boyd. 'The fucking R word.'

The always quiet Woodall is now entirely silent, either from strategy or fear.

'By this, I mean,' the President explains, 'that, whatever his party, whatever his platforms, each of the men who sat at this desk was the creation, and the creature, of the East Coast power élite.'

Boyd and Woodall exchange silent high fives.

'He hasn't said anything yet we can't spin,' says Boyd.

*

232

'But I was not the choice', their patron is insisting, 'of those bright white Yale and Harvard boys. Far from it. A database check we ran at the White House showed that the word "nuts" has appeared 189 times in major media pieces about me during and since the 1992 campaign. And they sure as hell weren't writing about my recipe for pecan pie.'

'Back home we always say,' drawls Boyd, in a twangy parody of Sanders, 'if people keep calling you nutty, you're either a chocolate bar or a prophet.'

Woodall chuckles, but he sees at once that this gag might serve one of two purposes in the book he eventually publishes. If Sanders survives, the anecdote will illustrate Boyd's disloyalty. If the President resigns or is impeached, Woodall can claim the joke as his own, demonstrating his instinctive distance from the guilty man at the time of his deceitful speech to the American people.

'There is only one reason that they call me nuts,' the President suggests. 'And that is because you made them nutty – nutty with anger that you finally got one of your people through their defences. And so, because the nuts thing didn't work against me in the campaign, now they call me worse than nuts. They call me sick. For legal reasons, it is not proper that I should comment on the specific allegations against me, until the current investigation of the Seattle Police Department is complete.'

'Of course, any first-year law student knows that isn't the position,' says Boyd.

'Sound not sense,' whispers Woodall. 'The American public hates lawyers, but is in awe of the law.'

'However,' the President stresses, 'I am permitted to say that there is no truth whatsoever in the charges. I would also say

233

that Recovered Memory Therapy – through which these allegations apparently emerged – is regarded by many distinguished medical professionals as liable to produce fantasy and factually unreliable testimony, through, I may say, no fault of the patient's.'

'That's good,' says Boyd. 'Diss the doctors, not the dame.'

'In her so-called evidence to the magazine', Sanders goes on, 'the patient remarks that child sexual abuse is, and I quote, the hidden sickness of America, end quote. In many cases, yes, it is. But not in this one. This case is about another hidden sickness in America: the revenge of the American media-political complex on the one president who was not theirs. You did not believe their stories about me during the campaign. I ask you not to believe them now. We think of coups, of revolutions against the state, as something that happens only in Latin America: with epaulettes, and reflecting sunglasses, and Kalashnikovs. But there is a coup, a silent coup, going on in this America, here and now, with Brooks Brothers button-down shirts, green eye shades, and microphone guns. In these dangerous times, I am grateful for the prayers and support of Joan, my wife, the best mother in America, and our four children. And for the prayers and support of you who put me here. *You* made my name, and I shall clear it, for *you*. Good night. And may God bless the United States of America.'

When the broadcast is over, Boyd and Woodall walk down the corridor to the Oval Office, expecting the door still to be locked. It is, however, open, as the television crew is leaving. There is a producer in button-down Brooks Brothers shirt; another man carrying a microphone gun.

Sanders is at the Nixon desk, a make-up assistant wiping his face with a cloth now deeply soiled orange. He notices Woodall and Boyd.

234

'Guys,' he says, 'no hard feelings about keeping you out of the loop on this thing. Back home, we say, when people shout bad things at you, shout back, don't waste time explaining to your friends. How was I?'

On this rare occasion, both men seem keen to reply, but Boyd is the quickest: 'It was a very clever speech, Mr President.'

'Best man on every base,' confirms Woodall.

'Al, Bob, clever's what lawyers do. I did what preachers do. I told God's truth.'

The make-up assistant leaves the room, the last of the television team to go. A burly Secret Service agent leans in and pulls the door shut.

Suddenly, Sanders crumples, his face, even under the residual television powder, looking sallow and pitted. The voice he speaks in is one they have never heard before: devoid of bounce and even accent.

'Guys, do you think we can save this thing?'

Here, for the first time, they see Sanders with no spin and no cunning: a man whose election, a historical impossibility six months before it happened, had redrawn the lines of his life, and who now must contemplate their erasure.

Boyd and Woodall hold a brief non-verbal conference, before the Chief of Staff opens one of the folders on his knee, and shakes out three stapled A4 sheets.

'Mr President, Al and I have considered a number of strategies for consolidating public confidence in you over this affair. The message of Nixon's Watergate and Carter's Iranian hostage crisis is that the Chief Executive must not be seen to have become a prisoner in Washington. One plan – which I would ask you to look at – is to take your message direct to the – well, what we might call the citadels of the East Coast élite. It shows that you are not afraid and it's also a kind of cleansing of the temples.'

'That was Our Lord's strategy, Bob.'

'Sir, we have drawn up a schedule of events this week, in Washington, Boston, and New York. Speeches, interviews, lunches with editors. We would envisage following up next week with a series of rallies and public forums in Real

America. But the idea of these appearances on the East Coast would be to take the battle into the enemy camp—'

'Or', Woodall jumps in, 'the bunker where the coup is being plotted.'

This last phrase engages Sanders, and he takes the piece of paper.

'I think I know what you're saying, Bob. Tonight went fine but, back home, we say, there's no point complaining about horse shit at a dog show.'

'Sir,' Boyd nicely improvises, as the President reads, 'we'll take you right to the arena of the horse show. The centrepiece of the week would be a major speech in Harvard on Thursday evening, at the Edward Kennedy School of Government.'

'I see that, Bob. They'd let me speak? At Harvard?'

'You're the President of the United States, sir.'

'Our idea, sir,' adds Woodall, keen to share what seems likely to be approbation, 'is that you will make a major policy speech, attacking those who are attempting to bring you down. But we also felt it might be wise to bring forward some of the themes and phrases from the State of the Union text.'

'"I am one of your family. You are one of my family. This is how it works,"' Boyd quotes from their earlier discussion.

'OK, boys, we'll put a *sold* sticker on that one. And the interview with the *Globe*, I suppose. But what's this other thing in Boston? Jack Kennedy's Library.'

'It's a rededication ceremony, sir. A new wing.'

'Al, I know what it is. I thought we turned them down.'

'We did, sir, when they first asked. Even though all the other living presidents had accepted. Because, at that time, we wished to emphasize your separation from that line of political descent. Now, there is a real fear that your absence from any group photograph might be interpreted as isolation.'

'You guys. To me, a picture is a picture.'

'There is an argument, sir,' Boyd continues, 'that your constant emphasis of how you are not a politician—'

'Bob, I'm not.'

'I wasn't being judgemental, Mr President. The point is that, by stressing this aspect, you may have denied yourself the historical protection of the presidency. Perhaps these guys need to be reminded that it is, after all, the President of the United States they're gunning for.'

'Bob, Al, let me think about this. You're asking me to think like a politician, and I can't do that. But maybe you could do it for me.'

'Mr President,' says Boyd, 'there is one other thing. We have a source at *America Now*. The word is that they're getting edgy about the Recovered Memory thing.'

'Well, now, there you . . .'

'But, sir . . .'

'Ah. Back home, we say, good news and fat women, it's the but you have to look out for.'

'Sir, they're working on another story about you.'

'Ah . . . What's this one? Me and Little Orphan Annie?'

'Mr President, the word is they're investigating rumours you pay $1,000 a month to a man in Houston.'

In the silence that follows, Boyd believes that his career is over. Sanders stares unblinkingly at him, twice raising his right hand from the desk, as if to strike someone or something, then letting it fall flat, the second time with a hard slap against the polished wood.

'They got that, Bob? They got hold of that?'

And then the President laughs; a great clatter of sound more fitting to an engine than a mouth.

'Well, if they got that, things are gonna get really interesting.'

Part Three

ALL OUR
LIVING LEADERS

51: Two People on the Beach

The tinted windows of the limousine lay a slight shade of grey over everything seen through them. Hyannis Port, out of season, does not take this added shadow well. The closed cafés, shops with whitewashed windows, and streets on which no cars are parked, already resemble the post-holocaust scenes in a nuclear movie. Jean's is the only vehicle, although the rumbling sea in the distance is a parody of heavy traffic; the bird calls the horns of stalled cars.

'Two minutes, Ms Norman,' Jean's driver informs her, as he turns left out of the empty, soundless town – where a few hopeful bouquets are arranged outside a flower shop – and heads down Sea Street, past a vast cemetery, heavy with American millionaires. Soon, she sees dunes and they turn onto Ocean Road.

'Take it slowly, Dan,' she says. 'I've never seen this.'

To her left is the public beach. She sees the rusting struts of the lifeguards' chairs, high as those of tennis umpires. To her right are the big seafront houses, pastel-coloured clapboard. They are mainly silent and shuttered, except for the occasional light in an upstairs room. Jean is uncertain whether this is a ruse to deter burglars, or if a few old widows are sitting out the winter, too doddery to reach the heat of Florida this year. In one or two of the gardens or drives, black workmen in windcheaters are doing repair work for absent employers who made it to the South.

The car passes a shuttered hut of blistered wood with a sign declaring it to be the BARNSTAPLE SHELLFISH INFORMATION OFFICE. The houses are getting bigger now. Their high fences have a garnish of barbed wire. The car turns left at a small white church, which seems to be floating on a sea of brown leaves. A large sign warns: DON'T EVEN THINK ABOUT PARKING.

'I guess that doesn't mean us,' says Dan, then adds declaratively, like a herald in a history film: 'The Kennedy compound!'

As they park, a young man with a neat black beard walks towards them across the grass verge.

'Good morning. David Boomer,' he says, leaning in through the passenger-side window, which the driver has wound down.

'Ms Monroe . . .'

'Norman.'

'Ms Norman, I'm very sorry. I'm glad to tell you, though, no press, no snoopers, no dune-walkers have been sighted near by. We *have* had two inquisitive seagulls, but the Secret Service have confirmed that they are birds.'

In the young man's crisp charm, Jean senses an embryonic politician. She steps out of the car and follows Boomer through a camouflaged door in the fence.

'The President is on the deck,' he tells her, when they are inside the main house on the compound.

'OK.'

He opens dusty double doors, and Jean suddenly feels herself to be in some political equivalent of *Sunset Boulevard*. She half expects to hear Jack mumbling: 'I'm ready for my photo opportunity, Mr Chief of Staff.' But, stepping out onto the splintered deck, she sees him, sitting at a summer table, on which there stands a steaming mug, painted with the presidential seal. He is reading a thick biography of FDR. Jean takes off her sunglasses.

'Sir,' says Boomer gently. He hesitates at the door, and Jean guesses that he is torn between his orders and the desire to witness the reunion. But he has turned and left, before Jack looks up.

'Marilyn!' he says, and stands and limps towards her. He is wearing black worsted trousers and a Boston Red Sox bomber jacket over a fluffy red sweater.

'I'm Jean now.'

'Oh, you'll always be Marilyn to me,' he says lightly, his old flirtatious manner intact.

'I'm serious,' she says. 'Old movie stars don't get government bodyguards.'

'OK. I'm sorry. Jean. I'm still Jack, by the way.'

His smile survives. Only the face has changed, the skin creased and thickened. He takes both of her hands and enfolds them gently in his. She quickly slips from the grip.

'You're quite safe, *Jean*.' He says her new name tentatively, testing the taste on his tongue. 'I really didn't know if you'd come.'

'Neither did I. Finally, I figured either I was too old to be hurt any more, or you were too old to hurt me. One of those.'

'Ah.'

'Why did you invite me?'

'It's a common enough impulse for the old, I imagine. Sorting things out. Isn't there an old phrase about putting your affairs in order? My Church has this expression as well: last things. The irritation of loose ends.'

'That I understand. I guess that's why I said yes.'

'It's not November weather yet. I thought we might walk on the beach.'

'That's fine.' She looks out across the untramped sand, towards the soundless houses. 'Not much of a party, this time of year, is it?'

'Ghost town. Yes, I like that. My kind of town, Hyannis is.'

He takes woollen gloves from the pockets of his coat. As he pulls them on, Jean notices that dark brown stripes stretch across his hands from between the bases of his fingers and thumbs towards his wrists. He becomes aware of her inspection.

'You're looking at my stripes? Addison's disease, one of the symptoms. Generally, it's in control with steroids. Though I must admit, when I heard I had to take them for the rest of my life, I kind of had visions of ending up running for Russia in the women's hundred metres.'

Jean, who had convinced herself that her visit was in a spirit of clinical curiosity, finds herself warming to him already. This has been her experience with every former lover re-encountered. For all the divorces, the family wars, this was, for her, the real story of the heart. The dumb tenacity of old attraction.

'I was on steroids through two administrations,' he says, 'and we kept it secret. These days, I probably couldn't get past the New Hampshire primary without the *Washington Post* splashing on Addison's. Sidebar by a Nobel-winning physician. It has often occurred to me that I would probably these days be unelectable, on health alone.'

'I've read that said. And . . . no . . .'

'No. Go on. And the women? I know. We were lucky to live when we did.'

She declines to respond to this proposition. They are walking on the beach now. The Atlantic is placid, and the sky above the sea divides into pinkish and silvery layers, a band of brightness just above the water, the way old medicines settle in their bottles into strips of different viscosity. The smell hovers somewhere between seaweed and sewage.

'Of course, the Pacific is my ocean,' says Jean. 'But this is cute too.'

On the dunes beyond, there is a stark contrast between two sleek crew-cut suited Secret Service men and the squat shaven-headed bomber-jacketed duo of her own Hollywood security.

Jean breaks the next uneasy silence of their meeting with: 'Are you looking forward to the ceremony this afternoon?'

'No. But it's part of the deal of having been President. Anyway, I'm just the sideshow now. With my five uncles.'

'Your uncles?'

'Oh, yes. Uncle Dick, Uncle Gerry, Uncle Jimmy, Uncle Ron, and Uncle George. I'm sorry, you're looking bewildered. Private joke. All five other former presidents are turning out for me. Their codename in the planning has been my uncles.'

'That's a pretty impressive show.'

'I guess. But you ain't seen nothing yet, as my Uncle Ron liked to say. Big Brother's dropping in as well.'

'Huh?'

'Sanders. He's chosen my ceremony for a damage-limitation exercise. I don't actually approve, but you don't say no to a President of the United States.'

'Yes, I think I remember you telling me that rule.'

'Oh, Maril— *Jean*, don't keep hitting on me for thirty years ago.'

'I said I'd be here. I didn't say I'd be sweet . . .'

'All right. All right. You're tougher than you were.'

'I hope so.'

They walk on in fragile silence. Then Jean, feeling that she has established that it is no longer a case of the president and the showgirl, relents, and says: 'What do you make of the Sanders stuff?'

'I don't think he did it. I think he's perverted *politics*, but that's all. But it's been scandal of the week since Watergate. If Mother Theresa of Calcutta was president, someone would find a drug-baron ex-husband somewhere, and the White House would deny it, and there'd be Congressional hearings, and no one would ever quite know, but it would affect her re-election.'

They have reached the end of the private beach. They watch the froth of the small breakers.

'Do you read what they write about you?' he asks.

'Do you?'

'Do I read what they write about you?'

'No. About you.'

'Don't worry, Jean, I was going to answer for myself. But you first.'

'My people tear out bits from magazines to shield me, though I usually get to see the stuff. But I was thinking on the way here. In one sense we have the same problem. In a strange way, I was sort of elected, voted into power. The studio never pushed me. It was the people who wanted me. And we both have the thing of being public property. But people can still have *me* as I was. The posters, the movies . . . Marilyn is trapped in history. They'll be happiest when I've gone and don't give them the contrast problem any more. You could say that they're waiting for me to die so that they can have my body.'

'Ah. I know what you mean. Political promise and achievement is disprovable, ruined by time. And birds shit on statues. But beauty can be frozen.'

She ignores what she assumes to be a compliment, and says: 'Do you read what they write about you?'

'No. In fact, I'm lying. Yes, every word. I know the biographies better than the people who wrote them. I could give recitals. You see, there is this problem. What are politicians to do after they leave office? Tend their gardens? That gets boring, so they tend their reputations. Dick Nixon spends a million dollars a year in legal fees, holding on to Watergate tapes and papers, delaying judgement. And I hear another Nixon story. He's attending the funeral of the Cardinal of New York, years after he resigned. He's going slowly up the steps of St Pat's. The reporters are shouting: 'Mr Nixon? A comment, please?' He just walks on, deaf as he was to his conscience. Then one of them, on a hunch, yells: "Mr President, sir?" Dick practically *skips* down the steps. Paint a picture of that and title it *The Former President*. Me, I let people call me what they want. And most of them don't need permission. The trick is not to panic. Reputations are so interchangeable. If I'd died, I'd be a hero. If Teddy had lived, he'd be a schmuck. The word news, we use it so much, I think we forget what it means. New. *New*. And history is just news shouted down a long line of people, many of them deaf. One day, they'll want something fresh on me, and maybe it will be that I wasn't such a schmuck after all. Ten, twenty years, some history professor in Vermont will go into print with a new view of my administration. And a history professor from New Hampshire will cautiously approve in the *New York Review of Books*. And then, a little later, the word "revisionism" appears in a little magazine. Reputation is a long game.'

'Do you . . . no, I . . .'

'Go on. Do I what?'

'Do you think Johnson or Nixon – someone else – would have done the same in Vietnam?'

'I've seen it argued that Lyndon wouldn't. But I have to believe that it would have happened, anyway. Vietnam was more the product of American history than individual whim, or so at least I must convince myself at night. You see, this is the problem. Everyone pretends they live in the present tense . . . am, are, is . . .'

'Will be . . . could be . . . that's how it always was for me.'

'How it always *was*. Yes, all right, the future tense, perhaps, for the young. My point is that after a certain age, we stop living in the present tense and live in the, well, the alternative present. Might have been, would have been, could have been . . .'

'You could be right. I mean, I know what you mean.'

'Indeed, in the early hours of the morning, I have considered any number of possibilities, including that we are dead and dreaming this.'

He is beginning to adopt the rhetorical manner she knows from his famous speeches. He is speaking for an audience of more than one. They have turned, and reversed their path along the sand, Jean following the lead of Jack's feet.

'Also,' he continues, 'a related problem, I often ask myself this, I don't know if you have a view . . . Why do we have to remember so much?'

'Oh, so we know who we are, and where we live, so we can get home at night. And find our loved ones. When we want to . . .'

'Look, Marilyn.'

'I was speaking generally. Even personally. The point I was going to make was that they programmed too much storage. No erase. We kind of miss a wipe facility.'

'Yeah. Sometimes I think . . . sometimes I think that the reason we remember everything, that we carry in our heads this record, this ridiculously detailed record, of all that we have done . . . sometimes I think it's proof that we'll be judged after we die.'

'Oh, Jack, don't be so Catholic. And, anyway, I mean . . .'

She has seen a logical flaw in his argument, but hesitates to express it, the old hierarchy of their minds re-asserting itself.

'I mean', she wills herself to object, 'what about people with Alzheimer's? According to your theory, they would all go to hell or get waved through the Pearly Gates on a technicality. Or people who are always late for appointments.'

'Like you.'

'Yes, all right. I'm better now.'

They are laughing, and he reaches across and links his arm in hers. She stiffens and is beginning to resist, but then she thinks that they are two old people and what can it matter now.

'Of course,' Jack says, 'I am aware of the paradox. I don't want to remember. But I want to be remembered. My own memories frighten me, but I spend my last days courting them in others.'

'Jack?' she says.

'Yes.'

'What do you think happens to us when we die?'

'Ah. You and me? We carry on in our absence, in forms we are forced into by other people. And, in honesty, we far prefer that to the alternative.'

'Do you know that old movie stars go to the salt mines?'

'Say what?'

'Yes, really. Fox – most of the other studios too – keep their archives in a salt mine in Kansas. Salt absorbs moisture, keeps the stock fresh.'

'Siberia.'

'Yeah. And it's the fans and the critics who decide if you ever come out.'

'Tell me about it. For the first year after Dallas, I thought I had been spared to accomplish something specific. Even my more hostile biographers acknowledge that this sense existed . . . this, this, what one of them calls I believe a "sense of grace" in America, of miracle, of *mission*. But I guess that I have come to see that it was just dumb luck. Good men die. Tyrants are spared to continue their tyrannies. There isn't a plan. And yet there are still very many times when I believe the opposite. I really don't know. I think more and more about chance . . .'

'Opportunity? Taking your chances?'

'No, no. A Kennedy? I was born with a silver presidency in my mouth, remember? No, the hand of fate. All that. Take Ronald Reagan, OK? Reagan's supporters, a lot of them were from the Bible Right?'

'Well, I voted for him. But that was actor solidarity and taxes.'

'Fine, but the point I'm making is, these Bible types think – they must – that Reagan survived assassination in '81 because God spared him.'

'And you know that Reagan nearly choked to death.'

'What? When?'

'On a peanut. 1972.'

'My God. The Lone Nut Theory.'

'That guy, one of his aides – Deaver, was it? – saved him. That German thing?'

'Heimlich's manoeuvre?'

'Right.'

'I didn't know that.'

'Gore Vidal told me. He read it in a book.'

'And Jimmy Carter was a peanut farmer. I guess there'll be some smart student somewhere writing a thesis on the peanut and the presidency. But, well, this is all ammunition for what I'm saying. And Catholics, I guess, we Catholics, such as I remain one, are supposed to think the same about John Paul II surviving the bullets. OK? So God *wanted* Dr Luther King to die, did he? I mean, Luther King was clergy, for Chrissake. Or look at it from the other side. Hitler. Now, Gordeler —'

'Who?'

'It doesn't matter who. He would have blown up Hitler on July 20th, 1944 – briefcase bomb – only someone moved the briefcase, quite by accident, further along the table. So God wanted Hitler to have another year?'

'Oh, sure. Why does God let bad things happen? You think you're the first to worry about this, Jack? Most of us figure it's one we'll leave until we see God, and ask him.'

The incoming water was making only cautious progress across the sand. There had been many such walks – usually solitary – in his years out of office. Sometimes the spume beating on the beach was so strong that it was like the plumes of smoke from a detonating bomb. On other occasions – such as today – the foam was as slight as champagne bubbles, although these days there was a strong chance that the effervescence was effluent.

'No, I don't mean: "Why does God let little children die?",' Jack goes on. 'I'm talking about chance. There's a small one in my life. I mean, apart from the times I might have died. Now, there's one hell of a lot of Catholics in

Wisconsin. Statistically, or do I mean demographically, this is the case. In 1960, the crucial Presidential primary was in Wisconsin. That's where I left Hubert Humphrey for dead. A Catholic candidate wins there, becomes our country's first, still only, Catholic president. You see how someone might begin to think? If Wisconsin had been Protestant, he might have been wiped off the slate. You tell yourself it's chaos – people tell you it's all random – but there are these details . . .'

'Oh, Jack, I know. I have this too, a little. In most of the books and articles about Marilyn, there's this one story. Of how, when Marilyn was a baby, this crazy woman – sometimes my mother, sometimes my aunt, occasionally a neighbour – tried to smother her with a pillow. Then someone else – mother, aunt, neighbour – dashes in at the right time, and saves her. Of course, the point of the story is the big what-if. Her whole existence becomes miraculous. The problem is, I have no idea now if the story is true. Sometimes, I remember it quite vividly, myself fighting for breath. Others, I recall it being invented by one of the studio flacks to give Marilyn mystique. I have no idea . . .'

'You talk about Marilyn in the third person.'

'Yes. I couldn't live with her. So I moved out.'

This, she realizes, has the feel of a curtain line, and the conversation falters. Jack, too, is preoccupied with the previous line of thought, which he resumes: 'There are always these two possibilities. Do you know, because of deadlines on election night – old technology, no computers then – reporters used to write up stories on polling day for both results. The printers set them both in type and pushed the button on the one that happened. So, there was a ghost story of Nixon's victory in 1960. A reporter once showed me a Xerox of a "McGovern Triumphs" piece from 1972. Dateline. Quotes. Everything was real except the facts. It nearly made you cry . . . More and more, I wonder how we live with this – that, in almost every moment, there are two possibilities.'

'Choice?'

'No, not choice. Because who chooses to be killed? To be unhappy? To lose? What I mean is, this daily sense that everything could go either way – of never knowing the end of the story. I once opened an exhibition of war art at the Smithsonian and the picture you did – I mean, I know nothing about painting – but it seemed to me that the picture you did if you had no imagination was the one of the soldier going off to war, the family grouped around the door. Glum mother, crying wife. And there's this instant sympathy because the point is: is he ever coming home? But it isn't just war. This is the shit deal of being human. Nobody who goes out of their door in the morning – nobody – actually *knows* they're coming home.'

'You mean, like crime and so on?'

'No, not crime. Or not just crime. I'm not being a politician now, making speeches about our lawless streets. I mean something – anything – could happen to them. They don't know that it won't.'

Jean feels herself lulled into the rhythm of their conversations of thirty years before: him the effortless lecturer, her the awe-struck stooge. So she says, with a slant of sarcasm in her voice: 'Well, yes, Jack. But, I mean, the vast majority of people who go out of their doors every morning – the vast majority – they do come home. More than in a war.'

'All right. *Statistically*. A government spokesman said: "The vast majority of those who leave their homes in the morning do come back at night." Statistically, we know we're coming home. But not certainly. This is the big question to me. How do we live with our . . . our . . . disposability? Knowing that any single minute could – theoretically – be our last? Why aren't we screaming?'

'Well, Jack, because of . . . because of stuff like . . . Look up your high school class when you're in your thirties. You haven't seen them for fifteen years . . .'

'And they'll mainly be alive? Is that what you were going to say?'

'Yes. Except one. There's usually one. Car crash. Leukaemia. Then, in your forties, more are missing. And so on. Finally, one or two are the last in the class.'

'Right. And we're getting there. We're getting to be the last in our class. So, what you're saying is, it's statistics that keep us sane?'

'Yeah. Likelihood . . .'

'Right. Opera singers and wine collectors fascinate me in this respect. They are people, you see, who live in the future. Jackie and I would book tenors and divas for the White House. We were known – as you may recall – for our courting of the artistic community.'

'Oh, I *recall*.'

'Ouch. Another free hit. You're sharp now.'

'I hope. I guess you preferred me blunt.'

'What was I saying? The point is, when we signed these people up for the White House, it would be made quite clear that they were making an exception for the President in diaries blocked to '67 or '68. Now, take wine buffs . . .'

'Oenophiles,' she suddenly blurts.

'Oh, bravo! Still reading dictionaries?'

In their lives in another time, he had been amused by her determination to learn and master words and knowledge.

'Don't fucking patronize me, Jack. We both had our best lines typed out by other people.'

'It's true. And politicians don't give screenplay credits. I'm sorry, Jean. But my point . . . my point. Opera singers and oenophiles. A Brahmin billionaire here recently showed me his cellar before dinner. This is a man of easily sixty, one by-pass at least behind him. Now the wines are labelled with drinking dates. '97, '98. A few not due to feel the corkscrew until the next century. And he showed me this collection with pride. Fear, I felt, would be more appropriate. Or regret. I buy wine, and I drink it. But a cellar. Like an opera singer's diary, it always seems to me a challenge to fate or God or whatever . . .'

They are approaching the steps to the deck. She slips her arm out of his, nervous of the house staff blabbing to *America Now*.

'What's your one biggest regret?' she asks.

But the confessional intimacy of their walk has gone. The public figure is being reconstructed for the ceremony in the afternoon, and Jack just laughs and says: 'Well, you know, I would really quite like to have had an airport called after me . . .'

52:   Apollo 2

Walking to the conference room, to interview the source for the Apollo 2 story, Thomson has the euphoria of a man with the rare combination of a large problem and a fast solution. The newspaper and magazine articles forming an escarpment on his desk – each of them raising another question about the reliability of Recovered Memory Therapy – will cease to be alarming if the forthcoming conversation proceeds as promised. His mind is, once more, a riot of book deals and Pulitzer Prizes.

'This is the nail', he rumbles to Washington, 'that fixes Sanders to the cross. And there won't *be* an Easter Sunday.'

Washington has often tried to instruct the Australian in modern American language rules – that a passing member of staff might judge such remarks discriminatory or offensive – but his lessons have clearly not adhered.

The conference room is a cold, stark box constructed from flimsy partitions. There is a table, scraped and pale, scalded by the salt of the many starlets' tears that have fallen on it during the life of *America Now*. Sitting at the table, dumbly juggling a mug of coffee, is a man in his forties, stocky and with neatly cropped salt-and-pepper hair.

'Jefferson Burgess,' he says, in a nicotine croak. 'Thank you for seeing me.'

'Thank *you*,' says the editor. 'I'm Jim Thomson. This is my deputy, Elliot Washington.'

Hands are shaken, coffees poured or refreshed, the tape recorder arranged on the table.

'I had to contact you,' Burgess explains. 'Soon as I read this stuff about Sanders. He wouldn't want me to tell you what I'm gonna say . . .' The two journalists smile at what they take as irony. 'But it's right that I do.'

'Mr Burgess,' says Thomson, already visualizing this scene in the movie of the 'Apollogate' affair, 'let's begin by establishing some facts. You are willing to confirm that Newton W. Sanders, currently the President of the United States, has paid into a private account in your name the sum of $1,000 each month for the last fifteen years?'

'Correct. That is, it's $1,000 now. It's been inflation-adjusted, obviously. But, yes, that's correct.'

'Why did the payments begin?'

'Because of something that happened between us.'

'When you were a child?'

'A *child*? Hell, no. I'd have been twenty-eight, twenty-nine, not that I see why it matters.'

Thomson tries to hide his disappointment at the absence of paedophilia from the narrative. But this will be enough. It is doubtful that Middle America is ready even for presidential homosexuality.

'Was Sanders a friend of yours, or of your family.'

'Hell, no. I don't think I'd ever heard of him until the restaurant.'

'The restaurant?'

'Yes. That's where it happened.'

53: All Our Living Leaders

Although the three occupants have entirely hostile blood groups, there is a happy family atmosphere in the apartment on the morning of November 25th. Consuela holds Nat on her knee, reading with him from a primer which consists of glossy pictures of household items, their names in big bold print beneath, for the child to repeat. With the instant mimicry of children innocent to expression, he does so with Hispanic intonations.

'Clack,' says Consuela.

'Clack,' repeats Nat.

Fraser, sitting at the desk on the opposite side of the room is also, in a sense, reading about clocks. Looking up from his book, and seeing the scene, Fraser thinks of 'family values', the phrase favoured by candidate Newton Sanders throughout his victorious campaign, although one which he will presumably be dropping from his rhetoric, given recent allegations.

'Da da da, la la la, li li li . . .'

All morning, Consuela has been singing what Fraser takes for Colombian counting songs or lullabies, although it is possible that their subject is money or luck, as the melodies began when he revealed to her the method by which she could gain a bonus fee of one thousand dollars.

'Just tik pitcher?' she asked.

'That's right. One picture of my kid with President Kennedy this morning. It means a lot to me.'

'Mr Kendy, you cousin, sumting, of Presdent Kendy?'

'What? Oh, no, we just have the same name,' says Fraser.

'But he means a lot to me. I get one picture of him holding Nat, you get the money.'

'How I do it?'

'Well, part of the money is for working that out. But, if I were you, I'd get there early, head down front by the wire, and slip Nat through. Even the goons aren't gonna shoot kids on sight.'

Since then, she has been singing. Now Fraser looks at his watch.

'Time,' he says. 'I'd say it was time you got going.'

He hands Consuela the camera, taken from the shelf of the cupboard, where his expensive field-glasses rest. She turns it over with a clouded brow.

'I hope I . . . Is easy?'

'Oh, yes. Just press the big red button.'

But, although Consuela cannot know this, the camera does not matter. There is, however, something else that does.

'Make sure he has the coat on, zipped right up. It's real coat weather today.'

'Yes. Mr Kendy . . . I get you picture.'

'I'd like that very much.'

The John F. Kennedy Presidential Library and Museum, designed by I. M. Pei, consists of three structures, distinct but linked.

At the rear of the building is a high triangular edifice in white stone, like a thick slice cut from a circular pie, or a book arranged to show fanned pages in a shop display. In front of this is a drum-shaped construction, of the same bleached concrete. These two parts of the design are linked by an oblong bridge, the end of which rests on top of the drum like the arm of an old-fashioned record player. Between the cake-portion and the drum, there stands another triangular slice, this one made of dark smoked glass framed in a lattice of steel. A low surrounding wall, also of white stone, runs down across lush grass towards the sea which laps the site on two sides. Terraced steps descend from the Library buildings to the grass.

For today only, the Secret Service has annotated Pei's design. A large planked platform has been set up parallel to the sea wall at the bottom of the garden area, facing back towards the steps and the Library buildings. Rows of chairs for dignitaries have been placed on the grass, in front of the platform. The wide areas of lawn on either side have been sectioned off with steel-mesh crash barriers, to hold the uninvited crowd. Admission to these pens is through a single entrance, where the door-frame shape of a metal detector is the only break in the metal fence.

Symbolic menace – psychological counter-attack – is everywhere. Motor boats with official markings – Police, Secret Service, Coastguard – rock across the rough hump-backed water in regular procession. Two helicopters throb above. Marksmen line the perimeter of the drum structure. State troopers and Boston police stand or patrol at points around the grounds.

'When I was a kid,' says Ford to Duke, as they flank one of the lines waiting to be checked by the metal detectors, 'seeing the President was a big, big thing. Kids here today, they're getting a fucking six-pack.'

At first, the police had believed that the rededication ceremony at the Library would be attended only by former Democratic Presidents Kennedy and Carter and the key-note speaker, the Governor of New York: a low-adrenalin assignment. Then, it had emerged that former Republican incumbents Nixon, Ford, Reagan, and Bush would also be attending, a tableau last seen in public at the opening of the Ronald W. Reagan Library and Museum in California in 1991. Although keen to view the museum of American leadership represented by the guests this afternoon, Officer Ford is distressed that the presence of former President Ford will solidify his nickname among his colleagues until retirement.

Now, this morning, the force was informed that President Sanders would also be present, as part of his strategy to counter scandal. For this reason, adrenalin, weaponry, and simple historical curiosity among officers have all risen to an exceptional level.

There is also unusual variety in the buttons and banners worn and carried by the crowd. Duke has spotted, on the lapels of old Bostonians, a *Kennedy Is Our Remedy* button from 1960, and a *Put Jack Back* from 1964. The banners include a 'Black Jack' from the anti-Vietnam days, and two reading *Tricky Dicky*, from the Watergate era. Others, aimed at Reagan and Bush, make reference to the Iran-Contra and Iraqgate illegal arms scandals of the 1980s. Already, Apollogate is growing slogans. *Lock Up Your Children*, warns one length of cardboard. *President Pervert*, a streamer accuses. But one hastily painted bed sheet insists: *Apollogate Is A Media Coup*. The banners and badges rustle and glint: a history of modern America in advocacy and protest.

Thick strings of saliva keep falling from the child's mouth. He is teething, his bite already one incisor sharper than on the smiling photographs his mother holds with failing hope at home in Newton, Maine.

'Oh, Nad, your nide noo code,' says Consuela, dabbing with a handkerchief at a saturated patch near the neck of the yellow jacket.

They have reached the metal detector. Consuela places her bag – which contains the camera, diapers, drinks, and cookies – on the conveyor belt that runs into the X-ray machine. She drops the apartment key and the few quarters from her pocket in the plastic dish handed to her by a woman in a dark blue suit, then carries the child through the scanner frame. The machine squeals. Consuela is asked to try again, which she does, but with the same result. The uniformed security guard looks closely at her and the child.

'I guess it might be his jacket,' she says. 'Kind of a heavy zipper. Try taking that off.'

When the woman tugs at the yellow cloth, and points to the X-ray machine, Consuela understands. Nat's jacket travels through on the conveyor belt. The child minder and her charge pass, this time silently, through the aluminium frame. On the other side, the jacket is handed back. The camera is carefully examined, turned over and sent through the machine as a separate item, but then is also returned.

Consuela carries Nat down the grassy slope towards the sea, then pushes through the crowd towards the control barrier closest to the platform.

'OK, Ms Norman, the usher will show you to your seat.'

Jean, in her smart disguise of dark blue wide-brimmed hat and honey-tinted glasses, follows the grey-suited student through the latticed glass wedge which is the central structure of the building: an entrance lobby giving access to the various exhibit halls of the museum. Like limousine windows, or sunglasses, the construction is opaque to outside eyes, but, from inside, allows a clear shining sight of sun and sea.

Jean is led through a door and out onto the grass, where three banks of seats have been arranged facing a platform, set with chairs and a lectern decorated with the presidential seal. To her left, Jean sees Governor Bill Clinton of Arkansas, the struggle to be dignified in defeat showing in his pouched eyes and lined face. In front of her, Jean recognizes Nancy Reagan, swaddled in furs. The former First Lady turns, then seeing that the new arrival is some unrecognizable nobody, looks away.

Meredith, halfway back in the gathering crowd at the right side of the stage, feels a sentence, and then a paragraph, of his biography seeding and accreting in his head.

> The museum was supposed to encapture, for future generations of Americans, his life. But a woman who had been a major part of it was not represented there at all. No portrait of her hung in its cool white halls. She was, however, present at the ceremony in person, in heavy disguise, amid the banked ranks of American establishment panjandrums.

Or perhaps it is 'panjandra'. He can check the plural later. Taking his video camera from his shoulder-bag, he aims it towards the rows of VIP seats, and records the faces arrayed there. Later, with electronic enhancement and archive comparison, he should be able to identify one of them as Marilyn.

A murmur of alertness rises in the crowd. Turning back towards the water, Meredith sees a series of boats speeding towards a pontoon bridge, just along the coast from the Library, watched and followed by helicopters. They are bringing the leaders in by sea.

For security reasons, the former presidents – known as 'the uncles' in Secret Service preparations for today – travel in separate boats from Boston Harbor to the landing pontoon on Columbia Point, where the Library stands.

In a holding room at a converted warehouse before boarding, they were briefly all together. There was little conversation. Nixon and Carter uneasily discussed the forthcoming non-racial elections in South Africa, which both had visited. Reagan became involved in a befuddled discussion with a waitress about whether or not the coffee was decaffeinated. Jack found himself chatting to Gerry Ford about back pain and chiropractics. Each man, he felt, was looking around the room, constructing a league table of reputations.

'All our living leaders have turned out for you today,' says Boomer on the boat, as the Library comes into view. 'It's a great tribute to you, sir.'

'Forgotten politicians,' says Jack. 'We're a small club, and we stick together. We stick together in the hope that one of us might not be forgotten.'

'Back home,' says President Sanders, waving to the crowd from the deck of the presidential launch as the sea spray shines his face, 'we always say, if you see someone waving to you from the water, chances are they're not just saying hello.'

In recent days, the Seattle aphorisms of which Boyd and Woodall have been advised have become increasingly pessimistic. Boyd fingers the waterproof folder in his hand, which contains the speech on which the newspapers are saying the President's future depends, successfully edited of any mention of reincarnation.

From a piece of raised ground on the University of Massachusetts campus, to the rear of the John F. Kennedy Library and Museum, Fraser watches through his field glasses. He focuses on Nixon and Ford, in their heavy charcoal overcoats, talking as they sit on the platform. Then he scans the crowds on both sides of the stage. Within a minute, he finds Consuela and the child, tight against barriers right down by the edge of the stage. He smiles. God bless America. People come to the country with scarcely a word of the language. But they understand money.

54: A Bigger Piece of Meat

'So there I am', says Jefferson Burgess to Thomson and Washington and the spooling tape, 'with a girlfriend. The men are eating steak, the girls are eating chicken. Now this is a real Texas restaurant. The steaks are like cross-sections of cows, if you know what I mean.'

Thomson and Washington, though worried that the story is taking a long time to move from beef to buggery, humour their informant by allowing him to continue.

'Then, suddenly, there's the most tremendous spluttering and coughing and all-round hollering from one of the other tables. And there's this guy who's half standing at the table, his hands up at his throat, and he's obviously choking.'

Thomson has a shivering premonition of the way the story will turn out, but he says only: 'And this was Newton Sanders?'

'As it turns out. But this is fifteen years ago, before anyone knows him from a hole in the ground. And he's nearly in a hole in the ground. Because this rich-looking dame is shouting: "He's dying. I love him and he's dying . . ." Kind of stuff you'd think that should be said in private.'

A last hope visits Thomson, and he asks: 'And this was Mrs Sanders?'

'Yeah. Oh, *yes*. Oh, I see. No, this ain't like one of those things you boys generally print. Oh, this was Mrs Sanders. Now, the thing is, various times in my life, for reasons you don't need to know, I've had time on my hands. Watched more afternoon TV than maybe some folks have. Now, on these things, they do themes, get people together in the studio. "Women Who Have Slept With Donkeys". Know the kind of thing? Well, one day, it was "People Who Have Saved People's Lives". Now, you had a bone marrow donor, and a guy who'd landed a 737 on one engine, and you had this man who'd saved another man from choking in a restaurant. And the host says, well, how? And the guy says he stood behind the other guy, put his arms around him and banged him in the midriff . . . Now, this stayed with me. And that's what I did in the restaurant, fifteen years ago. I saved the life of Newton Sanders.'

'Fuck,' says Thomson, who, for a moment, during the part about the guy standing behind the other guy and putting his arms around him, had become cheerful again.

'I know,' says Burgess. 'Don't think I haven't thought about it. There's two ways to it. Either God sent a piece of meat to stop Sanders one day being President, and I got in the way, or he sent me to make sure he did become President. That would be a strange God, though. I'll tell you, a lot of my friends say, though admittedly they're Bush Republicans, if only it had been a bigger piece of meat . . .'

Thomson swallows hard, as if experiencing a digestive crisis of his own.

'And this is why he pays you money?'

'Yes. Oh, he offered more. I took what I did, in the end, to make him go away. I wouldn't recommend it, you know, saving someone's life. They go all doggy on you. It's like having another kid suddenly. It was worse because Sanders, actually, I found, I didn't like. Perhaps it was what happened in the restaurant, but he seemed to become convinced he'd been spared for a purpose. It would be around then the folk in his company started getting little books of his thoughts with the Christmas bonus.'

This makes sense to Thomson. The miraculous escape was a recurring theme in the biographies of politicians. Often it was escape from poverty, but, many times also, from death. There had been one in Australia, who had walked safe from a commercial jet which had suffered total engine failure. There was George Bush, the only member of his World War II crew to survive a ditching in the sea, and carrying, friends said, a sense of mission all his life because of this apparent miracle.

Two of Richard Nixon's brothers had died, in beds beside him, from tuberculosis in their youth.

'So there you are, boys,' says Burgess. 'You asked me to tell you my story, and I have.'

'Yeah, thanks.'

Back in his office, Thomson looks at Washington and says: 'Take me to a steak restaurant! I'm going to eat a T-bone really fast. And I don't want to be resuscitated.'

55: A Child! How Charming!

At the John F. Kennedy Library and Museum, the Governor of New York is giving the warm-up oration.

'We live in a world', he is saying, his big hands beating the air for emphasis, 'in which the leader is offered no automatic respect, as once he was by the mere fact of elevation. A world in which the pressure on the elected – from economies, from the media, from the cynicism of the electorate – is perhaps greater than it has been at any time in human history. Yet nations must be led, and shall be led, and it is for us, as a nation and a people, to decide.'

America's leadership since 1960 sits behind the speaker on the platform: a line of old men, trembling slightly in the cold.

The child, keen to play the great and still unexplored game of walking, keeps kicking downwards, squashing his shoes into Consuela's stomach, trying to break her embrace, and squawking his boredom. 'Sshh, Nat, sssh,' she says, but she is not sure how much longer she can hold him, and fears attention in the respectful silence of the listening crowd.

Meredith sees Reagan, during the Governor's address on American leadership, pat back his wind-ruffled hair with one hand. He thinks he will write in his book, though, that Reagan consulted his watch. It is a legitimate interpretation of the gesture. He thinks he might also say that Nixon looked uncomfortable during the rhetoric on integrity.

*

To Fraser, through his field-glasses, the presidents are small men. He is still invigorated by the unexpected extra presences. He had calculated only for Kennedy, and the parade that preceded him felt at first like a mirage of ambitions. When Sanders appeared, he felt alarm, feeling that fate and history were on his side. Now he is impatient, waiting for the moment when the politicians leave the stage and come down and work the crowd, press the flesh.

'And so here today', says the Governor of New York, 'we rededicate – and unveil a new exhibit at – a building dedicated to a man who gave eight years as president, and has given seventy-six as a human being, to the ideal of strong, humane, and compassionate American leadership – John Fitzgerald Kennedy!'

Jack bows his head, as if in church, as the applause spreads through the audience, not strong enough to muffle the mocking commentary of the Vietnam veterans.

Consuela is allowing the child to hang from her hands, swinging him behind, then up, over, and in front of the crowd-control barrier, in a makeshift game. She hopes that this limited activity, of kicking and swinging, will satisfy and quieten him for a while. But her own hands are becoming greasy from the heat and friction of the boy's, and suddenly, in the second part of his arc, on the far side of the barrier, he slips from her grip, stumbles on the grass, halts in brief surprise at his liberation, then waddles away from Consuela's lunge.

In the magnified moons of his binoculars, Fraser sees the first flicker of the yellow coat and knows that his plan is abandoned, that he is perhaps being directed to a grander act, and that he has a moment to settle many destinies.

*

A laugh builds and thickens in the crowd as the child struts and stares in its strange new playground. The police and Secret Service look at each other, not drilled in responses to breaches of security as innocent as this, fearing legal action and accusation from the parents of the child if they should handle it too roughly. On the platform, the seven presidents smile indulgently. An aide – later identified as Robert F. Boyd, White House Chief of Staff – leans forward and speaks into the ear of President Sanders.

Behind the drawn drapes of the master bedroom of the Robinson house in Newton, Maine, CNN plays, with the sound turned down. The pictures – captioned LIVE FROM BOSTON – show the scenes at the ceremony where the American President will make his first major speech since the recent allegations against him. A man and a woman, fully dressed, lie on top of the crumpled duvet staring at the silent screen. She wears an airline complimentary night-flight eye-mask hitched up on her forehead. Two chunky brown pill bottles and a half-empty glass of water with a scummy film on top stand on the night table.

'Nat!' the woman shouts suddenly, pointing at the television screen, 'Nat! Nat!'

The man turns to her with an expression of agonized rationality, tender fear, and is about to speak, when he too glances at the screen.

'Oh my God!' he says, and reaches for the phone.

President Sanders rises to his feet, says something that two of the former presidents present will later report to have been, 'A child! How charming!' and walks across the platform, and down the small set of steps onto the grass. He jogs towards the child, who is giggling and skipping, picks him up, and turns towards the pen on the left of the stage where the photographers and television cameras are gathered.

*

Fraser, seeing this, feels guided, forced towards a story he never foresaw, but which now has inevitability. And so, focusing the field-glasses with one hand, he steadies the radio transmitter with the other.

The Robinsons of Newton, Maine, are permitted less than half a minute of elation and relief before they start screaming.

The first thing Duke feels after the explosion is the elation of his own survival. His next instinct is to look for Ford. Seeing his partner staggering to his feet at the rear of the VIP seats, he shouts: 'Gerry, let's get these people out of here!'

To their relief, they can see no dead. People are already half-rising amid the scattered chairs, dazed and deafened. The first guest the two policemen reach is a woman in her sixties, a victim, it seems, of nothing worse than bruised vanity, for she holds in her hands a wig and tinted glasses thrown off by the blast. Ford stares at her.

'Oh shit!' he says. 'You're Marilyn Monroe . . .'

In reply, she mumbles two words, which the pragmatic Duke will later claim were 'My back!' The romantic Ford, however, insists on translating this pained communication as 'Where's Jack?'

At this moment, though, Ford notices a bloodstain spreading at the front of his gut; a red, irregular lake on the shirt-cloth straining above his waist.

Through a freak electrical effect, the bomb activates the prompter screen attached to the lectern on the platform. The words of the President's speech unfurl in the air, unread.

Jack thinks that maybe his ribs are broken, from the force with which the agents pulled him off the platform. His current fear, though, is the possible irony of surviving a bomb only to

268

die in a motor boat smash, such is the speed with which he is being raced across the water back to Boston Harbor. Through the portholes, he can see two of the boats carrying the five other former presidents, making the same pace away from the scene of the assassination. Only the presidential launch remains moored there.

He has just been officially informed of the death of President Newton Sanders.

'The bomb was . . .?' Jack begins, reluctant to contemplate what he guesses to have been the method.

'The child, sir, yes,' the agent who brought him the news confirms. 'We assume. Detonated from a distance. Prime Minister Rajiv Gandhi of India was killed that way, although the carrier was an adult. We looked at it then. But we figured no one could get close enough to our man . . .'

'Except a child,' says Jack.

'Yeah. They've taken in the woman who was with the kid. The word is that she's a Russian. Sir?'

'Yes.'

'There's no Vice-President.'

'I know.'

'What happens now?'

'Well, either Congress recants and confirms Mr Diet Pepsi from Pittsburgh as President, which is on balance unlikely. Or the Speaker of the House becomes President for the rest of the term.'

'What a fuck— I'm sorry, sir. What a mess . . .'

'No, you're right. What a fucking mess . . .'

And so Jack has survived again. Escape, he finds, is both exhilarating and dismaying. Every human instinct, short of the chemical eccentricity of suicide, assumed an individual future. Yet each of us could be blown away in a moment.

Is this fate? To him, it has the feel of chaos. For the true horror of this afternoon is the ingenuity of cruelty. Society connived restraints – precautions, police forces, punishments – but all that happened was that new terrors were invented.

People talked of fate – meaning dumb chance – but the complication was that what they called fate worked itself out through human inspiration. Someone who died in a plane crash was a victim of chance, but also of engineering genius. If the plane had not been invented, they would not have perished in that way. Someone who died at the hands of an assassin was, in the same way, a victim of fate but also of human inspiration: of another person having the idea and the means.

Spreading chaos through the water by its haste, the boat, with JFK locked below, makes for safety.

56:   Boston Logan

On this day of assassination, the sky is dramatic and ominous at dusk. Above Boston Logan airport, the clouds are swellings of red and black, like the eye of a boxer stopped in the seventh with cuts. In an earlier century, the priests would have seized on this coincidence, but now it is regarded merely as chance; one stray chime in chaos.

At Logan – named after a Second World War hero – crowds are standing grouped around the television sets in the departure hall bars, tuned live to CNN.

Violence proceeds in a straight line, but the record develops. The Second World War was a radio and newsreel story. Vietnam was fought on recorded television. The Persian Gulf War was broadcast live from the battlefield. Oswald's shooting of President Kennedy was captured on radio and home movie. Hinckley's shots at President Reagan were recorded on video by television. The blowing up, by a person or persons unknown, of President Sanders was featured live on cable television.

On the televisions in the bars at Boston Logan, the President has already died again from all angles and at every speed. Watching the pictures, some people are weeping. More, however, are still and pale, the first in generations of Americans to be called on for such public mourning, although some, perhaps, those in their fifties and beyond, had the rehearsal of Dallas in 1963. The remorse is not, however, uniform. A fat young man in a baseball cap says loudly, as Sanders walks once more towards the skipping child: 'One photo opportunity too many.' People turn to him with violent

271

eyes as he walks smirkingly away. 'Fuck you,' one man hisses after him.

On television, the pundits look uncomfortable, perhaps for reasons other than grief. It is customary on these occasions to speak of continuity, but Sanders has no successor and no party. 'In a sense,' says one pale commentator on CNN, 'what you might call the apostolic line of governance of the Republic has come to an end. I frankly don't know where we go from here . . .'

To Fraser, standing at the back of one of the watching crowds, his boarding pass for Albuquerque dampening in his hand, this sounds apocalyptic. He feels dizzy with history, a man who woke up believing his destiny was to kill a former president and who, instead, was offered the opportunity to kill the President, to end the apostolic line of the governance of the Republic.

The airport has been closed for two hours, securing an enormous cordon of untouched air for the rushed departure of the former presidents and then the return to Washington of the remains of President Sanders on Air Force One. Now the brooding sky is crowding again with commuter planes. The flight information monitor, its long line of DELAYEDs reducing by the minute, shows that Fraser's plane is boarding, so he leaves the crowd of leaderless Americans – although CNN has just shown the Speaker of the House arriving at the White House – and walks with his heavy hold-all towards the departure gates.

Although the car heater is running, Ford sits huddled with his arms wrapped round his middle. He is trying to hide the stain on his quilted jacket, from where some flying fragment caught him at the library. He hopes that Duke will not see that he is injured. Ford does not want to leave the story yet. He calculates that food might distract him, and fumbles for another diabetic pretzel on the ledge.

'What strikes you', says Duke, who is driving, 'is that if the magazine had never made the accusations against Sanders, he would never have come to Boston, and he would never have died.'

'You're saying it's a conspiracy?'

'No, Gerry, I am *not*. I'm saying the opposite. I'm saying it's chance. The Minus Game. Did the assassin know Sanders was in Boston? A tip-off? Or was the target someone else instead? Kennedy?'

'They were saying on the television in the station that it points to a conspiracy.'

'They always say that. It's a form of therapy. And I'm saying maybe it doesn't. Although I see why people want to believe that.'

But their discussion is interrupted by a radio call, summoning them to an incident at Boston Logan airport.

Almost every passenger is being sent back through the metal detectors two or three times. At Idlewild once, during the Persian Gulf War, Fraser had triggered the tocsin with a single quarter forgotten in his pocket. The machine had been placed on its most sensitive setting. The technology seems to be as neurotic today, rejecting all who approach it.

Fraser drops just a few coins into the plastic dish he is handed for his suspicious objects on the landside of the frame. He carries no keys. Those for the Boston apartment are now in the city's sewage system, flushed with his own gaseous nervous shit down an airport toilet. His next destination is a New Mexico hotel.

He passes noiselessly through the detector at the first attempt, which he takes as an omen, until, on the other side, he sees a security goon removing his hold-all from the conveyor belt and carrying it to the examination table.

There, the man starts to unpack the bag, as Fraser stands and watches, with an attempted attitude of nonchalance and public-spirited understanding of the need for the procedure. The top layer comprises six or seven books about Time, although the titles are not read. Each book is shaken, its pages fanned, checking for hollows in the body of the text.

The volumes are stacked neatly on the table, followed out by a handful of neatly folded shirts, pants, hose. A denim sponge bag is untied and emptied. Fraser is asked to activate the electric razor, which he does.

Carefully repacking the toiletries, the guard reaches down deep into the valise. He removes a plastic laundry bag, wound twice around its inconsiderable contents. From this, he pulls out three pairs of petite jeans, two small sweatshirts, three pairs of tiny socks.

Fraser meets the man's curious look as steadily as he can. Assuming the Boston apartment would be the first place to be searched, he left no traceable purchases near there. He had felt horribly conspicuous in the baby shop the previous week, obsessed that his sterility and guilt somehow showed. His plan had been to ditch the bag of child clothes at the airport but, arriving there, he found the trash cans sealed, one of the police's immediate responses to the bomb.

'You travelling with a child, sir?'

'Oh, er, no. I'm flying out to meet my family. This is stuff my wife wanted from home . . .'

'Uh huh. Can I see your boarding pass, sir?'

'Can I ask why?'

'You understand, sir, on a day like this . . . we're being careful.'

Of course, thinks Fraser. Don't be stupid. Public duty.

'Yes, sure. I'm sorry. Day like this, as you say.'

The man looks at the strip of cardboard, then passes it back, repacks the bag, in the same order as before, with the bag of half-size garments at the base, then zips it closed.

'OK, Mr Fraser, thank you for your co-operation.'

When Duke and Ford arrive at the airport, they are directed, with three other pairs of officers who responded to the call, to the waiting area at Gate 14 in the domestic departures hall, where the suspect is about to board a flight to New Mexico, via Dallas.

They turn the corner, past the live lobster shop and the news and book store, piled high with an emergency afternoon edition of the *Boston Globe*, headlined: THE PRESIDENT IS DEAD. At the gate, they rapidly identify the suspect, one of few Caucasians among the mainly Hispanic passengers, and one of only two men young enough for a match with the blurred and flimsy photograph from the surveillance camera at the gate. The man is sitting, reading a book, a cardboard cup of a steaming substance in his hand. At his feet is a bag of the colour, size, and style described by the security guard who searched it.

As Ford and Dukakis approach the gate area from the left, two of their colleagues are moving in from the right. This sudden heavy presence is noticed by some of the waiting passengers, who gasp. Ford will later tell the inquiry that he believes that there were other guilty people at the gate, perhaps illegal immigrants. Dukakis will attribute the reaction to the heightened sense of fear and danger among Americans because of the assassination.

But, for whatever reason, the suspect looks up. He is facing Ford and Dukakis, who are still thirty feet away. The suspect checks his watch – like a passenger calculating whether there is time for a final errand before the flight – then picks up his bag, and turns right, walking very fast past the food court and along the shopping corridor. It is here that he sees the other two policemen. Ten amateur video tapes – shot by passengers carrying camcorders, would-be Zapruders – will later establish that the suspect tries to walk on, as if he has not seen the officers. Both policemen will later tell the inquiry that a warning was shouted to the man to stop. This is confirmed by sound enhancement of the amateur footage.

But the man starts to run, flattening two elderly passengers who block his path. The policemen will claim that, in pursuit, they gave a second warning, but this defence will be disputed by witnesses, and enhanced versions of the sound-tracks of four of the ten home videos – the other six camera-owners were too infirm to chase the later action – leave doubt about whether or not there was a shout before the shots.

Duke and Ford, arriving afterwards, clear a space around the scene, while their colleagues check the body. It is Ford who notes and bags the book, a battered paperback that fell from the suspect's hand and spun away across the airport marble. The book is called *A Brief History of Time*.

The man who had read it is dead, but his public life begins.

Part Four

IDLEWILD

57:   The Time Bandit

One reading of the life and career of Newton Sanders is that
it provides a pure illustration of the operation of chance.
Nearly obliterated in a Houston restaurant by overestimating
the machismo of his chewing mechanism, he was saved by
the chance expertise of a nearby diner. Lifted from non-
political obscurity to the presidency in an event which there
was a clear temptation to see as destiny, he was wiped out
when an assassin intent on killing someone else was surprised
to find Sanders in his sights. His life can be summarized as
three pieces of luck: two good, one bad.

This is not, though, a popular gloss on events in the
months after the assassination. Americans – a proud and
religious tribe – are alarmed by the bleakness of a universe of
chance. In a pure democracy of phenomena, no nation could
call itself blessed.

So the search for explanations, the hunt for understanding, begins. But, first, there are names. In the aftermath of
this catastrophe, journalism resembles medicine: unable to
reveal why a condition occurred, or how it might be reversed,
it proves adept at identifying and labelling.

Consuela Martinez, thirty-nine, is revealed as the adult
who accompanied the dead – and killing – child to the
ceremony at the Library. A Colombian citizen, she is reported
by some news sources, without official confirmation, to be
absent from tax and welfare records in America.

In the period when it is believed that this woman is the
power behind the plot, several newspapers and television
shows refer to her as 'The nanny from hell' and invoke the
phrase 'The Hand that Rocks the Cradle', the title of a recent

Hollywood movie about a psychopathic childminder. Soon, however, the FBI is briefing journalists that the woman was a dupe, and the story moves away from her. She will never merit a sole biography.

There will be three such volumes – though they are brief works, intended for young readers, in the manner of hagiographies of teenage saints – about Nat Robinson, aged two, who rapidly becomes a symbol of the impossibility of innocence in America. Six different groups and soloists record cover versions of 'Tears In Heaven', the song written by Eric Clapton after the tragic death of his own young son. Each record, CD, and mini-cassette sleeve features a picture of the Maine baby at his second, and last, birthday party. Within two weeks of the assassination, these half-dozen interpretations of the same song log-jam the first six places in the *Billboard* charts.

For the method of the child's death – and that of the President – the media generally favour the phrase 'baby bomb', although 'dynamite diaper' is also widely employed. It is generally agreed that the method of assassination – radio-controlled detonation from a distance of a coat lined with Semtex explosive – exploited the one weakness, sentimentality about children, in the presidential security screen constructed after Dallas in 1963.

But it is Anderson Kempinski Fraser, thirty-eight, who is most often named and labelled, and usually only in the opening paragraph with the designation and age released by the Boston Police and the FBI on the evening of his shooting by a police officer at Logan Airport.

One reading of the life of Anderson Fraser is that a planned assassination gave way to an opportunistic one. But this line has few buyers in America. A newspaper reports that 'Fraser' was born Yusuf Yusuf, near Baghdad, and was once a close associate of the son of President Saddam Hussein of Iraq. NBC has exclusive details of a two-year period spent in Israel, ostensibly as a student, but able, for some reason, to live far more lavishly than his peers at the University of Tel Aviv. Was he funded, perhaps, by Mossad? A television news magazine programme claims that Fraser was in love with Marilyn Monroe, and attempting to kill ex-President Kennedy, whom he viewed as a rival.

But, for all the hours and pages of news, the sense of investigation and pursuit, the anonymous assassin is fragmenting. Fraser is a naked mannequin, an empty page, and on him clothes are hung and lines inscribed. This is a democratic business. No one version seems to affect the plausibility of, or interest in, a rival line. In the aftermath of the assassination, a single detail sticks. Because of the book that fell from his hand when he was shot, and the related titles in his bag, and the duplicate volumes of the same works found at the Boston apartment where the abducted child was kept, Fraser becomes known as 'The Time Bandit'.

58: This Is How It Works

The President Newton Sanders Memorial in Arlington Cemetry in Washington, DC, is a curved wall of white tiles, seven feet high and with a bent length of fifteen feet.

Inscribed in black lettering on the inner surface are three lines from the speech that the President was due to deliver in Boston on the day of his assassination:

I AM ONE OF YOUR FAMILY.
YOU ARE ONE OF MY FAMILY.
THIS IS HOW IT WORKS.

The basic design is, without the teddy bear motifs, the one sketched by the late President for the putative tombs of the unknown children, the abortion crematoria, a policy initiative which he never lived to make public.

But Americans are not made aware of the origin of the structure. Nor will they know – until, perhaps, the late President's reputation is reconsidered some time in the next century – that the words preserved on this memorial held a quite different meaning for Newton Sanders than is taken away by those who gaze at it, and see only an exhortation to earthly harmony.

Only Boyd and Woodall, however, know of the late President's engagement with the idea of reincarnation. One day, perhaps, it will be lucrative or strategic for them to reveal it; to recant, in retrospective public television documentaries, interviewed with greying dignity at their Florida compounds. But, for the moment, respect plays – and pays – best.

Newton Sanders, martyred, is in the process of attaining sainthood. The three rapid biographies published during his 1992 campaign, now hastily reprinted with a weepy post-script, occupy the first three positions in the *New York Times* hardback non-fiction bestseller lists. Four television mini-series about his life – NBC's *A Brief Shining Light*, CBS's *The Death of a President*, ABC's *The Day America Died*, and Fox's *Newt!* – aired within three spring days. Two Hollywood movies are in preparation. Jack Lemmon has not yet said no to playing the slain leader.

Until the publication of the autumn catalogues, no one can be sure of the number of books about Sanders in preparation, but two titles already announced are *This Is How It Worked*, by Robert F. Boyd, and *I Was One of His Family* by Allan S. Woodall, intimate portraits of the late President by his two closest friends and advisers in the White House.

59:   Tricky Dicky

And one spring evening, Richard Milhous Nixon, the thirty-sixth or thirty-seventh President of the United States, is standing on his New Jersey terrace, admiring the sunset with a glass of mineral water in his hand. He has renounced alcohol in order to live longer. He is in mellow temper. The page proofs of his latest oracular, self-exonerating volume have arrived in the mail that day and await correction on his desk.

Suddenly, he stumbles, drops the tumbler he is holding.

After spending four days in a stroke-induced coma – having left prior orders that he should not be resuscitated if his intellectual faculties are impaired – he dies in a New York hospital, aged eighty-one.

He was the only American president to resign from office, doing so under threat of impeachment by Congress. Though denying knowledge of the break-in at Democratic National Headquarters organized by his campaign aides, admitting only limited complicity in a cover-up, his acceptance of a pardon from his successor Gerald Ford – 'for all crimes he has committed or may have committed' – may be logically regarded as a concession that such crimes existed. He spent a million dollars annually in the decades between his resignation and his death preventing the release of documents which might, if he indeed were innocent, have proved his purity; which might have crushed the judgement of some that he was a crook and an enemy of democracy.

But, when he dies at eighty-one, *Time* magazine describes him as 'the greatest figure of the post-war era'. The President of Russia, Boris Yeltsin, claims him as 'one of the greatest politicians'. Former President Ronald Reagan comments that Nixon's 'legacy' will 'continue to guide the forces of democracy for ever'. The former British Prime Minister Sir Edward Heath says: 'His policies were right in every way.'

Former President John F. Kennedy is not available for comment.

Richard Milhous Nixon is buried in the lawn of the little wooden house where he was born in Yorba Linda, California: now the site of his presidential library. All the living former presidents of the United States are present. In the funeral orations, Watergate is never mentioned. The day of the funeral is declared an occasion of national mourning.

Tricky Dicky has escaped his reputation.

60:   Second Shot

To Meredith's distress, Fraternelli's successor favours the same faded trattoria for business lunches, even for the ritual bacchanal to mark delivery of the manuscript. Perhaps an internal memorandum mandates the restaurant for all entertainment on expenses.

Meredith's new editor is Thomson, a capacious Australian, from whom Meredith catches a vague air of shame, like a priest with a dirty secret. The new man is, however, kinder with the wine than the American-Italian was, America having apparently diluted Italy in Fraternelli's genetic temperament.

'I'm an Australian. You're a Pom,' says the editor to the biographer. 'Let's show these limp-cocked Puritans how to lunch.'

'How is Fraternelli?' Meredith feels he ought to ask.

'He'll be fine. Nobody wants to get a stroke, but this was milder than his first. As he says himself, it sort of evens out his face. He's a good guy, Fraternelli. I'd dealt with him on serializations when I was elsewhere in the company. Some of the authors could have done with him looking less like a gangster, of course. Actually, he wasn't one of the company thugs. He even read books. Thrillers, mainly. But he read them, which is something in publishing these days, I'm discovering.'

The company which commissioned Meredith's book was once an independent publisher, but eighteen months previously was taken over by an entertainment conglomerate, comprising film, television, video, newspaper, and magazine interests. Fraternelli had previously been a film accountant.

Thomson, Meredith understood, was a former editor in the corporation's magazine division.

They order food. Thomson chooses stuffed veal shin. Meredith selects grilled sardines.

'You disappoint me. With your reputation, I was sure you'd want something stuffed.'

The writer laughts politely. 'So,' the publisher continues, 'what drew you to biography?'

Meredith keeps a prepared speech in response to this question, which he now delivers: 'I like to think of myself as an alternative historian. In two senses. By this, I mean that I am another kind of historian – as opposed to a journalist, I would say – but also that I offer an alternative to the official contemporary history. I question the record. That's why I've called this book *Marilyn and Jack: A Double Life*. A double life, obviously, in terms of being a twin biography, but also in the way in which they hid their true selves and the truth of their relationship from the American public.'

'Sounds good. Maybe I'll read it when it comes out in paperback. A *joke*. Well, it's fairly obvious what you should do next. The only difficult part is whether you do Sanders or Fraser, victim or killer. I'd say the markets are about the same size, so there's no financial downside either way. It's where you feel happiest, uh, artistically. We're actually looking for someone to do *American Martyr*, the story of how Sanders was murdered by the political and military establishment he challenged.'

'You think that's what happened?'

'We think there are a lot of people who want to read it. If you wanted to do something more critical on Sanders, you'd have to wait. See, reputation is like weather. The trick is guessing when it's going to change. You don't, you can't, think, "This guy's sunshine." You need to think: "Is he becoming rain?" Take Nixon. Who'd have thought it, but people are putting down their umbrellas. I tell you, the sun's coming round to him. I'd buy a *Saint Tricky, Nixon Resurrexit*, synopsis tomorrow, sight unseen. As an outsider, this is what amazes me about America. Even down Shit River, there are lifeboats. Of course the opposite is also true, as Kennedy found out. Even in Sun Valley, there are rats. But Shit River, Sun Valley, you gotta keep one eye on the weather. It may change. One day, who knows, you might even want a second shot at Kennedy. But Sanders, there aren't gonna be clouds around for years. And, of course, there are some you don't really need a weathercock. Like Marilyn. That hard-on's lasted thirty years. It's good for half a century. What is it about that piece of ass? It's got legs. No joke. But it's got legs . . .'

When the bottle of dessert wine is empty enough to throw back clenched reflections of the drinkers from its neck and upper body, Thomson reaches for the attaché case at his feet, and removes a sheet of glazed cardboard.

'I got them to do a mock-up of the cover.'

The book has been designed with a double jacket. The title and the author's name appear on both front and back. Only the photographs are different. One shows the breathy actress singing to the sexy president at his birthday gala in New York in 1961. The other – murky and furtive, taken by a photographer concealed behind a distant sand dune – shows the couple in old age, walking arm in arm on the beach at Hyannis Port in November 1993. Thomson does not mention it to the biographer, but this photograph – the only such image in existence – featured on the cover of the last edition of *America Now* he edited before the proprietor switched him to the books division of the empire.

'I take my hat off to you,' says Thomson. 'The story that they were still fucking was one of the ones I always wanted. Well, you got it.'

'Research,' says Meredith gravely, quartering a strawberry, then compressing a crescent of lemon above it, flinching as the cruel juice stings a small nick on his finger.

61: Pilgrim

Home in Oklahoma, Crick clicks the start key of his computer.
Since the assassination, the electronic message system used
by the Dealey Plaza Researchers has daily risked information
overload, conspiracy apocalypse. Crick's software uses the
icon of a small white envelope to reveal a message waiting.
Logging on these days, his screen generally resembles a
conventional mailbox at Christmas or a birthday.

He cracks open the icons one by one. Most of the messages
are responses from Columbia Point Researchers, that newly
formed subsection of the Dealey Plaza Researchers which will
concentrate on analysis of the Sanders assassination.

BANDIT, reads the first communication, addressing
Crick by his network log-on, SUGGEST THAT ROLE OF
CONSUELA MARTINEZ, CHILDMINDER, HAS NOT
BEEN PROPERLY EXAMINED. FBI ADMITS SHE
ILLEGAL IMMIGRANT. WHY NO DEPORTATION
ORDER? WHY IS THE US GOVERNMENT PROTECT-
ING HER? REGARDS, LONER.

BANDIT, another researcher has written, SOURCES IN
HAVANA SUGGEST THAT FRASER MAY HAVE
SPENT TIME IN CUBA. POSSIBLE LINK BETWEEN
FRASER AND LEE HARVEY OSWALD? SEEK THE
TRUTH. OYSTER.

BANDIT, requests a third electronic correspondent,
PLEASE CONFIRM IF 221193 – ASSASSINATION DATE
– IS PRIME NUMBER. MET YOU DALLAS. WARM
REGARDS, LASER.

BANDIT, a fourth conspirator informs him, WE MUST
CONSIDER POSSIBILITY THAT SANDERS KILLED

BY ALIEN AGENTS, ANGRY ABOUT HIS REVEL-
ATION OF EXTRA-TERRESTRIAL ENCOUNTER IN
SEATTLE. LONESTAR.

The fifth message is from Evaristi, under his network log-
on of FATHER. He has written: BANDIT, A BREAK-
THROUGH. HAVE DISCOVERED THAT ONE OF
WOMEN IN MIMI'S SORORITY AT TIME OF HER
DEATH IS NOW STUDYING AT FBI COLLEGE IN
QUANTICO. IF WAS LINKED WITH AGENCY WHILE
STUDENT, METHOD OF MIMI'S MURDER
BECOMES CLEAR. I THANK GOD FOR THIS ILLU-
MINATION. AND LOVE TO YOU, PROFESSOR.
FATHER.

There is, however, once again, no message from PIL-
GRIM, the email name of Kathy Malone. Crick asks his
computer to establish if the operator with that log-on is using
the network at the moment. Soon, his screen confirms:
PILGRIM ONLINE. He imagines her sitting at a desk in
her San Francisco home. It has four storeys, and a distant
view of the bay from her office at the top, he guesses. It is
built to roll with the shakes of an earthquake. Her mother's
crucifix hangs in the hall, more from tradition than religion.
He visualizes Kathy tapping at her keyboard, her legs
together under the desk, her vagina dry, uninspired by the
prospect of the entry – a rare and ritualized imposition this
decade, anyway – of her husband.

PILGRIM, he types, PLEASE RESPOND. I UNDER-
STAND, AS A CATHOLIC MYSELF, THAT WHAT YOU
ARE SUFFERING IS GUILT, AND THAT IS WHY YOU
ARE IGNORING MY MESSAGES. BUT WE HAVE NO
CAUSE FOR GUILT. DALLAS WAS SPECIAL. IT WAS
MEANT TO HAPPEN. I HAVE NO OTHER CLAIM ON
YOU EXCEPT TO MAINTAIN THIS BOND. PLEASE
RESPOND. WAITING, WITH ALL LOVE, BANDIT.

Trying to highlight the phrase *It was meant to happen*, but
unable to find the font he wants, he sends his voiceless
message down the telephone line. He does not, however,
expect a reply. Kathy checked out of the Dallas hotel early on
the morning after their encounter. He has heard nothing from

her since. Kathy Malone has turned back to the narrative of her marriage. Crick, however, has become convinced that he has glimpsed the possibility of an alternative existence. Waiting for the envelope icon of a response to appear on his screen, the professor unzips his jeans, and returns in his imagination to Dallas, November 22nd, 1993.

62:   Today Again

'Thanks, Willard. Sunbathing weather, huh? See you again in an hour. Monday morning on *Today*. Coming up in the next hour, former Secretary of State Henry Kissinger will be arguing that one of the consequences of the political vacuum in Washington following the assassination of the President has been the failure of the West to control Serbian aggression in Bosnia. And new hope for Americans who suffer from diabetes. But, first, it's a very great pleasure to welcome our special guest, Miss Marilyn Monroe. Hiya, Marilyn.'

'Hi, Katie.'

'You're looking great. Now you're here to talk about your first movie for thirteen years. Appropriately enough, it's called *She's Back!* What made you want to do it?'

'Well, it was the funniest script I'd been sent in ages. And I'd been away from movies a long time and well, you know . . .'

'Some of the critics have pointed out that you play an ageing Hollywood sex goddess.'

'Well, actually, in the film, she's dead. I don't know if the critics were trying to tell me something. Really, that's why I wanted to do the movie. It's about death, and how we only get one chance and . . . well, this is kind of a popular theme at the moment. I've just seen the new Peter Weir film, *Fearless*, and that's, like, a concept movie about mortality. Suddenly, all the stories are, like, about this thing.'

'Why do you think that is?'

'I don't know. I guess we haven't got death licked . . . or . . . let's say doctors and theologians haven't sorted this one out, so don't hold your breath that an actress will . . .'

Dumb will sell more tickets, so she gives them dumb. But it is a performance: Marilyn, not Jean.

'Now there's obviously a lot of concern about your co-star in the film after what happened last week – how is she?'

'I haven't spoken to her. I wrote, of course. I understand from her assistant that she was more mentally shaken up than physically injured. And, of course, there's an investigation going on into how this guy, this "stalker", isn't that an awful word, got onto the set of her new movie. She's a tough lady, and she'll get over it, but . . .'

'Part of the reality of being a movie star these days.'

'Well, yeah. The dangers change, I guess you'd say. In my time, movie stars killed themselves, one way or another, that was the threat. These days, other people try to kill them.'

'Right. Now, there's a new biography out to coincide with the release of the film.'

'Uh-oh. I was enjoying this . . .'

'We want to give you a chance to answer some of what the author Peter Meredith says. It's suggested in the book that you are a closet lesbian . . .'

'Katie, I've been married five times! That's quite a lot of rooms before you get to the closet.'

'Good answer. What have you learned about marriage?'

'That it doesn't always work.'

'Would you marry again?'

'Put it this way. I don't think the man has been born who could make me happy now. And if he hasn't been born yet, there'd be a sort of an age-gap problem by the time we got round to it.'

'The new book says you're back with JFK?'

'Yeah? As well as being a secret lesbian? I wish my life was as exciting to lead as it is to read about. The President and I talked for a while on a beach, one windy morning. We kept all our clothes on, and we are both rather old. It was the kind of date you could safely tell your mom all that happened.'

'Is it tough getting old?'

'Listen, it was no day at the beach being young.'

'Are you happy now?'

'Oh, yes. Oh yes.'

Dumb and happy is the best hope for the gross. Actress, act!

'Well, may you long continue to be an inspiration to those Americans who face adversity in their lives. Marilyn, we wish you luck with the new movie. See you again.'

'Thanks, Katie.'

'This is *Today* on NBC. And we'll be back after this station break.'

63: The Fly

One summer afternoon in the White House office they share
– retained as aides in the emergency administration of the
Speaker of the House, now the forty-second President – Boyd
and Woodall are disrupted in the writing of their memoirs by
the ducking and buzzing of a fly. The insect keeps settling
alternately on their rival stacks of foolscap: a loud and
indecisive browser, or fickle critic.

Boyd, the taller of the two, stalks it to a corner of the
room, then, with a Joe Di Maggio swipe of rolled memoir,
reduces the fly to a stain on a page recalling his early
involvement in politics. A few minutes later, back at his
keyboard, Boyd begins to shake with laughter.

'Oh, God,' whispers Woodall, 'your memoir is going to
have jokes?'

'No, no. I just realized. I killed the President . . .'

'What?'

'If Sanders was right about reincarnation, I reckon I just
saw him off again.'

He points to the spot of aphid paste on his curled top
sheet. Then both men tremble with feral and cathartic
laughter.

64: Professional Misconduct

At a Washington press conference called by her attorney, Diane Yapullo announces that she is withdrawing her previous allegations of sexual abuse against the late President Sanders.

It is now her belief, she tells the press, that she was wrongly prompted to construct the claims by her psychoanalyst during Recovered Memory Therapy. It is her intention to sue the therapist in question for professional misconduct and for the distress and harmful publicity to which she has been subjected.

At a press conference of his own in Seattle, Ms Yapullo's former therapist insists that her analysis was properly conducted, but admits that there is a possibility that the memories of abuse by Newton Sanders may represent denial and transference of an incident of assault by another male authority figure in his patient's past. He announces that he is counter-suing Ms Yapullo for defamation, loss of professional income, and for non-payment of fees.

65: Nam

One spring afternoon at Hyannis, Jack finally plays the tapes
from the new exhibits at his museum. The building will re-
open in two weeks, the bomb damage repaired and a small
memorial to the late President Sanders dug into the grass
where he died. Then the additional halls will admit their first
visitors, now perhaps drawn by morbid motives other than
those that would formerly have brought them.

The first cassette Jack watches is for the supplementary
exhibit called 'A Noble Mission Tragically Gone Wrong', a
line from Jack's final television address to the American
people at the end of his second administration in 1968. The
reference was to Vietnam. Previously featured only briefly in
the 'Foreign Policy' room of the museum, the war has now
been allowed, after long and strong opposition from the
former president, a small hall of its own. Jack was finally
persuaded, by a prominent liberal historian also summering
on Cape Cod, that any other approach was old-style Soviet.

The exhibit takes the form of photographs, declassified
memoranda, and a videotaped interview between Boomer
and Jack. He had taken the precaution of drawing up his own
questions but, arriving for the recording, found that Boomer's
own intended interrogation – immaculately word-processed
with supplementaries designated 'a' or 'b' of the main question number – was considerably softer.

On the tape, Boomer, now out of vision after a single
establishing mid-shot showing him with his clipboard, says:
'Mr President, have critics and historians been too harsh on
your handling of the Vietnam War?'

Jack replies: 'Well, obviously I think so. But I do have

serious arguments to support this view. Vietnam was a product of many things. It resulted from the American terror of Communism – a fear which may seem quaint to younger and subsequent generations, but which was a fact of the American psyche from the middle of this century, demonstrated, most famously, by the McCarthy hearings. Also, the generally perceived lesson of World War II was that aggression must never be rewarded. In that sense, you could say that Vietnam was a combination of a lesson *from* World War II and a lesson *to* World War III – no appeasement, least of all of Communism. Pushing this view, there was the power of the "military-industrial complex", against which President Eisenhower had warned, and which was a tangible pressure on all his successors. And there was the reality of political deal-making on the Hill. To some extent, there was a straight swap in Congress: the Civil Rights Act in exchange for holding the line in South Vietnam – left–right, liberal–redneck cancelling each other out. It wasn't pretty, but it was politics.'

'What is your response to those – such as the film-maker Oliver Stone – who have argued that the tragedy of Vietnam would not have happened under another president?'

'People are entitled to run other films of history in their head. We all do it. I can only say that the pressures I have just outlined – the need to be tough on Communism, the lessons of the war in Europe, the ambitions of the military, and the need to balance domestic liberalism with some other sign of toughness – would have affected any president.'

'Mr President, do you believe that Congress or the American people was ever misled over Vietnam?'

'I can honestly say that I think not. There were secrets. There always are in wars. But a secret is not a lie.'

This is, at best, disingenuous. Even while he answered, Jack's memory was flashing back fragments at him. Of the Gulf of Tonkin Resolution, by which, in August 1964, Congress permitted independent presidential action, without consultation, in South-East Asia. They had made much use of this power, although it soon became clear that the incident which had convinced Congress – a reported torpedo attack on an American aircraft carrier, which returned fire – was of low probity. He remembers Vice-President Johnson saying at a late-night meeting: 'Those damn sailors were taking shots at a lot of flying fishes.' This was one of their secrets, for years, as were the desperate meetings at the State Department, even on Election Day in 1964, discussing strategies for escalation of the war, although the electorate had been promised no increase in American involvement.

He did not, however, direct Boomer to these discrepancies. There is no room for purity in the pursuit of reputation.

66: Revisionism

A week after the release of *She's Back!*, a professor of cultural studies at a midwestern university contributes a more general essay about the movies of Marilyn Monroe to the Arts & Leisure section of the *Sunday New York Times*. In part, the article argues:

> Although Monroe's performance in *She's Back!* shows considerable comic technique, it is increasingly clear that her best film is *The K Brothers* (later re-released as *The Three Ruskateers*.) Though much ridiculed at the time of its release, in 1982, the film can now be seen to have been ahead of its time.
>
> With the distance of a decade, *The K Brothers* stands revealed as a post-modern masterpiece. Made—courageously—at the height of the Cold War between the United States and the Soviet Union, the film plays daringly with American stereotypes and prejudices about Russia. Key to this artistic scheme is Monroe's willingness to perform against age and against range as Grushenka. Although movie-goers and critics were generally too blinded by facile expectation to see it, the film showcases one of the most intriguing and subversive cinematic personalities of the past 30 years . . .

67: Wounding Review

Meredith commits his latest paragraph to the tiny but elephantine memory of his machine. He is transcribing early material for his next project: the first hostile biography of Nelson Mandela, currently South Africa's first black president and an international hero. But Mandela's sunshine will not last. Meredith's new publisher has made him understand this. He will be ready for the rain.

He taps the 'sleep' key of his laptop, and leaves his workroom. The income from *A Double Life* has bought him a corner apartment overlooking Central Park. Several times a day, he is drawn to survey his double-window-sized slice of New York, as if it were a work of art, which, to him, it is. He would never have paid for a painting what he happily spent on this perspective.

The implosion of the glass just below his eyeline – the webbing of its surface like water scattered by a stone – he at first takes to be the result of exactly that: a stone thrown from above or below. There is no time for him to consider the question of how a fifteenth-storey apartment might be vulnerable to such an assault before the wetness on his chest skin, and urgent protestations of the nerve-ends just beneath, convince him that the intruding object was a bullet.

Dialling for help, he smears the keypad with blood from the fingers that have just probed the hole. The muscles in his arm are pulsing, from impact and shock, and he misses two of the three emergency digits with his first palsied jabs.

But, even in this predicament, Meredith remains enough of a cultural commentator – finds enough space in his fading brain – to unpeel this scene of its meaning. In what may be his final deconstruction, he appreciates that he is living, perhaps dying, in a pure democracy of horrors. The character assassin who targeted the assassinated – Kennedy, Lennon – has himself succumbed to the gunman's bullet. It was so easy – particularly for an outsider like himself – to view America as a tragic mess. Yet there was a neatness here.

The last thought of Peter Meredith before he loses consciousness is how ideal this scene would be as a prologue to a biography of himself.

68: Fat is a Theological Issue

Duke turns the blue-and-white onto Newbury Street. They cruise past the exclusive boutiques. In Ford's second Father 'Beads' O'Reilly novel – the first has just been rejected by a third publisher – he has sited the first corpse here: a rich parishioner of the pastor-detective found stabbed in a fitting room while trying on a major-label ballgown.

It is Ford's first shift since his return from the injury sustained on the day of the Sanders assassination. A piece of shrapnel from the shattered platform lodged in one of his side-bags of fat. According to ballistics, Ford's corpulence was the perfect shock-absorber. If he had been thinner, the missile might have missed him and injured others. Without this flak-jacket of flab, his own vital organs or spinal cord might have been harmed. So his waistline saved himself and others.

Telling Duke this story, Ford concluded: 'I was meant to be this shape. God needed me fat.'

He plans to use this incident in any appeal against a fine resulting from his failure to reach the new regulation weight.

His first morning back has been boring. Duke doesn't seem to play the minus game these days. They have been arguing about the O'Connor Commission Report on the assassination of President Sanders. The Commission – the members of which include former Presidents Ford and Bush – has just released its finding that the assassination was carried out by a single fanatic acting alone.

'The problem is,' says Duke, 'there's still no motive.'

'Yes, there is.'

'What?'

'Time.'

'What?'

'That's why they call him The Time Bandit.'

'But what *about* Time? What was the motive?'

'I dunno. It bugged him, I suppose.'

'Well, great. That explains it, Gerry. Anyway, what do I care? I'm out of here. I start law school Tuesday.'

'What? Duke, ya kidding me.'

There is a long pause before the other policeman admits: 'In fact, I am. But I just wanted to see how it would sound. And, one day, I'll say it for real.'

But then the radio wants them for a homicide.

69: Idlewild

One of the options on the ballot paper in the district elections permits New Yorkers to vote for the American, living or dead, whose name they would like to be given to the city's Idlewild International Airport.

Among those who receive some support are former President Ronald Reagan, the Apollo 11 astronaut Neil Armstrong, the pop star Madonna, the movie actor Tom Cruise, the basketball hero Earvin 'Magic' Johnson, and the Reverend Sun Myung Moon, founder of the International Church of Scientology.

Finally, however, it is announced that Idlewild will in future be known as the Elvis A. Presley International Airport or, in the most likely abbreviation among the flying community, New York Presley.

70:   Poor Soul

And in Boston or Los Angeles, or somewhere far from home, stricken unawares, the emergency admission is wheeled in. The doctors, nurses, and orderlies scowl down until they see the face is famous.

'Oh my God,' someone says, 'it really is—'

'Nothing. We're getting nothing,' interrupts a doctor, as the line on the monitor flattens to a horizon, with no sunrise coming. Electricity is directed through the chest, but it finds no answering spark of life.

Looking down at the body, they think of the obituaries, the television funerals, the books, the documentaries, the assessments, the reputations.

A nurse says: 'Poor soul.'

Author's Note

Although my novel is a counter-history, it is intended that those details of John F. Kennedy's life up to November 22nd, 1963 and of Marilyn Monroe's until August 4th, 1962 are factually correct. For example, the actress did indeed express an ambition to appear in a film of *The Brothers Karamazov*.

For biographical details – and for hints as to how character and career might have developed in both cases – I was helped by a number of books. The most important Kennedy sources were: *The Death of a President* by William Manchester (Harper & Row, 1965); *A Thousand Days* by Arthur M. Schlesinger (Houghton Mifflin, 1965); *President Kennedy: Profile of Power* by Richard Reeves (Simon & Schuster, 1993); *JFK – Reckless Youth* by Nigel Hamilton (Random House, 1992); *The Killing of a President* by Robert J. Groden (Viking Penguin, 1993); and *The Kennedy Conspiracy* by Anthony Summers (McGraw-Hill, 1980).

On Monroe, I read with most interest the exhaustive *Marilyn Monroe: The Biography* by Donald Spoto (Random House, 1993) and, among the rather more speculative volumes, *Marilyn: The Last Take* by Peter Brown and Patte Barham (Dutton, 1992). *Goddess: The Secret Lives of Marilyn Monroe* by Anthony Summers (Macmillan, 1985) and *Conversations With Marilyn* by W. J. Weatherby (Paragon House, 1992) also provided various useful clues.

In imagining Kennedy's second term, I inevitably drew on the actual Johnson administration of that period. In this respect, I was indebted to *Vietnam: A History* by Stanley Karnow (Viking Penguin, 1991) and to the four-part television series *LBJ* (BBC/WNET/WGBH/1991).

And, although they draw necessarily different conclusions, the Dealey Plaza Researchers, in their symposium addresses, are mainly working from facts which stand in our reality too. For example, National Security Action Memorandum No. 263 exists. And the 'Who Shot JR?' episode of *Dallas* was indeed screened by CBS on the eve of the 18th anniversary of the shooting of John F. Kennedy.

In all cases, the responsibility for the uses to which the information has been put remains my own. Equally, Constance Garnett's Signet Classic translation of Dostoevsky's *The Brothers Karamazov* is in no way to blame for Jack Berettovich's rather loose adaptation of it in Chapter 24.

Extracts from Stephen Hawking's *Black Holes and Baby Universes* are used by kind permission of Writers House Inc.

I am extremely grateful to Antonia Couling, for much excellent research; and to Susan Feldman, David Stewart, Susan Banks, Cat Ledger, Roger Meredith, Charles Pattinson, Frank Lawson, and Sarah Lawson, who helped me in various ways.

Mark Lawson, February 1995